Dog politics

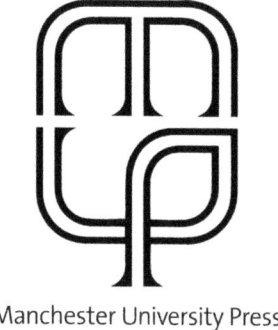

Manchester University Press

INSCRIPTIONS

Series editors
Des Fitzgerald and Amy Hinterberger

Editorial advisory board
Vivette García Deister, National Autonomous University of Mexico
John Gardner, Monash University, Australia
Maja Horst, Technical University of Denmark
Robert Kirk, Manchester, UK
Stéphanie Loyd, Laval University, Canada
Alice Mah, Warwick University, UK
Deboleena Roy, Emory University, USA
Hallam Stevens, Nanyang Technological University, Singapore
Niki Vermeulen, Edinburgh, UK
Megan Warin, Adelaide University, Australia
Malte Ziewitz, Cornell University, USA

Since the very earliest studies of scientific communities, we have known that texts and worlds are bound together. One of the most important ways to stabilise, organise and grow a laboratory, a group of scholars, even an entire intellectual community, is to write things down. As for science, so for the social studies of science: Inscriptions is a space for writing, recording and inscribing the most exciting current work in sociological and anthropological – and any related – studies of science.

The series foregrounds theoretically innovative and empirically rich interdisciplinary work that is emerging in the UK and internationally. It is self-consciously hospitable in terms of its approach to discipline (all areas of social sciences are considered), topic (we are interested in all scientific objects, including biomedical objects) and scale (books will include both fine-grained case studies and broad accounts of scientific cultures).

For readers, the series signals a new generation of scholarship captured in monograph form – tracking and analysing how science moves through our societies, cultures and lives. Employing innovative methodologies for investigating changing worlds, it is home to compelling new accounts of how science, technology, biomedicine and the environment translate and transform our social lives.

Dog politics

Species stories and the animal sciences

Mariam Motamedi Fraser

MANCHESTER UNIVERSITY PRESS

Copyright © Mariam Motamedi Fraser 2024

The right of Mariam Motamedi Fraser to be identified as the author of this work has been asserted in accordance with the Copyright, Designs and Patents Act 1988.

An electronic version of this book is also available under a Creative Commons (CC-BY-NC-ND) licence, which permits non-commercial use, distribution and reproduction provided the author(s) and Manchester University Press are fully cited and no modifications or adaptations are made. Details of the licence can be viewed at https://creativecommons.org/licenses/by-nc-nd/2.0/uk/

Published by Manchester University Press
Oxford Road, Manchester, M13 9PL

www.manchesteruniversitypress.co.uk

British Library Cataloguing-in-Publication Data
A catalogue record for this book is available from the British Library

ISBN 978 1 5261 7480 2 hardback

First published 2024

The publisher has no responsibility for the persistence or accuracy of URLs for any external or third-party internet websites referred to in this book, and does not guarantee that any content on such websites is, or will remain, accurate or appropriate.

Typeset by Newgen Publishing UK

To Monk
For Monk

Animals may indeed be supremely indifferent to the names we give them: but they are not indifferent to the naming of oppression.

> Lynda Birke, 'Naming names – or, what's in it for the animals?' (2009)

Contents

List of figures and tables	*page* viii
Preface	ix
Acknowledgements	xi
Introduction: Senta's howl	1
1 It's a dog's life and there's nothing natural about it	28
2 Dogs' species story	62
3 Vanishing animals: How to turn an individual dog into a species ambassador	91
4 Do dogs work? The labour of 'the bond'	123
5 Dog disputes: Scientific research with dogs	155
6 On the deathlessness of 'the dog': Species, 'race' and individuals	185
7 Dog politics	219
References	238
Index	260

Figures and tables

Figure

2.1 Darwin's transmutation diagram, 1837, Cambridge University Library, MS DAR 121, p. 36. Reproduced by kind permission of the Syndics of Cambridge University Library. MS DAR 121, 36. *page* 69

Tables

1.1 The standardised socialisation programme developed for puppies by Helen Vaterlaws-Whiteside and Amandine Hartmann. From Helen Vaterlaws-Whiteside and Amandine Hartmann, 'Improving puppy behavior using a new standardized socialization program', *Applied Animal Behaviour Science* 197 (2017): 55–61 (56). *page* 40

1.2 'The face of fear'. From Nicole Wilde, *Help for Your Fearful Dog: A Step-by-Step Guide to Helping Your Dog Conquer His Fears* (San Clarita: Phantom Publishing, 2006), 17. 46

Preface

A note on how this book came about, which is in large part through my work with The Dog Hub (www.thedoghub.co.uk/ (accessed September 2023). On account of its close association with the local authority of Camden, London, The Dog Hub, built and developed by Susan Close, offers an unusual – and potentially radical – model of support for dogs, handlers and communities. Since 2008, Camden Council has provided The Dog Hub with funding, a dedicated indoor space, and permission to work in all open spaces where dogs are allowed (such as parks). In return, The Dog Hub provides free, non-judgemental dog training, support and advice to anyone living or working in Camden. The Dog Hub liaises with and across nearly all the council's departments (especially housing, social services, parks and open spaces, reparation, supported living, police etc.) with the aim, on the one hand, of helping council staff to better understand dogs and their lives and, on the other, of responding to council requests for problem solving, which usually means preventing situations involving dogs from escalating out of control (escalation being nearly always detrimental to the dog). Over the past seven years, I have participated in Dog Hub activities in numerous capacities, including being a volunteer in dog classes; shadowing Susan on home visits; attending dog welfare stakeholder meetings; participating in reading groups with canine behavioural professionals; and, above all, being in the privileged position of sometime sounding-board for Susan when challenging issues arise. At the same time, I have been working on an advanced diploma (Ad.Dip.) in applied animal behaviour (canine).

My work with The Dog Hub and on the Ad.Dip. have together motivated this book. Inadvertently, they have highlighted to me how substantial is the gap, often, between what humans feel about the dogs with whom they live and/or work, and what those dogs, as far as it is possible to tell, are feeling. This gap can be identified across the social spectrum, and across many varied ways of being with dogs in different social settings. Although ultimately the gap cannot be closed, most of the dogs I have met would certainly benefit if it was at least narrowed. There is no substitute for practical, on-the-ground support, especially when it is aimed at understanding a dog's singularity, the organisation of their life as a whole and the relationships that shape it. My hope, however, is that this book too will change in some small way how we think about dogs, and therefore what we expect from them, and how we treat them.

Acknowledgements

My first thanks go to the dogs. To Rupert and Tom; to Husky, Kite and Nimbo; to Eddie; to Shadow, Finley and Daisy; to Seven, China and Io; to Cleo; to Juno; to Luna, Rafa and Diego; to Eric; to Azul; and to Cheidle. Thanks also to my more recent acquaintances Peggy and Django, Jessie, Charlie, Reggie, Nico, Lena, and Blake, all of whom have waited patiently (or seemingly patiently) while I rambled on to their humans about this book.

Some of the best parts of my life are shared with women with a passion for dogs, and these women, too, have for years put up patiently (or seemingly patiently) with conversations about this book, and have read various versions of it. Heartfelt thanks to Lisa Rabanal, especially for our weekly dog discussions, without which my life would be much diminished; to Emer Lenihan, whose insight and gentleness have supported both Monk and me through many challenges, outside as well as inside the veterinary clinic; and to Joanne Martin, my tutor, who has with great patience tolerated numerous interruptions to my Ad.Dip. (and also my lengthy essay answers). Above all, I am deeply grateful to Susan Close, who over the past eight years has taught me more about dogs and humans than it is possible to convey.

It is a profound privilege to have friends and colleagues who have been generous enough to look beyond the confusion on the page and to support me in clarifying my thinking. Grateful thanks to Celia Lury, Alberto Toscano, Martin Savransky, Sarah Pike, Lynn Turner, Charles Hirschkind, Maisie Tomlinson, Sonia Turcotte and Nick Millet. Thanks also to Tom Farsides, for sending me things to think about, including the work of Charles H. Turner, and to

Richard Burkhardt, whose extensive knowledge and personal kindness brought nuance to my understanding of ethology, and of the animal sciences more broadly. My thanks also to the anonymous reviewers of this book, in the USA and in the UK, for their careful and attentive reading. These comments made a real difference, raising the bar for this book right at the finish.

Every year I have taught students who have created worlds in which books such as this one and, more broadly, commitments to animals, can flourish. I am indebted to all the students who have participated in my undergraduate and master's animal modules at Goldsmiths. In particular, however, I want to thank the students on Thinking Animals 2017–2018, which was my first teaching class after an extended period of medical leave, for sharing, intensifying and enriching my excitement about and dedication to the module, and for all the work that we achieved together in that basement café in Bloomsbury. Sari Easton, you were right; we learned that the world is bigger and less lonely than we thought. I also want to extend special thanks to the three generations of students on the Ethics and Politics of Animals module (2021–2024), which is a core course on the M.A. in ecology, culture and society at Goldsmiths. The wide range of these students' disciplinary backgrounds and work experiences, coupled with their remarkable openness, warmth and integrity, has made a deep impression on me and on this book.

I was lucky enough to meet Laura Swift, the commissioning editor at Manchester University Press (MUP), somewhat by accident. Yet no author could have received better intellectual and practical support than I have had from her. I also want to thank the editors of the Inscriptions series at MUP, Des Fitzgerald and Amy Hinterberger, for welcoming me on board, and the teams at MUP and Newgen, and Sarah Cook, for turning these words into a book. Important thanks are due to Hugh Macnicol, Sarah Jackson, Monica Greco, and Dimitrios Giannoulopoulos for the immeasurable efforts that they made on my behalf, to ensure this book is available to a wider audience through Open Access. This means a huge amount to me, and they made it possible.

This book has been supported by old friends: Brenna Bhandar, Natalie Fenton, Yasmin Gunaratnam, Gholam Khiabany, Stephanie Lawler, Cath Le Couteur (who generously gave me the final line of this book), Nirmal Puwar, Nikolas Rose, Marsha Rosengarten and Evelyn Ruppert. And by new ones: Gail Davies, Charles Foster, Jay Griffiths, Engin Isen. It has been supported by my family, both immediate and extended, nearly all of whom have lived or live with dogs, especially Kayvaan and Rosanna, who are rarely seen without one (or two, or …). Finally, always, it has been supported by Michael Parker, who actively created, with love, humour and endurance, the many different kinds of spaces in our lives that this book demanded. And who read it all, transforming entire lines of thought with just a word or a sentence. I am so glad to be in your debt, Michael.

I said in the preface that this book was motivated by work. Also, it was motivated by love. By my love, of Monk.

Introduction: Senta's howl

> In over a quarter of a century of training I have never met an animal who turned out to be replaceable.
>
> (Hearne 1993: 2)

There is a story told about dogs, in the language of science. It is a story that usually, implicitly, claims to tell of all dogs, even though most of its central characters are dogs who live and work with humans in the Global North.[1] It says that dogs 'belong' in some way with humans, and that the principal manifestation of this belonging is dogs' responsiveness to humans. You and I might debate what kind of a dog a responsive dog is – is she a docile, biddable dog, or an engaged and lively dog? – but the bottom line is that a dog should be interested in the humans with whom they are closest. And, most often, dogs are. After all, their lives depend on it.

In his moving discussion of Beth in *Bad Dog: Pit Bull Politics and Multispecies Justice*, Harlan Weaver notes that, even though Beth's guardians said that they relinquished her for behavioural reasons (biting other dogs etc.), Weaver himself suspects it was more likely on account of her 'disinterest in humans' (Weaver 2021: 162). If Weaver is right, then Beth, who was euthanised, paid for that disinterest with her life. Beth is the touchstone for this book. This book will argue that, if Beth's death requires no ethical or political justification – that is, if the expectations that humans place on dogs, and the uses they make of them, pass largely without substantive comment – then this is in part because they are not perceived to be expectations and uses at all. For dogs belong with humans, so the story goes. Dogs, in fact, would not *be* dogs without humans.

The central claim of this book is that the lives of domesticated dogs in the Global North are in nearly all aspects shaped by a story that seeks to tie them irrevocably to humans and to naturalise dog–human intimacy. This story – broadly disseminated and embellished – originates in, and accrues its authority from, science: specifically, from a science of species that was invented much later than was dogs' invention of themselves. At the heart of this story, the heart out of which so many other dog stories are pumped, are scientific accounts of dogs' biological speciation – scientific accounts, that is, of how dogs came to be dogs. In this book, I will call such accounts dogs' 'species story'.

Speciation theories are key drivers of species stories not solely because they lay claim to how a group of individual animals came to be a species, but because these accounts of evolutionary becoming are often used to substantiate conceptions of what those animals are *today*. 'It matters', Donna Haraway writes, 'what matters we use to think other matters with; it matters what stories we tell to tell other stories with; it matters what knots knot knots, what thoughts think thoughts, what descriptions describe descriptions, what ties tie ties' (Haraway 2016: 12). And it surely does: as this book will illustrate, the story of how, precisely, a dog is understood to have become a dog contributes substantially to defining what a dog is expected to feel today; how a dog is expected to behave today; what treatment of dogs is justified today; and, above all, what about a dog passes almost unnoticed.

Species stories ascribe to groups of individual animals not just *any* history, or *any* set of characteristics, but histories and characteristics that are explicitly indexed to the concept of species in general and to 'their' mode of speciation in particular. In this way, species stories both foreground specific qualities as important *and* imply that they cannot, in any real sense, be transformed. There are other stories that bear on the ways the potentialities of animals are shaped but, given the authority of science, species stories usually represent themselves as the bottom line, the yardstick that defines the range and limits of an animal. This book will explore many different versions of dogs' species story. Nearly all of them consider dogs to be virtually incomprehensible without humans.

There are exceptions. In *A Dog's World: Imagining the Lives of Dogs in a World without Humans*, the bioethicist Jessica Pierce and ethologist Marc Bekoff pursue an experiment in 'speculative biology' (Pierce and Bekoff 2021: 8), which is to ask what would become of dogs in a world without humans. I will return to *A Dog's World* in Chapter 5. Suffice it to note here that the fact that Pierce and Bekoff feel obliged to explain the independent existence of dogs (independent of humans) by way of a science fiction scenario speaks volumes about the intractability of dogs' species story in canine science today. This book, *Dog Politics*, and Pierce and Bekoff's book, *A Dog's World*, are both critiques of how domesticated dogs are perceived and how they are treated on the basis of that perception. However, where *A Dog's World* seeks to augur change for dogs in the present by conjuring up an imaginary future, *Dog Politics* does so by challenging an imaginary past. Where *A Dog's World* contains its argument within the paradigm of species (just about), *Dog Politics* questions this paradigm. Where *A Dog's World* looks to those few scientific studies of free-ranging dogs for insight into 'who dogs are' (Pierce and Bekoff 2021: 11), *Dog Politics* engages critically with scientific studies of dogs 'who live in captivity' (Pierce and Bekoff 2021: 11).[2] Despite these significant differences, the agenda is similar: to loosen the human ties that bind the captive dog. 'Whatever would become of you without me?', their fictional owner asks. 'A lot!', whispers the dog in reply (Pierce and Bekoff 2021: 163).

Dog Politics rests on two assumptions: that species, in science and more broadly, is a core element in the conceptual architecture of thinking about animals, and that the exploitation of animals will continue to be the inevitable outcome of ethics and politics that refer back to species concepts. In this book, I will use the term *species thinking* purposely, as distinct from speciesism. I do so because, as Chapter 6 demonstrates, speciesism differs substantially from the term racism, and what the charge of racism is able to achieve, politically. Unlike the concept of racism, which is often a simultaneous effort to 'undo' the category of race, the concept of speciesism, I will argue, serves only to confirm animals as species. It seems impossible, at least for the time being, to wish species thinking away. Better, then, in my view – as a short-term strategy – to pay detailed critical attention to how species operate as stories. What forces does dogs' species story mobilise? What ways of living and dying does it shape? What relations, especially with humans, does it prescribe?

This book will argue that one of the most serious consequences of species thinking is that, once a species rank has been established, species gives no scientific, ethical or political reason to be interested in particularity. The form of particularity that I will be especially concerned with in this book is the particular individual. At worst, species thinking does not 'merely' displace the individual; rather, it erases this figure entirely, with the consequence that individuals appear to be endlessly substitutable, one for another. In a recent seminar, a student told me that for the entirety of his life, a heron had perched on the bank of a lough near his home. And that for the entirety of his life, his family had referred to this heron as Frank, based on the sound of the heron's call, *fraaa-aaank*. When he grew up (to be a marine ecologist), this student learned that the average life expectancy for a grey heron in the wild is five years.[3] The story is salutary: it illustrates how easily particular individuals, who live and die, can be eclipsed by 'immortal' species.

I will use the term 'individual' very often during the course of this book. By it, I mean a kind of banal individuality: an individuality that is roughly equivalent to non-species particularity; that assumes no specific qualities, capacities or experiences in advance; and that is not loaded with notions of, for example, 'personhood', 'agency', 'autonomy' etc. The important point about this individual, as I will explore in Chapters 5 and 7 especially, is that it is irreducibly singular – although not necessarily singular in any *exceptional* sense (on this distinction, see Chapter 3) – and, as such, is irreplaceable. Probably, this minimal conception is zoocentric: it refers to an individual 'who', who is born once; dies once; and, between these two existential poles, endures in the world uniquely. This minimal conception of individuality, which I will use in this book, is not intended to be a contribution to the question as to whether or not dogs are subjects. On this complex topic I have no theory of my own to propose.

Alfred North Whitehead's (1978; 1967) concept of an 'enduring concrete percipient' is my own preferred understanding of an 'individual'. However, I do not draw on this concept in this book, or even introduce it until Chapter 7. The reason for this 'omission' is that I want to avoid technical terms that have the potential to disguise the implications, for animals and especially for dogs, of species thinking. *Dog Politics* will argue ultimately that dogs' species story is a specific, entrenched and constraining *order* or *pattern* of becoming through which an idea of a dog is created.

This idea is made material through practices such as socialisation, through the identification of dogs' objections to their living conditions as problem behaviours, and through the endlessly reiterated song of 'the bond'. It is an altogether dazzling performance. So dazzling, in fact, that you can barely see the dog who stands in front of you. The individual dog. Haraway writes that Isabelle Stengers's cosmopolitics demands that 'decisions must take place somehow in the presence of those who will bear their consequences' (Haraway 2016: 12). Dogs' species story is the 'decision' – the decision in Whitehead's sense of the word (see Chapter 7) – that would shape an individual dog into an image of *all* dogs. I use 'the individual' in order to be clear about this, and about who it is that 'bears the consequences'.

By ridding themselves of the 'burden' of individuals, species categories are simultaneously evacuated of those animals who would bear testimony, with their lives and also, importantly, with their deaths, to the violent implications of species thinking. Today, dogs are considered to be among the best researched and most interesting animal subjects across a wide range of scientific disciplines, from contemporary psychology and ethology to evolutionary anthropology and comparative genetics. Yet their welfare issues are often narrowly defined: determined less by what is important to *that* individual dog; less by *that* individual dog's needs, wants, desires; and more by whether and how those issues impact upon the dog's relations with humans (see Chapters 1, 4 and 7). Dogs' species story accounts at least in part for this paradox: if dogs are, by definition, to be with humans, how significant can any welfare issue be, beyond how it affects the quality of that relationship?

This book argues, in essence, that the story of 'companionship' – companionship in its colloquial sense, not as Haraway understands it[4] – is *itself* 'the Greatest Story Ever Told' (Haraway 2003: 5). And that the implications of this story for dogs are equivocal at best. *Dog Politics* analyses how this story is woven into broader scientific shifts in understandings of species, animals and animal behaviours. These shifts both inform and were/are informed by transformative political events, including slavery and colonialism, the Second World War and its aftermath, and the emergence of anti-racist movements in the twentieth and twenty-first centuries. As well as exploring the consequences of dogs' species story for dogs, then, this book also uses dogs' species story as an empirical prism through which to refract a number of pressing topics pertaining to animals, and to how animals and animal behaviours are understood, in the animal sciences.

Animal sciences

In the title of this book, I use the term 'animal sciences' as a shorthand for the scientific study of animals. This focus on science means, in practice, that I will explore broad scientific debates that span several decades and disciplines – changing conceptions of evolution and inheritance, or of the relations between evolution and behaviour, would be examples here – as well as key scientific texts on dogs, and key scientific texts that use dogs to illustrate arguments about species and animal behaviours. I pay particular attention to evolutionary theory in the nineteenth century; to the complex triad of instinct, behaviour and 'intelligence' in the first part of the twentieth century; to the 'cognitive revolution' in the second part of the twentieth century; and to the continuing unfolding of that revolution's implications in the twenty-first century. Authors addressed in detail include Charles Darwin and George Romanes; Conwy Lloyd Morgan; Konrad Lorenz; contemporary ethologists such as Marc Bekoff; and researchers associated with the 'dog paper boom' (Horowitz 2014b: vi) of the 1990s, for instance Gregory Berns, Brian Hare, Alexandra Horowitz, Ádám Miklósi and Clive Wynne.

Dog Politics offers a granular analysis of scientific texts that crystallise some of the trends, developments and ruptures in ways of thinking about dogs, as well as about animals more broadly. It puts these ways of thinking into dialogue with contemporary animal studies literatures in particular, and with social and cultural theory more generally. Inevitably, the trends, developments and ruptures it addresses were shaped in part by the growing institutionalisation and professionalisation of science in the nineteenth and early twentieth century in Europe and North America (see Chapter 3 in particular), and by the splintering of the life sciences into numerous sub-disciplines in the twentieth and twenty-first centuries. Typically, the research for this book was led to articles published in scientific journals in the fields of evolutionary biology, evolutionary anthropology, genetics, archaeology, comparative psychology, behavioural science, and classical and contemporary ethology. In the end, however, at least with regard to conceptions of 'what is a dog?', these disciplinary distinctions turned out to be of less significance, to many contemporary canine scientists, than the differences between pre- and post-1990s approaches to dogs (as discussed in Chapter 5).

My reason for focusing on science at all is because it is the principal site in which concepts of species have been, and continue to be, developed and disputed. This matters, because scientific expertise remains, today, one of the most authoritative forms of knowledge about animals. Where dogs are concerned, its authority is arguably on the rise. In her discussion of the 'increased "scientification"' (Włodarczyk 2018: 230) of contemporary dog training, Justyna Włodarczyk argues that although dog training has always been influenced by science, the training–science relationship is now especially 'intense', as illustrated by the way that scientists write specifically *for* trainers and often 'moonlight' as trainers themselves (231). 'Wherever "science" will go now, dog training will follow' (231).

The authoritative status of science, as the historian Keith Thomas and many others have demonstrated, comes at a price. Specifically, the 'revolution in perception' (Thomas 1984: 70) that was the birth of modern science was won at the expense of the marginalisation of other ways of 'knowing' animals, whether they be the ways of people who live and/or work with animals, or of people who have non-scientific and/or non-western relations with animals and the natural world. Thomas describes an eighteenth-century ostler, who, 'after failing to answer a long series of questions put to him by a gentleman about the animal in his charge', exclaims ' "Ah, sir! … considering that I have lived thirteen years in a stable, tis surprising to think how *little* I knows of a horse" ' (Thomas 1984: 80–81, emphasis in the original). This historical marginalisation of 'ordinary people' (Thomas 1984: 70) is arguably on-going, and can be similarly identified today in the unstable working conditions and low pay of the majority of people who work with animals, but who are not deemed 'professionals': agricultural workers, dog walkers, people who run kennels and day care centres, many animal trainers, groomers, volunteers in the 'animal sector' etc. (for more details, see Coulter 2016: Chapter 1). Writing with Eddie

Sweat in mind – who was 'groom to the decorated and accomplished racehorse Secretariat' and who 'died in poverty' (Coulter 2016: 26) – Lawrence Scanlan writes: '[n]o one understands [the] horse better than an astute and caring groom, and no one gets less credit' (Scanlan in Coulter 2016: 30).[5]

By way of something of a sleight of hand, the sciences have historically claimed hegemony over the study of animals on not one but two grounds. The first is that theirs is the enquiry into biological processes and into behaviours that are believed to have their origins in these processes; the second that animals are nothing much *but* an aggregation of such processes and behaviours. These claims scale up the Cartesian mind/body dualism into a divided disciplinary landscape that is informed, profoundly, by human exceptionalism. To be crude: the (animal) body and the biological sciences belong together on the one hand, and the (human) mind and the social sciences and humanities belong together on the other.[6] Yet the 'naturalness' of this division has recently become less persuasive, as scientists take as their object of study topics that were once considered proper to the domain of the social sciences and humanities, and from which, 'necessarily', animals have long been excluded. These topics include not only consciousness and reason, but also culture and sociality, deception, awareness of time and of death, emotions (including grief and psychic trauma), intentionality, agency, beliefs, perception, attention, interpretation, meaning, aesthetics, experience, creativity, memory, morality and humour. It is unclear, to me, whether the boundaries that define biology are swelling in order to absorb these new topics, or whether these topics are bringing about the collapse of those boundaries. But perhaps it does not matter. Jeffrey Bussolini, sociologist, philosopher and historian of technology, argues that recent developments in critical ethology and cognitive science (but one might now add a range of other scientific disciplines to these two) promise a 'renaissance within *every* discipline – scientific, social scientific and humanities alike' (Bussolini 2013: 188; my emphasis).

That renaissance is especially evident in the work of the European 'philosophical ethologists', as Bussolini and his colleagues dub them (Buchanan *et al.* 2014: 1), who have generously interpreted, built upon, amplified and transformed the implications of these new developments in science. Among them is Vinciane Despret, to whose work *Dog Politics* is particularly indebted (see for instance Chapter 5). Like other philosophical ethologists, Despret illustrates how '[t]here is much to be gained from a mixed-methods approach [to the study of animals] that incorporates ideas from across the traditional divides of the natural sciences, social sciences, and humanities' (Buchanan *et al.* 2014: 2). Instead of holding these disciplines apart, Despret shows how relations with science might be built without compromise, 'to produce a broader field of inquiry within which animal mind and animal behavior can be more accurately interpreted' (Bussolini 2013: 188).

Despite more than a decade of efforts on the part of Bussolini and others, most of the philosophical ethologists unfortunately remain largely unrecognised among anglophone researchers.[7] But even without their work, non-science scholars today find justifiable reasons for learning from the life sciences. For example: in his engaging review of Eduardo Kohn's (2013) *How Forests Think*, Philippe Descola proposes that, in order to take Kohn's pansemiotic approach seriously, 'a real investigation of how nonhuman life forms *actually* deal with iconic and indexical signs' is required: 'where Kohn says that he was led by the Runa to infer that an organism was interpreting a sign, we would also have liked to know what investigations on, say, animal ethology, cognition, and perception, or on biomimetism, or on plant communication, had to say about it' (Descola 2014: 272, emphasis in the original). The expertise of biologists is problematic to be sure, but as Matthew Watson argues in his critique of Thom van Dooren's (2016) article 'Authentic crows' – which he perceives as less engaged with biologists and conservationists than was Van Dooren's (2014) *Flight Ways* – philosophical concepts such as performativity or becoming, while often helpful, are not in themselves a substitute for historical and ethnographic accounts of forms of life (Watson 2016: 166).

In short, the animal sciences must be taken seriously, for several important reasons. Nevertheless, some ambivalence is arguably justified, especially in the light of the longevity of disciplinary, conceptual and methodological trajectories, and the different ways they continue to give definition to the work of scientists. Although the persistence of species concepts is an exemplary illustration of this point – as this book will demonstrate – there is arguably a broader case to be brought against the colonisation of a field by way of any single concept or small cluster of concepts. (This is as relevant to social science and humanities scholarship as it is to science, which is in part why the promise of a multidisciplinary renaissance is so compelling). I make that broader case now by reflecting on the classical ethologist Konrad Lorenz's 'chronic preoccupation' (Kalikow 2020) with species, a preoccupation that probably contributed to Lorenz's decision to join the Nazi Party. Although it might be objected that Lorenz's life choices were exceptional, this is, I think, to miss the point. The point is that his choices illustrate the potential gravity of the consequences, both intellectual and political, that can follow from the pursuit of a restricted conceptual repertoire.

Lorenz's species thinking

The darker side of Lorenz's aversion to analysing the developmental aspects of behaviour – an aversion that I will address in Chapter 3 of this book – can be identified in his 'chronic preoccupation' (Kalikow 2020: 267) not merely with instincts but, more specifically, with the degeneration of instincts by way of domestication in animals and civilisation in humans. Informed perhaps by his early training in comparative anatomy, Lorenz identified what he believed was a 'homology between characteristics that animals have acquired during domestication and that humans have acquired through civilizing processes' (Benvegnú 2018: 5). Lorenz found a receptive audience for his preoccupation with degeneration in the Nationalsozialistische Deutsche Arbeiterpartei (NSDAP), of which he was a voluntary member. 'There can be no denying', the historian Richard Burkhardt writes, 'that [Lorenz] claimed on numerous occasions that his research and ideas on animal behavior had a contribution to make to the race-political aims of the Third Reich' (Burkhardt 2005: 232). Nor can there be any denying Lorenz's enthusiasm for the *Anschluss* in and of itself, quite apart from the professional opportunities it promised. Nor that Lorenz worked for the Office for Race Policy in 1942, where he contributed to an assessment of the offspring of 877 mixed Polish–German couples. Some of those offspring, on the basis of that assessment, were sent to concentration camps; others were assigned to forced

Germanisation. '[*I*]*nvirent* types', Lorenz wrote, 'threaten to penetrate the body of a people like the cells of a malignant tumor' (Lorenz in Burkhardt 2005: 244, emphasis in the original). Numerous scholars of science have since struggled with how to understand Lorenz's legacy. Boria Sax, for example, has argued that the connection between Lorenz's work and Nazi ideology tars the entirety of ethology, such that the history of the discipline – and indeed of all animal psychology – should be subject to reassessment, and its contemporary theories regarded with suspicion (Sax 1997).[8] On the other hand, Theodora Kalikow, who has been researching Lorenz's life and work since 1970, argues that it is 'too simple to dismiss Lorenz as "always a Nazi"' (Kalikow 2020: 271). Lorenz, she argues, was an opportunist who would attach his views on degeneration to whatever ideology was relevant in the moment: to fascism in the 1930s and 1940s; to antifascism as a prisoner of war in a Russian camp in the late 1940s;[9] to anti-capitalism in his book *On Aggression* (2002c [1963]) in the 1960s; to 'environmental stewardship' (Kalikow 2020: 271) in the 1980s. One might add psychoanalysis to this list. Marga Vicedo argues that Lorenz 'relied on his recognized scientific expertise to identify the mother as a main cause of degeneration … After World War II, it was no longer acceptable to blame morons for the degeneration of the race; but it was acceptable to blame mothers' (Vicedo 2009: 290). The point, in short, is that Lorenz was more firmly committed to the concept of degeneration than he was to Nazism *per se* (Kalikow 2020: 271).

But Lorenz's commitment to degeneration was surely tied up with his commitment to species – was possibly, even, a consequence of it. Degeneration, for Lorenz, is a cultural and/or genetic slide away, on account of the relaxation of natural selection, from – what? Arguably, from the best or some better way of being or embodying a species that, for Lorenz, was nearly always more 'natural' or more 'wild'. As I will discuss in Chapter 3, 'keeping animals' was illuminating to Lorenz because he believed that, under kept conditions, inherited species behavioural structures underwent 'abnormal' changes, or did not manifest at all. In his earlier work, Lorenz associated these 'abnormalities' with an animal's individual experience of captivity or ill health (Burkhardt 2005: 141). Later, he would associate them with 'the degenerative effects of domestication' (Burkhardt 2005: 142). In whatever sphere of life it occurs (politics, environmental degradation, mothering), degeneration, for Lorenz, always leads to extinction (the extinction of a species). Thus, despite the wide diversity of subjects to which Lorenz pinned the relevance of degeneration, the concept of species appears to be integral to them all.

Given Lorenz's views on the odious implications of domestication, one might expect him to identify dogs as the most degenerate animals of all. Yet when Lorenz writes that '[t]here is no domestic animal which has so radically altered its whole way of living, indeed its whole sphere of interests, that has become domestic in so true a sense as the dog' (Lorenz 2002b [1949]: ix), he writes admiringly. 'The most highly domesticated dogs', said Lorenz in *Man Meets Dog*, 'are generally the most free and adaptable in their behaviour' (Lorenz 2002b [1949]: 128). Lorenz's positive assessment of dogs' adaptability is unusual in his work. More commonly, Kalikow writes, Lorenz considered 'departures from the "pure" wild animal forms in domesticated animals only as degeneration and symptoms of decline; hardly ever, as Charles Otis Whitman and others had observed, as openings for creative new adaptations or novel opportunities for learning' (Kalikow 2020: 270).

Nevertheless, even if *Man Meets Dog* (2002a [1949]) – one of the best known of Lorenz's popular books – is exceptional with regard to Lorenz's position on the relationship between domestication and degeneration, Lorenz's clear preference for what he called 'Lupus dogs' introduces a chilling ambiguity to the book. In both *Man Meets Dog* and *King Solomon's Ring* (2002a [1949]), Lorenz identified two types of modern domesticated dogs, which he suggests are descended from two different ancestors: the golden jackal (*Canis aureus*) and the northern wolf (*Canis lupus*) (Lorenz 2002b [1949]: 1–18; Lorenz 2002a [1949]: 108–121). The descendants of *Canis aureus*, Lorenz argued, are the more 'intelligent', 'faithful' and conversable type of dog. '[B]ut for my own personal taste, all these dogs have lost too much of the primitive nature of the beast of prey. Owing to their extraordinary "humanness" they lack that charm of the natural which characterizes my wild "wolves"' (Lorenz 2002b [1949]: 130). It was Lorenz's belief 'that humans [perceive] wild forms as beautiful and domestic forms as ugly' (Burkhardt 2005: 250). He sought to illustrate this claim, in an article entitled 'Domestication-caused disruptions of species-specific behavior', by presenting 'pairs of pictures contrasting the wild forms with their domestic counterpart' (Burkhardt 2005: 250–251). In his correspondence with the biologist and ethologist Oskar Heinroth about the paper, Lorenz reported that he was planning to place an image of a wolf next to one of a pug. ' "Or should I take the bulldog?" ... "Stop! I'll take the Pekinese!" ' (Lorenz in Burkhardt 2005: 251). Although Heinroth disputed that this is how humans perceive wild and domesticated forms, Lorenz went ahead and, in the end, included thirty-five pictures or drawings in his article.[10]

Better or worse fidelity to an ideal species identity was profoundly racialised in Lorenz's work. As noted above, in Lorenz's view, as in the Nazi view, the 'better way' was the wild and natural way, which is why city people came under particular attack. 'Natural' was also more 'pure', which is why 'racial mixing' was identified by Lorenz as mutagenic (Kalikow 2020: 268). It is relevant in this context that the Nazis argued that Jewish people were not a people at all, not a 'distinct race, since they were allegedly so mixed that they had lost any primordial identity', nor were they considered to be 'integrated into any sort of landscape (biotic community or *organische Lebensgemeinschaft*)' (Sax 1997: 13). Behind the deportations and genocides of the Holocaust lay the Nazi basic unit of analysis: not the individual, which they scorned for being bourgeois, but the species, the breed, the race, the *Volk*.

It is surprising to learn, in view of contemporary scholarship, that Lorenz's *On Aggression* was one of Primo Levi's 'favourite readings' (Benvegnú 2018: 4) and that Levi cited it in an essay in support of his theory that 'racial intolerance has long-lost origins that are not only pre-historic, but pre-human' (Levi in Benvegnú 2018: 4). This suggests that Levi, who was suspicious toward 'intellectuals who had had any kind of official involvement with the Nazi regime', probably did not know of Lorenz's history (Benvegnú 2018: 5). Levi drew particularly, in his essay, on Lorenz's chapter on rats, as he did in an interview in 1981, where he commented 'that what Lorenz tells about aggression among different tribes of rats … is appalling, in conclusion it is the gas chambers' (Levi in Benvegnú 2018: 5).

Perhaps the rats chapter in *On Aggression* was significant to Levi because it offers the clearest example of what Lorenz calls ' "evil" in the real sense of the word' (Lorenz 2002c [1963]: 152).

His description here is striking, because *On Aggression* was expressly intended to dispute what Lorenz identified as the 'classic psychoanaly[tic]' conception of aggression as 'a diabolical, destructive principle' (44). In opposition to this principle, he sought to account for aggression either in terms of a species-preserving instinct (such as the even distribution of animals over a territory, selection for the strongest or brood defence (Lorenz 2002c [1963]: Chapter 3)), or in terms of an aggressive drive becoming 'derailed under conditions of civilisation' (27) (intraspecific competition between humans under commercial conditions would be an example here (38–39, 237)). Since rat 'tribe' aggression falls into neither of these two categories, and since Lorenz admits that he cannot identify any other external selection factor that could explain it, he concludes that 'it is quite possible that the group hate between rat-clans is really a diabolical invention which serves no good purpose' (158).

The appeal of this analysis to Levi is understandable. So horrific was Nazi racism and its consequences that it obliged Levi to cast his net widely for an origin of or explanation for it. For me, however, the fact that 'evil' is Lorenz's only answer to behaviour, when behaviour cannot be answered for by species, is indicative of how restricted and restrictive Lorenz's thinking had become, and how dysfunctional. Critiques of Lorenz most often focus, rightly, on the *kinds* of concepts he deployed, and the *kinds* of arguments he made. Also significant, however, as I noted earlier, is their *narrowness*. I take the title of this introduction, 'Senta's howl', from an anecdote told by Lorenz in *Man Meets Dog* (Lorenz 2002b [1949]: 124). Senta was Lorenz's own dog, and the 'long wolf-like howl' (124) she sounded concludes one of Lorenz's experiments, in which he 'planted' a dingo pup into Senta's litter and then watched as Senta battled with what he describes as the conflict between the 'brood-tending instinct' and the 'brood-defence instinct'. I will return to Senta's howl in Chapter 3. For now, I ask it to stand as both a protest and a caution. As a protest and a caution against reductionism, against single-concept explanations (instincts, species), and against the imperialistic assumption that animals' behaviours can be explained by any single discipline or field. After all, to suggest – as Lorenz did – that just one concept, or just a handful of concepts, or just one discipline, or just one field, could ever answer for *human* life, would be nothing less than a moral outrage.

Studies of and with animals

What can be done to avert the colonisation of a discipline or set of disciplines by a single concept, or a bundle of related concepts? The breadth and depth of a mature discipline[11] may ward against this to some degree. But a single discipline, no matter how broad and deep it is, cannot suffice in itself against conceptual reductionism, in part on account of 'the fact', as Cary Wolfe writes, 'that (by definition) *no* discourse, no discipline, can make transparent the conditions of its own observations' (Wolfe 2010: 116, emphasis in the original). In a commemorative special issue of *Animal Biology* on Nikolaas Tinbergen's famous 'four questions' paper (Tinbergen 2005 [1963]), entitled 'Four decades on from the "four questions"', the zoologist Aubrey Manning wrote: '[e]thology's enormous contribution was to reawaken the serious study of any animal behaviour, taking into account the selection pressures imposed by the environment in which it has evolved. In this sense it continues to dominate animal behaviour studies; we are all ethologists now' (Manning 2005: 289). I have to disagree. When it comes to research with animals, we are not all ethologists now, and nor, more importantly, should we be.

'Ethology is at work', Jocelyn Porcher and Tiphaine Schmitt write, 'where sociology would do better' (Porcher and Schmitt 2012: 56). Porcher makes this statement in the context of her analysis of cow labour and, for sure, the questions raised by her research – 'Do cows have a subjective interest in work? Does work enhance their sensibility, their intelligence, and their capacity to experience life? Can cows derive from work what humans derive from it?' (Porcher and Schmitt 2012: 56) – benefit from the insights of a discipline (sociology) that has long investigated and analysed experiences of work and the social, political and affective forces that organise work. But much of the productive direction of Porcher's research, as Porcher herself would be the first to admit, was shaped by the farmers themselves (Despret 2008), whose knowledges are among those that have been marginalised throughout the history of the natural and life sciences. And it was shaped also by the cows, whose species story differs from that of dogs, and whose contribution, therefore, is specific to their modes of becoming 'cow' (see Chapter 4). All these knowledges – of ethology *and* sociology *and* farmers *and* this group of cows *and* ... – are arguably necessary to avert the perilous consequences that potentially follow from an unyielding commitment to an overly narrow conceptual (and methodological) framework. Together, in part *because* they are potentially competing, conflicting and contradictory, these 'knowledges' can do more than expose each other's conditions of possibility. They can also invent the 'problem' they are addressing differently (Motamedi Fraser 2012). In this book, the problem is species thinking.

At the beginning of the twentieth century, Burkhardt writes, '[i]t was highly plausible to claim a role for the study of animal lives and behavior within the broader whole of the life sciences, but exactly where such work would fit – be it epistemologically, methodologically, or institutionally – was by no means a foregone conclusion' (Burkhardt 2005: 3). Today, as I have already indicated, it is not *quite* as plausible, or obvious, that the life sciences, and biology in particular, are the only or the proper home for the study of animals and animal behaviours. To be clear: I am not opposed to the scientific study of animals. On the contrary, I welcome it. The issue is rather the domination of the study of animals by scientists, which often excludes alternative conceptions of and relations with animals. The story of dogs' becoming, with its real-life implications for dogs – which is the focus of this book – illustrates the harsh consequences that often flow from such exclusion, in practice.

There are alternative traditions in science – minor traditions – to draw on. The work of Charles H. Turner (1865–1923), the first African American to publish in the journal *Science* (Abramson 2009: 346), was distinguished by its focus on individual insects who do not follow species scripts. 'Psychological notes upon the gallery spider', published in 1892 in *Journal of Comparative Neurology*, is an entrancing read (Turner 1892). In it, the twenty-five-year-old Turner, who had only just, in that same year, received his M.Sc. from the University of Cincinnati, describes thirty-six instances of spiders building webs under natural conditions and in controlled experiments of his own devising. In the article, Turner illustrates that '[u]nder the same external conditions, individuals of the same species construct dissimilar webs' and 'that under the same external conditions the same individual constructs webs that are quite different' (Turner 1892: 109). 'Was this web', Turner asks again and again, 'the result of blind instinct? I think not' (96).

One explanation for Turner's obscurity is that he was ahead of time – more than a century ahead – with regard to scientific thinking on animal cognition, emotions and intentionality. Despite his momentous achievements – including sixty-seven scientific papers, many of which were cited by luminaries such as Edward Thorndike, John Broadus Watson, Margaret Washburn, Theodore C. Schneirla and Karl von Frisch (Abramson 2009: 347; Dona and Chittka 2020: 530) – Turner never secured a professorship in a major university. Instead, as William E. B. Du Bois rightly laments, he 'died in a high school of neglect and overwork' (Du Bois in Abramson 2009: 248). A fuller explanation, therefore, might be that Turner was ahead of his time because the racist discrimination he faced prevented him from *shaping* his time, and from creating a different kind of inheritance (Despret 2015b) for future animal investigators. Where would an inheritance, bequeathed by an entomologist who disputes that species scripts can answer for individual animal behaviours, lead?

Chapter outlines

The remainder of this introduction outlines the contents of the book, chapter by chapter. These chapters can be read independently of each other. Together, however, they deepen the argument of *Dog Politics*, which is to be found in the book as a whole. Chapter 1 opens with a brief discussion of the elision of dog 'intelligence' with dog obedience to humans. It situates this elision in the context of a long European history in which the perception of dogs as useful animals had a part to play in colonial 'civilising' projects and, relatedly, in the development of scientific racism. But then I ask: are we not done with obedience today? Drawing on Justyna Włodarczyk's research on 'affirmative biopolitics' in contemporary dog training – in which 'having fun' and 'dog happiness' apparently mark a new and more positive chapter in dog–human relations – I suggest, somewhat counterintuitively, that the answer to this question is no.

This sets the scene for the major part of the discussion in Chapter 1, which is intended as a first step toward the de-naturalisation of dogs' species story. Drawing on research by canine scientists and canine behavioural professionals – with a methodological comment on my use of this research in this chapter – my focus here will lie on the considerable and not always successful efforts that are required, on the parts of both humans and dogs, to ensure that dogs' 'destiny' (with humans) is realised. I do this by way of an analysis of dog socialisation (its origins, its 'deity' status, its complexity) and the consequences of the failure of socialisation for dogs (dogs' so-called 'behavioural problems'). The troubles that were seen to have pursued the cohort of dogs who were born and raised during the COVID-19 pandemic (2019–2023) – the so-called 'pandemic puppies' – should not, I argue, be considered exceptional; rather, they shine an exceptionally bright light on the routine intolerability that characterises the conditions under which many domesticated dogs live in the Global North. Finally, I also address in this chapter the roles played by canine behavioural professionals in highlighting, mediating and sometimes repairing the gap between the widespread 'fascination' (Włodarczyk 2018: 231) with dogs, and how dogs live in practice.

Chapter 2 turns to dogs' species story itself. This is the story of 'how dogs became dogs' as it is understood, discussed and debated in the fields of genetics, archaeology, behavioural ecology and canine science. One of the most significant elements of this story concerns the relation between dog speciation and dog domestication. Did dogs become dogs *before* they were domesticated? Or did dogs become dogs *by way of* domestication? The answer to this question is important because, if it is the latter – and most scientists favour the latter explanation – then this is a story that conflates speciation with domestication and, in that gesture, installs humans at the very heart of the evolutionary becoming of dogs. But is it true? Chapter 2 is an interrogation of how proof of dog speciation/domestication is established, what evidence exists to support it, and what role dogs themselves play in disrupting it. In all, the aim of this chapter is to illustrate that dogs' species story is told with unwarranted confidence. But it is also to demonstrate, importantly, that it is a story that wields substantial power, authority and influence.

It is worth noting also that Chapter 2 is bookended by two interrelated topics that are important to *Dog Politics*: time, and the relations between species and 'race'. Chapter 2 begins with a discussion of why Darwin's theory of evolution – or rather, why Darwin's presentation of his theory to his Victorian public, which greatly relied on dogs – lends itself to such confusion with regard to the evolutionary relations between species (to the relations between, for example, dogs and wolves). Part of the answer, as I will illustrate, lies in the difficult-to-grasp distinction between evolution as processes that occur *over* time, and evolution as the product *of* time. In Chapter 6, I return to examine the significance of this distinction in detail, as it shapes both historical and contemporary conceptions of, and analyses of the relations between, species and 'race'. My discussion at the end of Chapter 2 is preliminary to this. It illustrates how easily (if not how inevitably) species and 'race' can be conflated, when the different temporal scales of biological speciation and political racialisation are not available to distinguish them. This is what happens in Raymond and Lorna Coppinger's (2016) theory of dog speciation, in which the identities and durations of species and of 'race' are rendered equivalent by the ecological niche.

One of the reasons why it is important to unpack dogs' species story in all its dimensions – empirical, theoretical, methodological, political, ethical etc. – is that, like all species stories, it plays an important role in explaining dog behaviours *today*. Conversely, 'the ways dogs behave today' is often used to fine-tune and firm up their species story. Chapter 3 thus addresses some of the ways that species identities and behaviours come to be connected to each other in science, and with what implications for animals as individuals. Since this connection is usually understood to be generic (all species identities and behaviours are linked in this or that way), I use dogs here only by way of example. The chapter explores three foundational traditions in the scientific study of animals: classical ethology; comparative psychology; and 'anecdotalism', which, although associated with Charles Darwin and Georges Romanes, continues to trouble contemporary canine science and, in particular, contemporary canine ethology. In some ways, these traditions could not be more different from each other. I will be touching, for example, on some of the postwar political conflicts between classical ethology and comparative psychology, conflicts that informed and were informed by their differing conceptions of the species–behaviour relation. As for anecdotalism: so different is it from every other school of thinking, one might imagine that it stands outside science altogether. But this is precisely my point in Chapter 3: despite the rifts that apparently separate their theories, methodologies and politics, these traditions are united in at least one thing, which is their reliance on species as the final explanation of animal behaviour, and their subsequent transformation of individual animals into species ambassadors.

Chapter 4 returns me to the particularity of dogs' species story. Having addressed, in Chapter 2, how scientists debate this story among themselves, and, in Chapter 3, some of the nuances of the species–behaviour relation, I bring these analyses together to examine what happens when scientists take their positions on dogs out into the public domain. My focus in the first part of Chapter 4 is on two popular science books: *The Genius of Dogs: Discovering the Unique Intelligence of Man's Best Friend* (Hare and Woods 2020a), co-authored by Vanessa Woods and the evolutionary anthropologist Brian Hare (who is credited with being among those scientists who, in the late 1990s, kickstarted the contemporary interest in canine research), and *Dog Is Love: The Science of Why and How Your Dog Loves You* (Wynne 2020a), by the behaviourist Clive Wynne. These books – both of which are representative of a genre – are important because they give flesh to the abstract debates that characterise scientific accounts of dog speciation and, in doing so, expatiate their implications for dogs in practice. As well as addressing the empirical implications that follow for dogs, this chapter also interrogates their political consequences.

Chief among those consequences is that dogs' labour for and with humans, a labour that includes companionship, is rendered entirely 'natural'. Not the work itself – hardly 'natural', to seek out an explosive – but the *being* with humans: this is natural, so natural that the significance of what, specifically, a dog is *doing* with humans all but dissolves. Rather than describe dogs' labour as 'work without a subject', therefore – which is Jocelyn Porcher's description of labour that is wrongly seen to be instinctive – I will argue that dogs are 'subjects without work'. Although I draw on Porcher's theory of animal labour to make this case and to explore its implications, the particularity of dogs' species story, as it is described for example by the scientists I explore in the first half of this chapter, also forces me to critique it, and to critique Porcher's implicit assumption that her account of labour applies equally to all domesticated animals. Animals are made into species differently. The distinct story by which dogs are made into species – and ascribed particular characteristics (the propensity to 'bond'), skills ('genius communication') and needs ('love') – transforms, in my view negatively, the meaning of the human–animal 'link' that Porcher claims gives value to the labour of domesticated animals. How, for dogs, can 'the link' that is established through work be a *route* into a 'second nature' when their species story defines that link/bond as the very *essence* of their nature? Debates about animal labour are complex and multifaceted, as the conclusion of this chapter acknowledges. I note here that while labour, in my view, cannot and should not wholly define the relations between humans and domesticated animals, as Porcher proposes, it can offer some useful insights into how the lives of domesticated animals are organised. Attention to the *time* of labour in particular, I suggest, is especially helpful with regard to understanding the lives of dogs, who often spend a lifetime servicing 'the bond'.

Previous chapters have addressed the serious trouble that dogs' species story makes for dogs. In Chapter 5, I turn to the trouble that the story makes for scientists – for the very scientists who are writing it. Dogs' evolutionary, genetic and social 'convergence' with humans, the zoologist James Serpell writes, places 'the dog in an unusual position relative to other animals' (Serpell 2017: 302). One site where this 'convergence' makes a difference, according to canine scientists, is in canine science itself. For 'the bond' is unquestionably compromising in numerous kinds of ways. It is a problem to see dogs as 'outside' nature, for instance, but it is equally a problem to see human social life as the 'natural' environment for dogs. The formation of dog–researcher relationships has consequences for research, but so does evading such relationships. And so on. In Chapter 5 I move back and forth between the methodological problems raised by scientific research with dogs – regarding, for example, what kinds of generalisable claims are possible, given that 'bonds' are in practice usually specific and relational – and Vinciane Despret's model of 'polite' research. I do so because polite research similarly addresses itself (albeit for different reasons) to the roles that *particular* social and non-social relations play in enabling or not the capabilities and characteristics of an animal research subject. One question above all motivates this discussion: how do these methodological debates contribute to strengthening or undoing dogs' species story?

Dogs' species story raises methodological issues not only for those scientists who are committed to it, but also for those who oppose it. In the second part of the chapter, I analyse what methodological implications follow from the efforts of bioethicist Jessica Pierce and ethologist Marc Bekoff to distance themselves from any biological category or concept that leads to generalisations about dogs, including the generalisation that dogs cannot be understood without reference to humans. In place of generalisation, and like Despret, Pierce and Bekoff rarely fail to foreground the scientific significance of particularity. But where, for Pierce and Bekoff, particularity assumes the form of a particular, non-relational, individual, for Despret, the form of the individual is the product of a particular apparatus, and its relations. Where do these seemingly irreconcilable positions leave dogs? The third part of this chapter finds, in the space between an uncritical conception of individuality on the one hand, and intersubjectivity on the other, another figure of methodological significance: not the individual subject whose capabilities are independent of the research apparatus, nor the relational subject whose capabilities are defined by the apparatus, but rather a minimal individual whose importance lies less in any capability or characteristic at all, and more in an irreducible singularity that is itself a form of 'resistance' to scientific experimentation and explanation. I illustrate this argument, and ask what broader conclusions might issue from it for dogs' species story, through an analysis of Martin Seligman's controversial 'learned helplessness' experiments, which are tragically illuminating precisely on account of their cruelty.

Chapters 1 through 5 refer to the concept of species without attempting to define it. In the final analysis chapter in this book, Chapter 6, I address species concepts directly, and therefore also concepts of 'race'. As many theorists have illustrated, species and 'race' have been historically, and are today, bound up in each other. This chapter explores how changing notions of species and of 'race' in science shape the forms and directions that the prejudicial exchanges between them will take. The advent of population thinking is especially significant here, I will argue, because although population thinking could, potentially, have transformed the meaning of the categories of both species and 'race', in the event it did not. Instead, population thinking contributed to the de-biologisation and politicisation of 'race,' and to the contraction of its temporality to the specific durations of forms of racialisation and racism. Species, by contrast, continues today to languish almost wholly in biology, and in the yawning time of evolutionary change. One consequence is that species (especially zoological species) appear to be effectively 'fixed'.

In Chapter 6, I twice excavate the political significance of these contemporary differences between species and 'race'. First, by way of a critical analysis of two readings of Darwin's famous parasol anecdote, which describes 'the behaviour of a dog on a sunny afternoon' (Chidester 2009: 64). These readings are illuminating on account of their worryingly optimistic conclusions – or more specifically, on account of the *reason* for their optimism, which is possible only because the authors fail to appreciate the implications of the different ways that species and 'race', and especially the temporal relations between them, were conceived of in the nineteenth century, as compared to how they are conceived of today. Second, I ask how the consequences of these contemporary differences bear on a specific group of dogs, a group of pit bull types, which has been much discussed in animal studies literature, and in the public domain more broadly. This is the Michael Vick dog fighting controversy.

As well as demonstrating the violent real-life repercussions of the traffic between racism and speciesism for humans and for dogs (as they both overlap and differ), my discussion in this chapter represents the beginning of an answer to a question that has thus far lain silent in this book: if species categories erase the relevance of particularity, by what routes are animals enabled to 'recover' it? Drawing on Foucault's analysis of racist biopower, I argue that the racialisation of pit bull types as 'black' (Kim 2015) and as 'white' (Weaver 2021) represent a rebarbative individuation and individualisation, respectively, of them. What is significant here is that, either way, the dogs are reconstituted as individual constituents of a population – of a population of dangerous dogs or, alternatively, of a population of dogs at risk of an unjust death. This change of assignment (from species to populations, or, more accurately, to populations as well as to species) serves to lift these dogs out of the 'deathlessness' of species and to confer on them the 'privilege' of a death that either counts, or matters. I should record here that this argument is not intended to replace ostensibly fixed biological species with temporary and contingent politicised populations (as I discuss in Chapter 7). Rather, it is an attempt to better illuminate, by way of the contrast between them, how species categories operate in practice, and with what implications for animals.

The concluding chapter of *Dog Politics* reflects on the core themes and issues raised by the book as a whole. It pivots around Lynda Birke's question, posed in her article 'Naming names – or, what's in it for the animals?' (Birke 2009), as to what animals have to gain from animal studies research. My own answer begins by returning, once again, to the individual. What exactly, I ask, is problematic about this figure in animal studies, and in social and cultural theory more broadly? What is problematic about it for humans, and what for animals? What alternatives are available? In keeping with the subject of this book, I confine my discussion of these questions to the individual as it is understood, by social scientists, to have been constituted or dismantled in and through science. I explore the Cartesian individual subject as the representative figure for modern science, a figure cleaved from animals, and the potential threat to that subject from the direction of evolutionary developmental biology that insists that 'we have never been individuals' (Gilbert *et al.* 2012: 336).

Challenges to biological individuality are important in themselves, and also lend force and vitality to social science understandings of 'the world' (or worlds, or worldings) in terms of becomings, relatings, entanglement etc. Nevertheless, having defined again what I consider to be at stake in the figure of the individual for animals – and why, therefore, I am loath to lose it – I find my own, less problematic, alternative both to the individual modern subject and to relational entanglement in Alfred Whitehead's concept of an enduring percipient (Whitehead 1978, 1967). The concept of an enduring percipient is especially valuable in the context of this chapter because it offers something of a 'rough guide to relevance', a guide to anticipating whether and how an event might become relevant from an individual's 'point of view'. I use this guide to return once again to Birke's question, and to ask what's in it for the animals, in these debates about the individual and relationality in the sciences and especially the social sciences. The final parts of this chapter and this book explore again how species thinking, in erasing the significance of animals as individuals, simultaneously erases a most important source of evidence of violence against them: their very 'selves', their bodies, their lives, their deaths. What then is to be done with species? I respond to this question by reflecting on the value of different ways of challenging species, and on what my own understanding of 'species stories' offers in this regard. *Dog Politics* closes, as it must, with a discussion of dogs and humans, and what the 'reconstruct[ion] [of] our relations' (Delon 2020: 172) might involve. My focus here lies on love, and on the problems human love of dogs poses for dogs.

Notes

1 In Chapter 5, I will explore the limitations and problems (especially the methodological problems) that are raised by the concentration of scientific research on these particular dogs, for scientists and more broadly.
2 Although the vast bulk of scientific research focuses on captive dogs, such dogs constitute only 15–20 per cent of the total global dog population, which probably numbers around 1 billion. See Coppinger and Coppinger (2016: Chapter 2) and Pierce and Bekoff (2021: 26–28, 168–171n) for detailed discussions of numbers of dogs in the world, and how they are counted.
3 My thanks to Alexander McMaster for giving me permission to recount his story.
4 When Haraway discusses 'companion species', she is hardly referring to companionship between two individuals of different species (!). On the contrary, for her, 'companion species' signifies '[a] bestiary of agencies, kinds of relatings, and scores of time [that] trump the imaginings of even the most baroque cosmologists' (Haraway 2003: 6).
5 This is not to suggest that 'folk expertise' (Delon 2020: 169) is necessarily better for animals than other forms of expertise. As Nicolas Delon notes, people who work with animals might not be best positioned to interpret animal signals because the work itself, with its '[s]pecific aims, values and needs', may 'shape what signals to pay attention to' (Delon 2020: 169; see also D'Souza *et al.* 2020: 108).
6 So engrained is this division that many scientists today appear not to be aware that animals are studied across numerous 'non-life-science'

disciplines. I have recently been involved in an interesting and illuminating dialogue with a well-known animal welfare behaviourist, who mentioned in passing that they had no idea that there was so much interest in animals beyond the sciences.
7 One of the reviewers of this book, for instance, noted anecdotally that few US colleagues in animal studies or anthrozoology would be familiar with their work. It is welcome news indeed, therefore, that Matthew Chrulew – who, along with Bussolini and Brett Buchanan, edited three special issues of the journal *Angelaki* on the scholarship of Despret, Dominique Lestel and Roberto Marchesini (see Buchanan *et al.* (2014) for a general introduction to this project) – is now editor of the Animalities series at Edinburgh University Press, which will soon be translating and publishing some of Despret's, Lestel's and Jocelyn Porcher's books into English (on Porcher, see especially Chapter 4 of this book).
8 In partial response to this, I think it is worth recalling that, even though Lorenz's name often appears to be synonymous with ethology (Buchanan 2008: 37), ethology cannot be reduced to Lorenz. Animal psychology flourished under National Socialism. But National Socialism was neither witness to the birth of ethology – the name was first coined in 1902 (Burkhardt 2005: 3) – nor was it the moment during which its key, enduring concepts were developed. This moment might alternatively be located in the mid-1950s, when Nikolaas Tinbergen, in rich appreciation of critiques of his and Lorenz's early work, defined ethology as '*the biological study of behaviour*' (Tinbergen 2005 [1963]: 299, emphasis in the original) and identified, in his four questions (of causation, survival value, ontogeny and evolution), what such a study would include. It is also worth noting that Karl von Frisch and Tinbergen – the two other recipients of the 1973 Nobel Prize – had very different experiences of the war (see for example Kalikow (2020): 269 on Frisch, and Burkhardt (2005): 374 on Tinbergen).
9 For a short account of Lorenz's experience of being a prisoner of war, see Sokolov and Baskin (1993).
10 This article is one of a series that Lorenz published in 1940, which scholars consider to be 'particularly noteworthy as examples of [Lorenz's] efforts to highlight the ideological value of his research' to Nazism (Burkhardt 2005: 250). Sax argues that the ideas in these articles formed the basis of Lorenz's 'popularizations' (Sax 1997: 18). Certainly, the 'before' and 'after' sketches of 'overbred' Chows that Lorenz includes in *Man Meets Dog* (Lorenz 2000b [1949]: 87) bears some testimony to this.

11 Which ethology was well on its way to becoming by the time Tinbergen wrote 'On aims and methods of ethology' in 1963. In it, Tinbergen admitted that his and Lorenz's early models of innate behaviour had been both too sweeping and too simplified, that they had not attended enough to learning, and that the study of 'causes', usually understood as internal physiological motives, had taken too much precedence over the study of survival (Tinbergen 2005 [1963]); Burkhardt 2005: 426–434).

1

It's a dog's life and there's nothing natural about it

[I]f a dog is deemed untrainable, he may find himself on 'death row'.
(Włodarczyk 2018: 233)

Everywhere domesticated dogs are found, they are stitched into human hearts. But are humans stitched into dogs' hearts? Countless celebrations of 'the dog–human bond' suggest that they are. Yet 'the bond' does not come easily. While the entirety of *Dog Politics* seeks to denaturalise, in different ways, the kernel of dogs' species story – which is that being with humans is somehow dogs' destiny – this chapter focuses specifically on the considerable *effort* that is required, on the parts of both humans and dogs, to ensure this 'destiny' is realised (with greater or lesser success). I set the scene for this discussion in the first part of this chapter, by briefly exploring changes in conceptions of dog–human relations as they are refracted through the lens of dog training. While the direction of change in theories and practices of dog training – from 'dominating' a dog, say, to positively 'encouraging' a dog – is certainly to be welcomed, my argument here will be that, as far as 'the bond' is concerned, there may not be as much difference between them as one first imagines. This is not to deny that 'bonds' can be built between some humans and some dogs under some conditions. Nevertheless, the scores and force of stories celebrating the happy naturalisation of the 'dog–human bond' can become grating in view of the reality of many dogs' lives.

Where is evidence of this reality to be found? In the second part of this chapter, I look to research published in scientific journals, and to books, articles, blogs and videos produced by behavioural professionals for each other and for dog owners, for a detailed (but not exhaustive) analysis of how dogs are coping, or not, with contemporary life in the Global North. After offering a methodological comment on my use of these texts, this second part focuses on one key issue in particular, which is human-controlled dog socialisation (from now on, 'socialisation') and the consequences that follow from inadequate socialisation ('behavioural problems').[1] Socialisation has been of keen interest to scientists since at least the 1950s and 1960s, as I will illustrate. It also, however, became a matter of considerable public concern during and following the COVID-19 pandemic (2019–2023). I close the second part of this chapter, on socialisation, with a discussion of the so-called 'pandemic puppies'. Although many have argued that this cohort of dogs is uniquely distinguished from pre- (and post-) pandemic dog populations, my own view is that striking similarities can be identified between them. My point, therefore, will not be that some dogs, such as the pandemic puppies, are inadequately socialised (although they often are), but that the pandemic puppy phenomenon illustrates how very few dogs can be socialised 'enough' to cope with the demands that are placed upon them today. The chapter concludes with a brief reflection on the insights that canine behavioural professionals, and especially dog trainers, can offer as they navigate between popular and scientific perceptions of dogs and dog–human relations, and the harsh truths of dog despair. In all, the aim of this chapter is to begin to cast doubt on the 'naturalness' of the dog–human bond by offering a pragmatic account of the work that is necessary to (try to) secure it, and the price that many dogs pay for living with it.

'Are we having fun yet?'[2]

In 1994, the psychologist Stanley Coren wrote a book called *The Intelligence of Dogs* (Coren 2006). In Chapter 10, he ranked breeds of dogs according to their 'working or obedience intelligence'. Although the chapter is one of several that measure different dog breeds against different types of intelligence, it is the working or obedience list specifically that has been widely disseminated. Even a most cursory search on Google reveals that, twenty-eight years after the original publication date of the book, numerous 'petsites' uncritically reproduce Coren's order and, moreover, extend working or obedience intelligence to 'intelligence' in general. Some established trainers, too, apparently endorse the ranking without qualification (Millan 2020). On Coren's list, Border Collies assume first position, Afghan Hounds last (Coren 2006: 182–183).

What kind of 'intelligence' is working or obedience intelligence? Coren writes:

> What [working or obedience intelligence] means is that the dogs are not simply taught tricks; rather, the specific exercises tested in the obedience ring should serve to indicate the trainability of dogs and their willingness to perform under the control of their human masters.
> (Coren 2006: 186)

The reason Coren refers to the 'obedience ring' here is because, having established the impossibility of empirically testing the requisite number of dogs to gain a scientifically valid answer to the question of breed intelligence,[3] he turned to data generated by the American Kennel Club (AKC) obedience trials. These data make a reasonable substitute, Coren argued, because the AKC obedience trials 'test exactly the same behaviors that define working and obedience intelligence' (Coren 2006: 186). On finding all the various methods of analysing the data to be flawed (186–189), Coren decided instead to base his ranking on the testimony of 199 AKC judges, who filled in a 'fairly long and complicated' questionnaire and, in 25 per cent of cases, provided additional notes. He followed this up with twenty-four telephone interviews (189).

One might object at this point that the only claim that Coren can make with confidence is this: Border Collies who are entered into AKC competitions (i.e. Border Collies who share the characteristic of being companion and/or working dogs raised and trained by guardians who hold AKC values), in the opinion of a small number of people, all of whom are guaranteed by their positions as AKC judges to posit a uniform conception of obedience, performed better against other AKC purebred dogs[4] in AKC trials when measured within constrained parameters (e.g. heel, sit, lie down, stand, stay, retrieve, high jump, broad jump etc.). The narrowness and specificity of the data on which Coren's conclusions are based, which includes the narrowness of his definition of 'intelligence', is rarely if ever mentioned on the websites that do or do not cite it. I will return to why this might be, and to why the ranking continues to be reproduced, below.

In England, dog breeds have historically served as a mark not only of social rank (Ritvo 1987; Thomas 1984; Worboys *et al.* 2018), but also of 'civilisation'. In this context, the *utility* of dogs has been key to assessments of their 'intelligence'. For example: in her analysis of the important parts played by animals in the seventeenth-century colonisation of New England and the Chesapeake colonies of Virginia and Maryland, Virginia DeJohn Anderson describes how English colonists looked down on 'Indian' dogs for, among other things, being barely tame, bred with foxes or wolves, and howling rather than barking (Anderson 2004: 34; see also Chaplin 2003: 146). These dogs 'did not sound like English dogs, and failed to act as colonists thought that dogs should' (Anderson 2004: 34). Two centuries later, John Campebell, a Scottish missionary in South Africa, would decry Boer dogs for being 'only useful as watchers':

> A shepherd's dog from Britain would have assisted us more in driving our spare cattle than a thousand African ones. It would be well if some of these were sent over to instruct African dogs to be more useful to their masters. Perhaps were the people here to witness their sagacity, they would suspect they were rational beings.
> (Campebell in Van Sittert and Swart 2008: 7)

Campebell's portrait of African dogs was unusual, Lance van Sittert and Sandra Swart write, only insofar as it was 'directed against Boers rather than Africans in this instance' (Van Sittert and Swart 2008: 7). Otherwise, it accurately reflected his more general 'contempt for the natives' want of industry, [which was] expressed through disdain for their slothful dogs' (7). Accounts of slothful if not 'lawless' dogs, no less than those of slothful if not 'lawless' people, served to rationalise and justify ' "the white man's burden" of civilizing and moralizing local "savages" ' (Suen 2015: 104).[5] As Ritvo dryly summarises it, 'the extent of canine servitude was an index of the advance of civilization' (Ritvo 1987: 20).

The issue of utility also played an important role in nineteenth-century debates about which animals were closest to humans (who were irremovably lodged at the apex of the natural kingdom). Dogs, among other animals, offered an alternative animal–human 'alliance' that served to 'displace apes from their awkward proximity'

(Ritvo 2000: 849). '[T]he issue was not simply taxonomical', Ritvo argues: '[i]n question was the more fundamental principle of whether animals should be ranked according to their utility to humankind, as literal servants or as instructive analogues, or according to some other standard' (Ritvo 1987: 35). Apes, who had been assaulting the human–animal boundary since at least 1699 (Ritvo 2000: 849), were possessed of an intelligence that was of use only to themselves (Ritvo 1987: 35). By contrast, '[a] somewhat circular calculation made the most sagacious animals the best servants. So dogs might not only rival apes in the mental competition, but surpass them – closest to their masters in mind as well as in domicile' (Ritvo 2000: 850). As I will be discussing in Chapter 6, dogs were not *the* central players in the development of nineteenth-century racist science, but they nonetheless cast as bright a light on the traffic among 'race', class and species as did chimpanzees and apes.

In view of this history, one might consider the most significant aspect of Coren's ranking to be not the particular breeds that populate it, and in what order, but the criteria that inform it. It is notable that six of the 'least intelligent' breeds – Afghan Hounds, Basenjis, Borzois, Bloodhounds, Beagles and Basset Hounds – are bred to work independently. If servitude – or some metaphor for it – undergirds the definition of intelligence, these dogs never had an AKC chance. Unlike Coren's report on the breeds that make the best guard dogs (Coren 2006: 142–143), to take just one example of his other rankings, the working or obedience rank describes and speaks most explicitly and directly to an established conception of dog–human relations: of a conception, indeed, that is entrenched historically. Of all the skills dogs have, it is their skills with humans, sometimes translated as servitude, sometimes utility, sometimes obedience, that define an 'intelligent' dog.

And yet, as Justyna Włodarczyk argues in her book *Genealogy of Obedience*, contemporary companion dog training 'bears witness to the death of obedience' (Włodarczyk 2018: 230). Behaviourism can take much of the credit for this, Włodarczyk writes, for in place of 'obedience to a human's will or the dog's natural submission', post-behaviourist trainers 'would speak of generalization of a cue; history of reinforcement, etc.' (Włodarczyk 2018: 230). In Włodarczyk's Foucauldian analysis of the genealogy of dog training in North America, B. F. Skinner's behaviourism marks the turning point between disciplinary techniques that 'mold and shape the body', and postdisciplinary 'techniques of control' that 'focus on creating motivation for the subject to behave in particular ways and not others' (Włodarczyk 2018: 155; on behaviourism, see Chapter 3 in this book). Somewhat counterintuitively – but nevertheless persuasively – Włodarczyk argues further that radical behaviourism, now largely rejected in the North American companion dog world, made possible a new, twenty-first century, 'affirmative biopolitics', in which reinforcement, the bedrock of behaviourism, is now deployed not as 'motivation for the subject to *behave* in particular ways' (Włodarczyk 2018: 155; my emphasis) but as motivation for the subject to *feel* in particular ways. Radical behaviourism, in other words, was the midwife of the change 'from discipline's focus on affecting the individual body to the postdisciplinary techniques of modulating affects' (155).

Central to this affirmative biopolitics – to 'the relocation of the activity of training from the paradigm of utility to that of affect' (Włodarczyk 2018: 207) – are two connected ideas, often portrayed as an ethics: 'fun', and the importance of dog 'happiness' (202), which is to be achieved by way of 'letting the dog be a dog' (Donaldson in Włodarczyk 2018: 200). Translated, this means not controlling a dog's instincts (as behaviourists sought to do), but rather 'understanding' and 'harnessing' them to enjoyable ends. This explains why, Włodarczyk continues, affirmative biopolitics is '[c]haracteristically ... accompanied by the emergence of numerous canine-related leisure and sports activities' (Włodarczyk 2018: 24–25). 'Play' transforms the dog–human relation from one of servitude and mastery into, apparently, a relationship of mutual engagement or 'co-becoming'. Włodarczyk cites Donna Haraway by way of example: 'both players make each other up in the flesh. Their principal task is to learn to be in the same game [agility], to learn to see each other, to move as someone new of whom neither can be alone' (Haraway in Włodarczyk 2018: 25).

But there is more to it than this. Rather than train a dog to be more 'civilized' (as discussed above) – rather than train him 'to become a bit less *zoë* and a bit more *bios*' (Włodarczyk 2018: 210) – the aim of this biopolitics is to erase '[the human/animal] boundary altogether through the affirmation of *zoë* as constitutive for *bios*' (211).

Now, owning a dog is way to own dogness itself, to 'be more dog' oneself, as Włodarczyk puts it (24). Agility is exemplary 'fun' (or *zoë*) because it captures the very essence of 'dogness': 'enthusiasm, exuberance, energy, sociability' (215). The human who participates in agility participates 'in an activity that oozes dogness' (215).

One might be somewhat suspicious of this ethics of 'fun', given that a key purpose of play in a lot of dog training literature, even while couched in the language of bonding and relationship enrichment, seems to be to introduce or further reinforce socialisation to humans (see below on socialisation) and training. Or more accurately: to introduce relationship enrichment *as* socialisation and training. Karen London and Patricia McConnell's (2008) book on play, *Play Together, Stay Together: Happy and Healthy Play between People and Dogs*, is aptly named in this regard. Clearly, 'fun' does not leave much room for thinking about how 'relations of communication are not external but immanent to relations of power' (Patton 2003: 91). It also does not leave much room for thinking about – indeed it seems to actively mitigate against thinking about – an arguably more engrained and enduring power relation that is expressed not solely in the power of humans *over* dogs (e.g. the power to define what is a game, and what is and is not positive play), but in the *assumption* that it is a dog's preference, under almost any circumstances, to be with humans. As Włodarczyk notes, '[t]he empirical research carried out on humans' motivation for participating in these events [agility etc.] reveals that humans take the dog's personal preferences into account while choosing the training activity they will both engage in' (Włodarczyk 2018: 25). Listed dog preferences are for digging holes, say, or catching balls; they are not the preference for dog–human participation itself, which is not in question.

But what if a dog's preference is *not* to participate? Or to rephrase that: does agility ooze dogness for dogs? The answer is: not always. Turid Rugaas, a Norwegian dog trainer best known for her work on canine body language and especially dogs' 'calming signals', offers the following painful example of Shiba, 'a Border Collie agility dog, [who] became slower and slower on the agility course. The owner ran around, jumped up and down, waved her arms and yelled a lot to encourage the dog. In the end, Shiba hardly moved around the agility field because she was trying so hard to calm her owner' (Rugaas 2006: 34). And this from a Border Collie who, as we know from Coren's ranking, is *the most intelligent* dog (the dog, that is, who is most responsive to humans). Arguably, the 'death of obedience' explains in part why the details of Coren's study are rarely referenced. The idea that intelligence is defined, to quote again, by dogs' 'willingness to perform under the control of their human masters', recalls an unflattering relation between dogs and humans. Yet the ranking itself continues to be reproduced, passing virtually into folklore. I conjecture that this is because, in the end, it does not matter whether the relation is one of servitude, obedience or fun, or whether its purpose is utility or affect: what matters is the so-called dog–human bond, which can be naturalised as well by 'fun' as it can by obedience.

Pause for a methodological observation

The second part of this chapter will be dedicated to exploring some of the demanding work that is required, on the parts of both dogs and humans, to produce 'the bond', and to some of the practical implications, for dogs, when their lives are shaped by expectations regarding it. As I noted in the introduction to this chapter, I draw here primarily on scientific research, and on texts produced by behavioural professionals. A word is in order, therefore, with regard to how I am approaching this material, especially given that, in the rest of this book, it will be subject to extensive critique.

Although *Dog Politics* focuses on how this body of work mostly, usually, promotes a constrained and limited 'order of becoming' to which dogs are obliged to conform, there are plenty of other reasons for criticising it: for its scientisation of knowledges of dogs, for its medicalisation of dogs' experiences, for the disingenuity of its protestations of 'care'. Moreover, as both Harlan Weaver (2021) and Katja Guenther (2020) illustrate, the 'problems' with 'problem' dogs cannot be separated from the racist, classist and heteronormative prejudices that shape perceptions of the humans with whom such dogs are often associated, as well as perceptions of their ability, or not, to provide normative standards and types of 'care' (such as socialisation), 'home' and 'family'.

Nevertheless, while this literature must rightly be criticised, especially for its endorsement of narrow and hegemonic conceptions of humans, of dogs and of human–dog relationships, when read for the 'wrong' reasons, it offers rich insight into *how* dogs are currently living with humans, by what means and at what price (for dogs). In other words, I do not believe that one has to accept the terms within which the arguments are framed, or even their diagnoses of and conclusions with regard to dogs' behaviours, to recognise the dog distress that is being documented here. This is why this material convincingly – if mostly inadvertently – illustrates the three points that I want to make in what follows. These are: that the dog–human relationship, the relationship that is deemed almost to be given in nature, in fact depends on an enormous amount of labour, especially during the early part of a dog's life; that, despite this early labour, the ability of dogs to live with or alongside humans is never fully achieved and thus requires *on-going* investment; and finally, that even with these efforts, many dogs still cannot 'adapt' themselves to human social and physical arrangements.

Socialisation

As Dinesh Wadiwel argues, 'biopolitical forms of violence' apply as much to companion animals as they do to agricultural animals. He writes:

> While companion animals are not routinely exposed to the life and death scenario of food production, the overt domination directed toward companion animals in urban societies is suggestive of different conflict zones: these sites of friction include routine controls over reproduction and sexuality; the use of forced bodily modification (such as microchipping), discipline, and training; total controls over diet, movement, living spaces, and sociality; and quite arbitrary regimes of disposability that accompany the politics of pet industries.
> (Wadiwel 2018: 541)

The experiential dimensions of this regime, for dogs, are multiple and overlapping. Lack of control over movement, for example, means that dogs are often not in a position to reject enforced modes and moments of sociality, whether with humans or dogs and other animals. Consider a most banal scenario: two women are walking at a brisk pace down a street, each with a dog on leash. The street is busy, there is a lot of activity, and the dogs are jostled by obstacles and passing people. The women are talking to each other, changing the hand in which they hold the leash as the dogs move behind them, in front of them, and then finally between them, in an attempt to find some security. Between the womens' legs, the two dogs cannot help but bump into each other. As they move along, one of them tries repeatedly to put his paw and then his jaws around the neck of the other. The other dog turns his head away, turns again, turns again, until eventually he stiffens and freezes. His owner feels his resistance through the leash and, without looking down, jerks him along.

Although it would be possible to write at length about any one of the conflict zones that Wadiwel identifies, I choose to focus on processes of socialisation (which I assume comes under Wadiwel's category 'discipline'), for two reasons. First, because socialisation plays a major role – if not *the* major role – in facilitating (or rather attempting to facilitate) the modes of living that characterise the biopolitical governance of companion and/or working dogs in the Global North. Socialisation is a demand that few dogs are in a position – biologically, behaviourally, physically or socially – to refuse and, for those who do, the consequences are likely to be deathly. Socialisation *creates* dependence in dogs and then offers them tools, often inadequate, to try to navigate it. Second, while the socialisation of dogs must rightly be criticised for being intrinsic to a broader scheme of violence, *lack* of socialisation has serious implications for individual dogs not only in terms of relinquishment and death, but also in terms of a life lived, among other things, in fear, anxiety and frustration.

Wadiwel's observation regarding biopolitical forms of violence is relevant to many kinds of companion animals. Dogs, however, bear the additional burden of the narrative of 'the bond', which not only naturalises dog–human relationships, but also transforms dogs who have justifiable problems with humans into problem dogs ('fearful dogs', 'aggressive dogs' etc.). Scientists and behavioural professionals recognise this, noting that 'problem' behaviours are often 'coping mechanisms' (Polgár et al. 2019: 9), not 'truly aberrant', but rather 'an adaptive response to an aberrant environment' (Lindsay 2001: 134; see also Lindsay 2001: 39–43). As the welfare scientists Robert Hubrecht and his colleagues argue: 'despite the dog's special status, and remarkable new research on its cognitive abilities, and genetics, the dog is still under-represented in welfare research when compared with farm animals and other species such as rodents used in research' (Hubrecht *et al.* 2017: 293). This should perhaps not be surprising. Just *being with* humans is often understood to be welfare enough (see also Chapter 7 of this book). If it isn't, the answer today is found not in the transformation of the dog–human relationship, but in more socialisation to it. Socialisation is often perceived both as the cause of 'problem' dog behaviours (bad socialisation) and the solution (good socialisation).

Dogs may or may not be born with a disposition toward humans. This is a matter of debate, which I will address in Chapters 2 and 4. Regardless of whether they are or not, the first few weeks and months of dogs' lives are seen to be crucial with regard to the socialisation of dogs to other dogs, to humans and other animals, and to some of the environments and experiences to which they will be obliged to become accustomed. Over this period, Steven Lindsay (author of the monumental three-volume *Handbook of Applied Dog Behavior and Training*) writes: 'an average puppy will probably learn more than during the remaining course of its lifetime, forming a lasting emotional and cognitive schemata of the social and physical environment' (Lindsay 2000: 35). Although there is research on conspecific socialisation – for instance: what happens if puppies are removed from the dam and the litter too soon? (Pierantoni *et al.* 2011); what happens if they are removed too late? (Jokinen *et al.* 2017) – socialisation to humans has been the subject of extensive and meticulous research.

The notion of a 'sensitive period' – or sensitive periods – can be traced to John Scott and John Fuller's (1965) classic study *Genetics and the Social Behavior of the Dog*.[6] Like other studies conducted during the 1950s and 1960s, Scott and Fuller 'sought to determine the upper and lower boundaries of early socialisation and so define the ideal period during which puppies were most sensitive to external stimuli' (McEvoy *et al.* 2022: 19). Most socialisation protocols today are based on this early research, which usually took the form of isolation experiments. This is just one reason why the 'deity status' (Overall 1997: 13) ascribed to socialisation periods is problematic: Scott and Fuller are probably the only scientists to achieve comparability across different dogs and groups of dogs on account of the conditions under which they kept their research dogs (in confinement) (Fugazza and Miklósi 2014: 184). Or, as McEvoy *et al.* explain: '[t]his means that their value in telling us what is necessary for normal development is limited as we cannot distinguish the trauma caused by isolation, from the positive effects of human exposure' (McEvoy *et al.* 2022: 21). Nevertheless, even if these developmental periods are not, after all, 'a genetically programmed timetable' (Lindsay 2000: 35), they are widely believed to provide a rough roadmap for socialisation. Today, the time frame for primary socialisation is generally considered to be between three and twelve weeks of age (McEvoy *et al.* 2022: 19) (although see below for more detail).

A veritable industry now supports and investigates these complex and fragile sensitive periods – fragile, perhaps, on account of their complexity. For example: drawing on Scott and Fuller, the veterinarian and applied animal behaviourist Karen Overall suggests that unless dogs are introduced to humans between week 5 and weeks 7–12, they are likely to be fearful of people in later life (Overall 1997: 13). This is not to suggest that dogs should not be exposed to humans before that time, only that '[t]he specified time frame ... implies that dogs are not sufficiently neurologically and behaviorally focused on people in initiate interaction with people before 5 to 7 weeks' (Overall 1997: 13). The point Overall is making here, about socialisation, is that development and growth are simultaneously biological and behavioural: the puppy needs to be exposed to stimuli at a time when it is meaningful in both these respects. This is why so much research on dogs attempts to address the question as to what constitutes too early, too late, too little or too much exposure to novel stimuli. Exposing puppies to severe fear can, during the developmental stage, enhance it (Overall 1997: 212). Socialisation programmes offer guidelines with regard to the timing of the introduction of stimuli (and what kinds of stimuli), but breeders, owners and trainers are also advised to go at the pace set by the puppy themself. Signs of hesitancy or negativity on the puppy's part indicate that a socialisation programme may need to be adapted (e.g. to go more cautiously). But then again, it is also important not to overprotect puppies, since underexposure can have seriously damaging consequences later in life, which cannot necessarily be undone (Vaterlaws-Whiteside and Hartmann 2017: 56).

The painstaking attention to detail that characterises investigations into maximally effective dog socialisation cannot be overestimated. Table 1.1, to take just one example, describes a five-week socialisation programme devised by Helen Vaterlaws-Whiteside and Amandine Hartmann (2017), who are based at the Guide Dogs National Breeding Centre in Warwickshire, England. According to this schedule, socialisation begins from week 0. Since the puppy's eyes and ears will be closed, the programme seeks to accustom puppies to the touch and smell of human contact by either holding puppies' bodies close to different materials (wool, nylon, fleece) – for thirty seconds – or stroking them gently with them (with a soft towel, a rubber glove, a child's toothbrush). Over the next four weeks, the puppy is exposed to some of the most common sounds in the human household. Visual stimulation and 'interactions with people' begin in week 2. Such interactions include restraint, which is possibly stressful. Yet stress, and its role in the socialisation process, is itself the topic of sizeable research. In her research on the socialisation of military dogs, Carmen Battaglia conducted experiments that she claims illustrate that puppies who are removed from the nest for three minutes each day during the first five to ten days of life are 'better able to withstand stress' as adults (Battaglia 2009: 203). Battaglia is building on the work of Michael Fox and others, who claim that early stress leads to 'resistance [to stress], emotional stability and improved learning ability' (Fox in Lindsay 2000: 39). Others, including Lindsay, suggest that such conclusions are conjectural (Lindsay 2000: 39).

Table 1.1 The standardised socialisation programme developed for puppies by Helen Vaterlaws-Whiteside and Amandine Hartmann. The table contains details of the stimuli applied as part of the trial socialisation programme. 'X' marks the age at application in weeks.

Theme	Stimulation activity	Weeks					
		0	1	2	3	4	5
Tactile stimuli	Velcro collar worn during socialisation session	X	X	X	X	X	X
	Puppy picked up	X	X				
	Puppy stroked gently with fingers	X	X				
	Puppy's body touched (head, body, tail, legs and paws)	X	X	X	X	X	X

Table 1.1 (Cont.)

Theme	Stimulation activity	0	1	2	3	4	5
	Puppy held close to a woollen jumper for 30 s	X	X				
	Puppy held close to a nylon T-shirt for 30 s	X	X				
	Puppy held close to fleece material for 30 s	X	X				
	Puppy's body gently stroked with a soft towel	X	X				
	Puppy's body gently stroked with a rubber glove	X	X				
	Puppy's body gently stroked with a soft child's toothbrush	X	X				
	Puppy encouraged to move over carpet			X	X	X	X
	Puppy encouraged to move over rubber matting			X	X	X	X
	Puppy encouraged to move over a reusable shopping bag				X	X	X
Auditory stimuli	Paper bag rustled gently near puppy		X				
	Plastic bag rustled gently near puppy		X				
	Keys jangled gently near puppy			X			
	Mobile ring (on lowest volume) near puppy			X	X		
	Gentle clapping near puppy				X	X	
	Mobile phone ring (on medium volume) near puppy					X	
	Rolling noisy items (e.g. filled toy) within puppy's reach, i.e. in the pen					X	X

(*continued*)

Table 1.1 (Cont.)

Theme	Stimulation activity	0	1	2	3	4	5
	Rolling noisy items out of puppy's reach, i.e. outside the pen					X	X
	Mobile ring (on standard volume) near the puppy						X
Visual stimuli	Puppy put in front of a television screen			X			
	Rolling items (e.g. ball) within puppy's reach, i.e. in the pen			X	X		
	Rolling items out of puppy's reach, i.e. outside the pen			X	X		
	Items hung above stimulation area (e.g. tinsel)			X	X	X	X
	Slowly opening and closing an umbrella in view of the puppy					X	
	Introduction of a mirror					X	
	Opening and closing an umbrella in view of the puppy						X
	Encourage exploration of mirror						X
Interaction with people	Puppy picked up and carried around kennel			X			
	Puppy stroked by hand			X			
	Puppy's ears and teeth gently examined			X	X	X	X
	One-to-one play session (soft toy and squeaky toy for a total of 3 min)			X			

Table 1.1 (Cont.)

Theme	Stimulation activity	0	1	2	3	4	5
	Puppy picked up and carried to stimulation kennel				X	X	X
	Puppy gently restrained for 5 s				X		
	One-to-one play session (soft toy, squeaky toy and tug toy for 3 min)				X	X	X
	Researcher wears a hat/sunglasses/back pack				X	X	X
	Puppy gently restrained for 15 s					X	
	Hiding a toy and encouraging the puppy to find it					X	X
	Puppy gently restrained for 20 s						X
Interaction with the environment	Puppy carried around outside (block run)				X		
	Experience concrete surface outside					X	X
	Experience grass surface outside					X	X
	Experience rubber surface outside					X	X
	Encourage puppy to climb over an obstacle					X	X
	Encourage puppy to move in and out of doorways						X
	Gently place a towel over the puppy and let it find its way out						X

Source: Vaterlaws-Whiteside and Hartmann (2017: 56).

Reading between the lines, a good part of socialisation programmes is designed to help a dog to manage their emotions, especially in the face of competing emotional demands upon them. As the veterinarian and ethologist Iben Meyer and his colleagues note, '[t]he "ideal dog" is expected to be social and friendly, both calm and energetic, and easy to train' (Meyer *et al.* 2022: 2). Above all, however, they must never be angry. In *Mine!*, a training book on resource guarding, trainer Jean Donaldson begins by reminding her reader that '[o]ur expectations of dogs are *very* high … The standard we have set for them is one we would consider absurd for any other species of animal, including ourselves. We want no aggressive behavior directed at humans, of even the most ritualized sort, at any time, over the entire course of the dog's life' (Donaldson 2002: 2, emphasis in the original). And in case her reader hasn't quite grasped the point: this is 'exactly like you … [n]ever once losing your temper' (2).

Donaldson is not suggesting that resource-guarding is not a problem. After all, it may be a symptom of a deeper unhappiness in a dog, of a mistrustful relationship between a dog and their handler, and it is also a serious welfare insult for dogs, since 'aggression' is one of the main reasons given for relinquishment. Nevertheless, what Donaldson is intimating here is that resource-guarding is perceived as a behavioural problem in part *because* dogs are not permitted to express anger (except when guarding something of value to humans that is under human threat). Given how often, during the day, an average dog experiences 'hassle' from which they cannot escape (from children; from other dogs; from owners obstructing, yanking, shouting, petting etc.), and how much time they spend in suspended dependence (waiting for food, for company, for attention, to go out, to go home, to play, to evacuate), and how curbed are their pleasures (running, sniffing, eating shit, splashing in mud, rolling in whatever-whatever etc.), it is perhaps surprising how rarely dogs react with anger (McConnell 2017: para. 4). Dogs are obliged to be 'happy', zoologist and dog trainer Patricia McConnell argues (critically), unless they are 'sad … [because] they are missing us' (McConnell 2017: para. 6).

'[B]eing left alone for many hours is something that has to be learned' (Meyer *et al.* 2022: 2). Like other things that must be learned, this is a learning that obliges dogs to reconcile at least two antithetical emotional dispositions: dependence upon humans, and the ability to tolerate potentially extensive periods of isolation from them. This gives (or should give) pause for reflection: a dog's warm welcome on the owner's return, often cited as one of the key rewards of human dog ownership, comes at a potentially high cost for the dog. A reported 5–30 per cent of dogs suffer separation anxiety, Meyer *et al.* write, but that figure, they also propose, is probably much higher, given that separation anxiety may not leave any evidence of itself, or because owners don't recognise evidence of it, or because owners don't consider it to be something that needs to be addressed (Meyer *et al.* 2022: 2).[7] As the behaviourist Suzanne Clothier notes, owners are more likely to identify and attend to a dog's physical discomfort and pain than they are to their cognitive and emotional distress (Clothier 2018; Young 2003: 76). Similarly, Hubrecht, Wickens and Kirkwood argue that '[p]eople are far more likely to see behaviors that directly affect humans, such as aggression, as severe and problematic compared to those that primarily affect the dog, such as fearfulness' (Hubrecht *et al.* 2017: 279). Fearful dogs receive less help (Hubrecht *et al.* 2017: 279).

What is the purpose of the science of socialisation? For humans, one of the main aims of this body of research appears to be predictive: how can we predict which puppies are likely to grow into adult dogs who will meet the criteria for, say, laboratory research (Boxall *et al.* 2004), military work (Battaglia 2009), assistance work (Mai *et al.* 2021) or companion work (Dietz *et al.* 2018)? Economic considerations are at least as important as, if not more important than, the welfare of the dog (e.g. Berns *et al.* 2017). In the domestic setting, the purpose is largely to avoid owner-assessed 'intolerable' dog behaviours that potentially lead to relinquishment and euthanasia. On-going 'canine behaviour problems' are one of the main reasons why 3.3 million dogs in the USA are relinquished each year, nearly one-quarter of whom (670,000 dogs) are euthanised (Dinwoodie *et al.* 2019: 63). Yet what dog, Meyer *et al.* ask, can tolerate the conditions under which they are required to live? (Meyer *et al.* 2022: 3).

What indeed becomes of the dog who is *not* 'socialised' (enough)? Fear looms large (Puurunen 2020). In evolutionary terms, fear is understood to have 'direct fitness consequences' (Wheat *et al.*

2019). Which is to say that an animal (including a human) who does not experience fear may not be able to anticipate or recognise danger and risk. Becoming less afraid of humans is often seen as a marker of domestication; it is itself an 'evolutionary pressure' (Meyer *et al.* 2022: 2; see Chapter 2 of this book). Yet it appears that a lot of dogs are afraid a lot of the time. In her book on treating fear in dogs, canine behaviour specialist Nicole Wilde begins by establishing a spectrum of fears. She classifies object-specific fear, for example, as 'moderate'. What does object-specific fear include? Among other fears, it may include fear of objects (e.g. sunglasses) and individuals (e.g. children), of a particular kind of motion (e.g. the car), of a particular environment (e.g. the vet), of strangers, of dogs, of separation or of touch (e.g. brushing and grooming); and non-social fears (e.g. fear of loud noises such as thunder, or fear of novel objects, surfaces, heights etc.). What does fear in a dog look like? Wilde provides a chart (Table 1.2).

Positive exposure to an enriched environment is not in itself a guarantee that a dog will not become fearful either when they are a puppy or later in life. As well as lack of adequate socialisation

Table 1.2 'The face of fear'.

Common audible signals	Common visible signals	Miscellaneous subtle signals
whining	dilated pupils	sweaty paw pads
whimpering	tensed muscles	shedding fur/dandruff
growling	trembling	'clingy'/leaning on owner
barking	pacing	restlessness/hyperactivity
howling	extreme salivation/	vigilantly scans environment
screaming	drooling *or*	shallow breathing or panting
	decreased salivation	'shaking off' (as if wet)
	rapid or very slow	stretching
	blinking	moving very slowly
	yawning	

Extreme anal sac expression, loss of bladder/sphincter control, vomiting

Source: Wilde (2006: 17).

and/or lack of on-going socialisation, other causes of fear include abuse, trauma and medical illness. Fear can also be idiopathic. Or it may be genetic (i.e. it may be heritable). Since the genomic sequencing of a purebred Boxer, Tasha, in 2004, the evolutionary convergence between dogs and humans has been understood to pertain not solely to behaviours (see Chapters 2, 4 and 5), but also to physiology, disease, disease presentation and clinical response.[8] So it is that fearful Pointers have been bred as a model for human anxiety disorders (Serpell *et al.* 2017: 107). Fear is reinforcing: a successful coping strategy (successful from the dog's point of view) is likely to be repeated. A behaviour that was once performed defensively, such as a posture or bark, can morph and even escalate into something that looks like 'aggression' (Wilde 2006: Chapter 1; Bradshaw and Rooney 2017: 139).

In a recent study, behaviour 'problems' were identified by Finnish owners in more than 85 per cent of 4,114 dogs (Dinwoodie *et al.* 2019: 67).[9] This study explicitly excluded owners who were motivated to participate because they believed their dog had a behaviour problem (63). The 'problem' behaviours identified were: 'fear/anxiety, aggression, jumping, excessive barking, coprophagia, obsessive-compulsive/compulsive behaviors, house soiling, rolling in repulsive materials, overactivity/hyperactivity, destructive behavior, running away/escaping, and mounting/humping' (Dinwoodie *et al.* 2019: 64).[10] The study is interesting because its aim was to investigate comorbidity, and startling because nearly every behaviour on the list was associated with fear and/or anxiety. One routine scientific response to this is to insist on more socialisation. Socialisation, recognised to be of singular importance during a puppy's developmental period, is now considered to be significant throughout a dog's life:

> The term 'enrichment' has come to mean the positive sum of experiences that have a cumulative effect on the individual. Enrichment experiences typically involve exposure to a wide variety of interesting, novel and exciting experiences with regular opportunities to freely investigate, manipulate, and interact with humans and other species. In many respects enrichment is an extension of socialization and lasts a lifetime.
>
> (Battaglia 2009: 209)

Socialisation, in short, is never finished, as studies exploring the negative effects of kennelling on already socialised dogs demonstrate especially well (e.g. Polgár *et al.* 2019). (See also below on the effects of the COVID-19 pandemic on adult dogs.)

The 'need' for on-going socialisation and training is revealing at a more prosaic level. Clothier writes:

> When I let quick drops and steady stays slip, *they* let it slip as well not because they are lazy or resistant dogs but *because it does not matter to them*. It only matters to me, and thus it is my responsibility to maintain a high level of awareness about this, and my obligation to remain invested in maintenance of the behavior. If I am unaware of my responsibility and blame the dogs, who do not understand the importance of the behavior as one way to keep them safe in their world, then I might slip over the edge and justify using force, placing the blame on the dogs and not on myself where it belongs.
>
> (Clothier 2005: 232, emphasis in the original)

In other words, don't blame the dog, who probably gives not a fig about sitting or downing or returning on cue, if you haven't insisted on reminding her that *you* do. Clothier is making an important point here. On-going socialisation matters to humans rather than to dogs, but the consequences that follow from its failure are borne by dogs. One of the reasons continued socialisation, enrichment and training are of concern to behavioural professionals – and why they should also be of concern to owners and handlers – is that, as Clothier says here, it keeps dogs safe. Safe from what? Principally, safe from humans: from human expectations, prejudices and aggressive behaviours toward dogs, many of which are consolidated in law. In the UK, a dog can be seized on the grounds that 'it causes fear or apprehension to a person' (DEFRA 2009: 2). A dog may live their life in fear of a human, humans or a human environment, as long as this fear has no consequences for humans. A human may fear a dog, perhaps for only a moment, and there will be consequences in law for the dog.

Pandemic puppies

In this final part of my discussion of socialisation, I explore what might be learned from the 'pandemic puppy' phenomenon, which brought the issue (of dog socialisation) to public attention.

More than 3 million animals were bought as pets during lockdown in the UK, with a particular demand for puppies (BBC 2021). This huge escalation in demand transformed breeding into an even more profitable business. Individual dogs could sell, for example, for as much as £9,000 (Munke 2023). Unsurprisingly, the number of puppies imported into the UK increased by more than 100 per cent (Brand *et al.* 2022: 20). Research suggests that people who bought a puppy during the pandemic 'were more likely to be first-time dog owners' (Packer *et al.* 2021: 1; see also PDSA 2021: 5);[11] that 10 per cent of pandemic puppy owners bought on impulse; and that 40 per cent bought a dog for how they look, rather than what they need (Menke 2023). At the same time, routine supports for puppy owners and their puppies, and especially for puppy socialisation, were withdrawn or compromised. These were the conditions that defined, and will probably continue to define, the lives of the pandemic puppies. What to me is especially disquieting, however, is that many of the problems faced by this cohort are widely shared by pre- (and post-) pandemic dog populations. This suggests that the pandemic did not create wholly new problems, so much as intensify and spotlight long-standing ones. In particular, the COVID-19 pandemic illuminated how much work is required to pull a dog 'up' onto the dog–human 'bond wagon', and how easy it is for any dog to fall from or to be pushed off it.

In their review of canine socialisation, Victoria McEvoy *et al.* write that:

> [t]here are currently six defined sensitive periods in early canine development: (1) the prenatal period (9 week gestation period) (2) the neonatal period (birth to 2 weeks of age) (3) the transition period (2–3 weeks of age) (4) the socialisation period (3–12 weeks of age) (5) the juvenile period (12 weeks to 6 months of age), and (6) the pubertal period (7–24 months).
>
> (McEvoy *et al.* 2022: 2)

One of the implications that follows from this understanding of dogs' developmental periods is that '[r]esponsibility for proper exposure to age-appropriate socialisation … starts with the breeder' (McEvoy *et al.* 2022: 2). Many European countries, including the UK, oblige breeders to socialise their puppies, and indeed to 'prove' to potential buyers that they have done so by showing them the puppy interacting with their mother, in their place of birth. The socialisation of puppies is not, however, often enforced in law and, as McEvoy *et al.* note, 'the largest puppy trade network in western Europe imports puppies from Hungary and Slovakia, which have no guidelines regarding dog breeding or socialisation' (McEvoy *et al.* 2022: 2).

Prior to the pandemic, a report by the Kennel Club indicated that, out of the 9 million UK dog population, 1 million had been bought by owners who had not seen the puppy in advance, and that 630,000 puppies had been delivered to the door (Kennel Club 2018: para. 7). This means that buyers had had no opportunity to see the environment in which the puppy was born and raised, or to see the puppy with their dam and litter. In short, they had no opportunity to learn anything about the puppy's early socialisation. It was hoped that such practices would be brought to an end by Lucy's Law, which was published on 6 April 2020. Lucy's law – named after a Cavalier King Charles Spaniel who was rescued from a puppy farm – banned the commercial third-party sale of puppies and kittens in an effort to ensure that potential owners buy puppies directly from a licensed breeder or adopt from a rescue shelter.

Lucy's Law commenced twelve days after lockdown measures in the UK came legally into force. But in the confusion surrounding these emergency measures, especially with regard to travel restrictions, puppy buyers found themselves able to meet sellers half-way, or to have puppies delivered to their homes. Claire Brand and her colleagues at the Royal Veterinary College (RVC) describe the consequences:

> [D]uring the pandemic, puppies were more likely to be viewed virtually (e.g., online video calls or pre-recorded videos/photos), and to be collected from outside their breeder's property, at a meeting place between the breeder's and new owner's properties or delivered directly to their new owner. [This] puppy-buying process risked prospective owners purchasing puppies from breeders who may have been using pandemic restrictions as a 'smokescreen' to either hide the unsuitable environments that puppies were raised in, or as a cover-up for the illegal importation of puppies from outside the UK to meet demand.
>
> (Brand *et al.* 2022: 2)

'"Click and collect" type purchases', as Ed Hayes, Head of Policy and Public Affairs at the Kennel Club puts it (Kennel Club 2021: para. 10), are often associated with intensive dog breeding (IDB) – also called 'puppy mills', 'puppy farms' or commercial breeding establishments (CBEs). Puppy farmers raise puppies as cheaply as possible, and dispatch them from their litters as quickly as possible. The detriments to dog welfare are manifold. To take just two examples: first, as has been extensively documented, the in-breeding of pedigree dogs has led the diversity of their gene pools to become diminished, leading in turn to 'genetically based deformities, diseases and disadvantages' (Bradshaw 2012: xxi) that can shape the entirety of a dog's life. Although it is poor compensation, mandatory screening – both phenotypic and genetic – is at least intended to 'weed out' 'genetically-caused behavioural and medical issues' (Wauthier and Williams 2018: 76). Such screening is unlikely to occur on a puppy farm. Second, quality of maternal care – considered by some to be more important than any other kind of socialisation (Dietz *et al.* 2018; Pierantoni *et al.* 2011) – can be severely compromised in puppy farms. Breeding bitches are forced to breed continuously, which causes physiological and emotional stress in the dam, creates stress sensitivity in her infants, and affects the amount and quality of care that infants receive in the neonatal period (Wauthier and Williams 2018: 76). When breeding bitches are no longer able to breed, they are 'discarded'.

Puppies born into CBEs unquestionably endure one of the worst starts in life. Regardless of whether one laughs at, weeps over, or decries scientific preoccupation with socialisation, an impoverished environment during the period when puppies are open to new stimuli, coupled with distressing transportation experiences while puppies are likely to be especially fearful – from eastern Europe, puppies might often travel 'several days, by road' (Brand *et al.* 2022: 2) – can only make it more difficult for a puppy to transition into human social life. Research suggests that dogs sourced from CBEs, on account of their 'inadequate socialisation', 'express more adverse behaviours as adults', and that the main behavioural disorders displayed are 'increased fear, aggression, anxiety, and separation-related behaviours, as well as attention-seeking behaviours and heightened sensitivity to touch' (McEvoy *et al.* 2022: 2). It is noteworthy, however, that dogs who emerge from these extreme conditions have characteristics in common not only with pandemic puppies who were *not* bought through 'click and collect', but also with already established (i.e. pre-pandemic) dog populations.

For example: during the pandemic, routine supports – such as conspecific socialisation, training classes, veterinary care and habituation to visits to the vet – were jeopardised for all new puppies. Although, as noted by Brand *et al.*, '[d]ata on the impact of the COVID-19 pandemic on puppy development are sparse' (Brand *et al.* 2022: 2), the People's Dispensary for Sick Animals (PDSA)'s Animal Wellbeing report (PAW) of 2021 indicated that 27 per cent of the dogs acquired after March 2020 – *without* discrimination as to how they were obtained – were 'showing behaviours that could be related to lack of socialisation' (PDSA 2021: 5), while 18 per cent 'show[ed] signs of distress when … left alone' (11). With regard to the commonalities between companion dogs procured prior to and during the pandemic, the PDSA reports here that 22 per cent of dogs acquired before March 2020 'have shown new behaviours' (11), and that these behaviours include: 'barking or vocalising for more than one minute at someone out the window', 'new signs of distress when left alone', 'new signs of fear' and 'new growling, snapping, or biting towards unfamiliar dogs' (11). In their article entitled 'Changes to adult dog social behaviour during and after COVID-19 lockdowns in England', Holly Boardman and Mark Farnworth ascribe such new behaviours to lack of socialisation for adult dogs during the pandemic, leading to 'an increase in aggression and fear-related behaviours' (Boardman and Farnworth 2022: 10). In keeping with my claim that the pandemic did not create new problems but rather highlighted long-standing ones, the authors further suggest that such behaviours would have come about *anyway*, if only more slowly (10).

'[W]e've got a whole cohort of dogs', writes the Dogs Trust operations director Adam Clowes, 'that started life in not the real world, and as life starts to return to normal those dogs and their owners are struggling to cope' (Clowes in Wollaston 2021: para. 7). But Clowes's protest could be read backwards: 'the real world' for dogs is *normally* a tough one, which requires a huge amount of on-going human regulation, structural organisation and professional support to make it possible. This is why the troubles I have been describing are not solely the troubles of those puppies whose early developmental periods were disrupted, for one reason or another, by the COVID-19 pandemic. Consider, for instance, separation anxiety: to be sure, pandemic puppies – whether they were born and raised in CBEs or not – are in an especially difficult position with regard to the issue of separation because they have been obliged to make the transition from rarely, if ever, being alone to often being alone. 'Post'-pandemic, the RVC called urgently for 'enhanced support mechanisms' (Packer *et al*. 2021: 23) that might prevent pandemic puppy owners from relinquishing their dogs. These support mechanisms include, notably, dog care and dog walkers, so that dogs are not 'left alone for long periods of time', and training for dogs so that they can be 'left alone without distress' (Packer *et al*. 2021: 23).[12] Nevertheless, these dogs are *joining* vast numbers of dogs who share their anxiety: the RVC suggests that pre-pandemic figures regarding the numbers of dogs suffering from separation-related behaviours could be anywhere between one-fifth (Packer *et al*. 2021: 23) and one half (Brand *et al*. 2022: 2) of the total UK dog population, while the RSPCA puts that figure closer to 80 per cent (RSPCA 2023: para. 2).

The COVID-19 pandemic was significant on two counts: it illuminated the consequences of the partial withdrawal of socialisation mechanisms for dogs, and it also showed those consequences to be relevant not only to dogs born during the pandemic, but also to dogs born before the pandemic began, i.e. to many adult dogs. In other words, it made visible the on-going necessity of socialisation throughout a dog's life and, as can be identified in the problems shared across different dog populations, how inadequate that socialisation often is. If there is one area, however, where the pandemic puppies are arguably distinctive, it is the young age at which they are being euthanised. In a sobering presentation at a meeting on dangerous dogs organised by the Public Policy Exchange, Sara Munke, who has been rehoming dogs for forty-six years and who is currently manager of the Chilterns Dog Rescue Society, reported that vets are saying that, as a result of the pandemic, 'a generation of dogs has been lost' (Munke 2023). By this vets mean that a generation of young dogs are being euthanised because they cannot adapt to life with humans at all, never mind to a life of 'the bond'.[13]

Keeping it real

In the UK, behavioural professionals often find themselves operating in the space between dog owners, scientists, dog welfare stakeholders, social services and the police. They may of course occupy more than one of these roles themselves and, like everyone else, they contribute to and shape debates about dogs. Having said that, behavioural professionals are arguably uniquely positioned as the group principally tasked with transforming changing ideas about dogs, and changing ideas about how a dog–human relationship 'should be', into material practice. As such, they are well positioned to witness the discrepancies between what people say and/or believe about their relationships with dogs, and the reality of dogs' lives on the ground.

In the present moment, as Justyna Włodarczyk argues, and as I illustrated earlier, 'the guiding principle of so much contemporary thought and practice' is characterised by a generalised 'fascination with animality' (Włodarczyk 2018: 231). With regard to dogs, Włodarczyk continues, this fascination manifests itself – in canine science, in the popular media and among dog owners – as a 'belief in canine genius' (Włodarczyk 2018: 231). It is notable that Włodarczyk excludes behavioural professionals, and especially dog trainers, from this list. Far from being 'fascinated', dog trainers, she writes, ' "keep it real" ' (Włodarczyk 2018: 231). 'Keeping it real' does not necessarily mean taking a strong, public, 'political' stance on dogs, however. Dog trainers 'are not (and most likely will never be) at the forefront of a revolution. Any revolution, really. They have dogs to take care of' (Włodarczyk 2018: 227). Nevertheless, Włodarczyk is not arguing that dog trainers are *a*political. On the contrary, she conceives of this group as Foucauldian 'truth-tellers' (Włodarczyk 2018: 227), and it is *because* 'they are committed to the truth' that they 'shine a critical lens on mainstream discourses about dogs' (Włodarczyk 2018: 227). Critical, and deflating. By way of example, Włodarczyk notes that 'genius' behaviours can be taught using fairly mechanical tools that draw on basic models of stimulus/response (see Chapter 3 of this book).

In my own experience, 'keeping it real' is less likely to involve the use of basic models of stimulus/response to disestablish a mistaken belief in canine genius, and more likely to involve these and other similar techniques to address the behavioural problems that often follow from dog despair. Separation anxiety, for example, might be mitigated using systematic desensitisation and relaxation protocols. Fear might be addressed with operant conditioning (teaching the dog to do something else in the presence of the stimulus they fear) or counter-conditioning (changing the dog's emotional response to the stimulus). Just as importantly, 'keeping it real' means working with owners and handlers who, while extolling the dog–human bond, often prefer to consider a problem – such as 'my dog barks at every moving object that passes the living room window' – atomistically, rather than as testimony to the myriad difficulties a dog might be struggling with on account of how their life as a whole is organised. I will return to this point below.

Of course, it is unrealistic to expect *all* dog trainers to be 'truth-tellers', especially given that dog training, which is unregulated in the UK, is a potentially lucrative business. For example: in keeping with an affirmative biopolitics (which seeks to 'manipulate affects'), Włodarczyk argues that the shift toward positive reinforcement training in the 1990s and early 2000s was and continues to be motivated in large part by what Nicole Shukin calls 'feeling power': 'a fantasy of mutual human–canine interspecies love and devotion' (Włodarczyk 2018: 19). Positive reinforcement training, at its most basic, refers to training that rewards a dog for what she does 'right', rather than punishing her for what she does 'wrong', and in the process strengthens the dog–owner relationship. The fantasy of mutual human–canine interspecies love and devotion has led many owners to seek out trainers who adopt what is sometimes called 'purely positive' training methods, and for some dog trainers, consequently, to identify themselves in this way, even though 'purely positive' is an almost unintelligible concept.[14]

To explain: operant conditioning is a theory that claims to be able to account for how behaviours are strengthened or extinguished. Operant conditioning is usually based on four quadrants, two positive, two negative. 'Positive', in this context, means that something is given; 'negative', that something is taken away. Where most conscientious professional trainers recognise and make explicit the inevitability of the use of negative punishment (withholding something the dog wants, like a treat) alongside positive reinforcement when training,[15] it is politic not to draw attention to the fact that, outside the classroom, owners themselves regularly use not only positive reinforcement and negative punishment, but also positive punishment and negative reinforcement, the two quadrants of operant conditioning that are commonly associated with aversive-based training (Casey *et al*. 2021: 12).

My discussion here is intended to be pragmatic. I am not addressing difficult questions regarding the philosophical 'honesty' or 'dishonesty' of operant conditioning;[16] what ethical issues are raised by different training methods; and what they tell, explicitly or implicitly, about the politics of dog–human relations. Rather, I am using operant conditioning instrumentally, as a lens through which to draw attention to the discrepancies between discourses of 'feeling power', which trainers may exploit, and routine handler/owner interactions with dogs, which are likely to invoke plenty of 'unpleasant stimuli' over the course of a single day (bearing in mind that what constitutes a 'positive' or 'aversive' stimulus will vary from one dog to another). Positive punishment tends to call to mind physically disciplinary techniques, such as hitting a dog, or using a prong or electric shock collar. Yet (to take a common example), simply applying leash pressure to a dog would also be an example of positive punishment, relieving leash pressure an example of negative reinforcement. What is significant, here, is that the unpalatable realities of many dogs' lives are set to the tune of positive reinforcement that, in the spirit of affirmative biopolitics, operates as a 'technology of love' (Włodarczyk 2018: 231). This makes 'resistance to power' more difficult for a dog, and more difficult for a human to recognise (Włodarczyk 2018: 145).

Owners often approach behavioural professionals for help with a single behavioural 'problem'. In response, nearly all behavioural professionals will conduct a full review of a dog's medical and behavioural history, and also ask detailed questions – often several times, from different angles – about the routines and relationships that characterise a dog's life. Why? Because, usually, it is this holistic picture that gives insight into the so-called 'isolated' issue. But as a canine behavioural specialist recently commented to me: owners generally want a quick fix. Yet even the quick fix can be tricky for owners, and for this professionals pay a heavy price in terms of their own welfare. 'One of the factors implicated in trainer burnout', trainer Jean Donaldson writes, is the 'steady stream of cases that would be routine fixes if only the owner were up to the program' (Donaldson 2002: 19). Some owners, of course, *are* up to 'the program', although it is striking that descriptions of such challenges sustain 'an entire genre of narratives written by owners of dogs deemed "unsavable"' (Włodarczyk 2018: 233). This suggests that so exceptional and remarkable is the event of an owner doing the work to 'save' a dog, that, when it occurs, it merits a book.

While there is an extensive literature documenting the high levels of stress, depression, anxiety and suicide in the veterinary profession (e.g. Platt *et al.* 2012), especially among vets who work with companion animals in the USA (Tomasi *et al.* 2019: 106), as Tamsin Durston notes in her book *Emotional Well-Being for Animal Professionals*, 'other professional groups, such as the dog training instructor community, simply haven't been studied' (Durston 2022: 4–5). People who work in animal protection and welfare are witness to much human and animal suffering, and can themselves, in turn, suffer intense psychological trauma. Thus it is that Rochelle Stevenson and Celeste Morales recommend that trauma-informed practices be implemented in this sector (Stevenson and Morales 2022). Behavioural professionals, particularly those whose work is not confined to the private sphere, are similarly placed with regard to the organisational, operational and emotional pressures of their work. Key among those pressures is the knowledge that, on account of how they have been bred, raised and/or treated, many dogs 'can be rescued' but cannot, 'ultimately, be saved' (Munke 2023).

Conclusion

In 2022, a rather technical article on the balance of disease predispositions and disease protections in Pugs, published in the scientific journal *Canine Medicine and Genetics*, hit the media headlines. Devised by Dan O'Neill, who is based at the RVC, the study sought to plug the 'information gaps about the health of Pugs relative to the general population of dogs' (O'Neill *et al.* 2022: 3). To this end, the researchers collected clinical data on 16,218 Pugs and 889,326 non-Pugs under primary veterinary care during the year 2016. They concluded, shockingly, that the health differences between Pugs and all other dogs have diverged so greatly that 'the Pug breed can no longer be considered as a typical dog from the perspective of its disorder profile' (O'Neill *et al.* 2022: 9).

The welfare crisis that is affecting Pugs and other brachycephalic breeds is called extreme conformation. As the British Veterinary Association (BVA) explains (rather understatedly): '[a]nimals with extremes of conformation have an exaggerated body shape, structure, or appearance which can negatively affect their health and welfare' (BVA 2023: para. 1). The O'Neill *et al.* study illustrated that Pugs' conformation is so extreme, and so extreme are the disorder consequences of that conformation, that they can no longer be considered a typical dog.

It is probably the use of this word 'typical' that ensured that the study reached the headlines (e.g. BBC 2022). Problematically however, in my view, the word – or rather, the description '*not* typical' – serves to cordon off the brachycephalic breeds, and to imply that the problems they are obliged to contend with are uniquely different from the problems of all other domesticated dogs. Is this so? Rather than claim that Pugs are extremely exceptional and therefore not typical, I would alternatively argue that they are extreme in their typicality, i.e. that they are *extremely typical*.[17] By this I mean that the breed typifies the extremity that often characterises the relationship between domesticated dogs and humans, whether this is recognised across other areas of dogs' lives or not. This is the face of 'the bond'.

My aim in this chapter has been to gesture toward how much work is involved in creating the dog–human 'bond', and how difficult that work mostly is, for dogs. My argument is *not* that the lives of the domesticated dogs in the Global North, that population of companion and working dogs that constitute the main subjects of canine scientific research, would be improved if, say, all dogs were well socialised, dogs were left alone less often, dogs were not seen to be discardable consumer objects, owners' limitations were more explicitly recognised, dogs were enabled to be more 'doggy', dogs were not expected always to be 'under control', there were fewer restrictions on dogs in public spaces etc. Although 'the contemporary emergency' (Rich 1986: 259) demands that all these issues, and many further issues, be urgently addressed, the more fundamental point of *Dog Politics* is that the notion of a 'special relationship' between dogs and humans, authorised and justified by dogs' species story, contributes substantially not only to creating these conditions in the first place, but also to finding them to be in some way par for the dog–human course. It may take a 'quantum leap' (Rich 1986: 259) to undo this.

The problems facing domesticated dogs are complex, and dogs' species story could not begin to account for them. Nevertheless, this story carries significant weight as a broad framework that informs the politics of dogs' lives with humans. It gives shape to and impacts on, for example, policy decisions regarding dog welfare; the topics that canine scientists consider important or unimportant to research; owner conceptions of what constitutes 'normal' dog–human relations; and, relatedly, what quality of life it is necessary to provide for dogs. This book continues to address these kinds of issues. Its primary focus, however, lies on the 'frame' itself, i.e. the story. It is to the story, to dogs' species story, that I turn next.

Notes

1 Although human-controlled socialisation is the focus of this chapter, I am not suggesting that dogs do not socialise themselves. Street dogs, clearly, are largely responsible for their own socialisation, but it is also the case that the socialisation of companion animals could not succeed without the participation of the dogs themselves, however unequal the terms of their engagement with that process.
2 Włodarczyk (2018: 207).
3 A problem that Dognition.com, which is connected to Duke University's Canine Cognition Centre, believes it has resolved through citizen science. I will return to Dognition.com in Chapter 4.
4 Mixed-breed dogs were not registered with the AKC until 2009, and were not allowed to compete in trials until 2010.
5 On the co-option of dogs in colonial and postcolonial projects – and on the often deathly consequences of this co-option for 'native' dogs – see for example Doble (2020) and Van Sittert and Swart (2008).
6 In fact, Scott and Fuller referred to these as 'critical' periods of development (see especially Scott and Fuller (1965: Chapter 5)). Today, they are more commonly described as 'sensitive', on account of the perceived 'plasticity of behaviour and preferences' (McEvoy *et al.* 2022: 2).

7 I also think this figure is likely to be higher. I will return to figures for separation anxiety and separation-related behaviours below.
8 Dogs have more diseases 'than any other species, with the exception of man' (Starkey *et al.* 2005: 112). More than half of canine genetic diseases (numbering about 350) have an equivalent human disease (Hayward *et al.* 2016: 2). As a result, dogs have been marked out as an especially significant model for human disease (Lindblad-Toh 2012: 256).
9 This figure roughly matches that given by Jessica Pierce and Marc Bekoff for the number of dogs with 'behavioral problems' in the United States – 80 per cent (Pierce and Bekoff 2021: 150).
10 Not all these behaviours are necessarily problematic from a dog's point of view. Current research suggests, for example, that coprophagia is 'a normal dog behaviour' (Case 2022: 30).
11 See Packer *et al.*'s (2021) well-publicised research report on the characteristics that defined pandemic puppy purchasers during the period 23 March–31 December 2020, as compared with puppy purchasers over the same period in 2019.
12 It is worth noting that, during the pandemic in the UK, 5 per cent of dogs acquired before March 2020 were said by their owners to be 'spending more time in quiet areas of the home' (PDSA 2021: 11). One wonders what was the experience of the pandemic puppies in this regard, even if the lockdown conditions in which they were raised ultimately lent themselves to separation anxiety.
13 See also Brand *et al.* (2022: 2) on the euthanasia of pandemic dogs under three years old on the grounds of 'undesirable behaviours' such as the display of non-social fear, social fearfulness and aggression.
14 There can be good reason to deploy solely positive reinforcement training, for example when working with extremely traumatised dogs. Training programmes that seek to do this, however, have to be devised with great care and executed with exacting attention to detail.
15 See for example Alexander (2006) on the Karen Pryor clicker training website, or the celebrity dog trainer Victoria Stilwell's (2017) blog 'Why I'm not (and never have been) a purely positive dog trainer'.
16 See Włodarczyk's excellent discussion of Vicki Hearne and B. F. Skinner by way of example (Włodarczyk 2018: 183–191).
17 This is not in any way to diminish the very serious problems that Pugs and other brachycephalic breeds suffer. So serious are the health consequences of these breeds (which include, for instance, French Bulldogs, English Bulldogs, Shih Tzus, Chow Chows, Pekingeses, Boxers, Cavalier King Charles Spaniels), they have rightly become a

matter of considerable professional concern, as illustrated, for example, by the British Veterinary Association's #BreedtoBreathe campaign. In the UK, a Brachycephalic Working Group (BWG) has been established, which brings together a significant number of major UK dog welfare stakeholders, such as the British Veterinary Association, the Dogs Trust, the RVC, DEFRA, the RSPCA etc. The BWG have a simple message for the public: 'stop and think before buying a flat-faced dog' (BWG 2022: 1).

2

Dogs' species story

> An international team of scientists has just identified what they believe is the world's first known dog, which was a large and toothy canine that lived 31,700 years ago and subsisted on a diet of horse, musk ox and reindeer.
>
> (NBC Science 2008: para. 1)

Let me begin this chapter with the 'dog-is-wolf' thesis, which is one variant of dogs' species story. I will return to this variant in more detail, and to several others, below. For now, I want simply to gesture to how significant are the implications, for dogs, of a story such as this, which will shape how dogs are understood and also, therefore, how they are trained and treated.

The anthrozoologist John Bradshaw writes: '[o]bservations of captive wolf packs have led not only to mistaken assessments of wolf behaviour, but also to fundamental misunderstandings about the structure of wolf families themselves, misunderstandings that have warped the popular conception of dogs as well' (Bradshaw 2012: 24). Bradshaw is referring here to how descriptions of breeding pairs of wolves as 'alpha males' and 'alpha females' have led to the misconception that wolves live in strictly hierarchical packs and how, in fidelity to this tale of wolf pack 'mentality', owners have been encouraged to 'impress their own "alpha" status on their dog' (Bradshaw 2012: 24). In other words, as well as being a misdescription of wolves, who live peaceably in family groups when not being held captive (Mech 1999, 2000), the dog-is-wolf story has given rise to the notion that dogs *must* be dominated because otherwise they themselves will attempt to become the 'leader' of the human household/pack (Charles *et al.* 2021).

Colonel Konrad Most (1878–1954), who trained dogs for the German police and military from 1906 onwards (but also trained working and sporting dogs toward the end of his life), occupies much of his reader's time, in his classic book *Training Dogs: A Manual* (2001 [1955]), with descriptions of how to use a switch on a dog. For Most, it is *because* the dog is a pack animal that he or she can be trained to live with humans at all: '[e]ver since the dog lived in a state of nature, as a wild animal of wolf type in packs, the pack instinct, or sociable impulse, has dwelt within him ... A dog's dependence on man is the expression of his pack instinct' (Most 2001 [1955]: 72). And it is on account of this also that he justifies 'training' a dog into complete submission:

> As in a pack of dogs, the order of hierarchy in a man and dog combination can only be established by physical force, that is, by an actual struggle, in which the man is instantly victorious. Such a result can only be brought about by convincing the dog of the absolute physical superiority of the man.
> (Most 2001 [1955]: 35)

Most is just one in a long history of animal trainers, which includes Barbara Woodhouse and Cesar Millan, who have encouraged owners to believe that a good relationship with their dog is characterised by the dog's total surrender.[1] Sophia Yin, a veterinarian, applied animal behaviourist, and pioneer of techniques designed to handle dogs without stress, offers this interpretation of Millan on film, grooming a small dog while simultaneously rhapsodising about the benefits of being the pack leader:

> It's man against a Miniature Poodle–Maltese mix as the popular trainer, Cesar Millan, pits his skill against a curly-haired, football-sized dog that hates being groomed. He brushes the dog's face and head as the dog stands, seemingly willingly, except for the subtle twitch of his upper lip. 'That's the beauty of becoming a pack leader', says Millan. 'Because anything they used to dislike, they learn to like, because they have no choice'. The owner looks on, her face lit with the joy of what she sees as a miracle before her eyes ... But then, as Millan stops to adjust the leash, the dog explodes with the emotion his earlier lip curl had warned lay below. He screams and bares his teeth – holding his mouth wide open like a shield studded with sharp white stones. The puffy white alligator flails his head and bites the fingers of

Millan's right hand ... [then] mouth agape in a tense threat, and feet up and clawing in full defense fight-mode – bites Millan again.

(Yin 2009: 17)

Although contemporary canine ethologist Alexandra Horowitz does not mention trainers such as Millan by name, it is likely that their controversial training techniques are uppermost in her mind when she redescribes 'family' dogs as members not of a pack, but of a gang (Horowitz 2012: 60–61). That is, as members of a group who are defined by their various, potentially intimate, associations with each other, and not by hierarchy.

I start with the dog-is-wolf variant of dogs' species story because it is an especially clear illustration and dramatisation of the material implications, for dogs today, of apparently neutral accounts of biological speciation that are said to have unfolded anywhere between 135,000 and 11,000 years ago (maybe). I will address the consequences of this story in other chapters. In this chapter, my concern is with the story itself. Like nearly every other variant of dogs' species story, the dog-is-wolf thesis is underpinned by a single, distinguishing feature, which is that the becoming of the species 'dog' is fundamentally inseparable from humans. This does not mean that the relationship between dogs and humans is one of *co*-becoming, however, because, across most scientific disciplines, dogs' species story does not pertain to both dogs and humans *at the species level*. While scientists concede that dogs may have put some 'cultural' pressure on humans, may even have 'civilised' them (that is, enabled them to become 'civilised'), for the most part the becoming of dogs as a species, in dogs' species story, leaves *Homo sapiens* untouched and intact.[2] As I will illustrate in Chapter 4 especially, this renders the 'relationality' of the dog–human configuration somewhat peculiar, for it appears to characterise only one side of the dyad – the dogs' side. While *some* humans might feel a deep dog–human connection (be it emotional, affective, biochemical or whatever), this is not a requirement of being a human. That connection, however, according to dogs' species story, *is* a requirement of being a dog. This makes dogs' relationality, at the species level, curiously unrelational.

Broadly speaking, dogs' species story (in nearly all its variants) is based on three interconnected claims: first, that dogs are the original domesticates (their domestication precedes the agricultural revolution); second, that the speciation of dogs is connected to, if not synonymous with, their domestication; third, that the parallel evolution of dogs and humans places dogs in a unique relation to humans. *Canis familiaris*. Named by Carl Linnaeus in the first volume of the tenth edition of *Systema naturae* (1758) and originating from the Latin *familia*, meaning household. Dogs are of the human household. This chapter explores these claims as they are recounted in contemporary genetics, archaeology, ecology and other science disciplines. While some of this recounting is said by scientists to be 'controversial', to my mind it is so only in the details. The broad thrust of the story is consistent across disciplines. This chapter explores this story and asks what evidence exists for it.

As a first step toward this analysis, I begin with the role that dogs are understood to have played in enabling Charles Darwin to articulate his theory of evolution by natural selection both to himself and to his Victorian public. Darwin's representation of his theory, and especially his representation of the two conceptions of time that inform it, contributed to the vexed linguistic, conceptual and political inheritance that he bequeathed to future evolutionary researchers. I will address this troubled legacy – especially as it relates to the issue of variability – in much greater detail in Chapter 6. I introduce it here in anticipation of that, but also because it provides a broad frame for much of the discussion that follows in this chapter.

Dogs and Darwin

In *Darwin's Sacred Cause: Race, Slavery, and the Quest for Human Origins*, authors Adrian Desmond and James Moore (2009) pay particular attention to how Darwin's relationships with dogs shaped his thinking on evolution. 'Hounds were Darwin's forte', they write (Desmond and Moore 2009: 309); '[d]ogs ... were [for Darwin] a microcosm of nature' (258). It should come as no surprise that dogs were Darwin's forte, for Darwin was born into a class, a country and a century in which dogs had accrued considerable emotional, social, cultural, symbolic and commercial value. Although, in England, 'the maintenance of idle animals', as Harriet Ritvo puts it – i.e. pet keeping – had originally been the privilege of courtiers and wealthy religious orders (Ritvo 1987: 85), by the sixteenth and seventeenth centuries it was 'a normal feature of the middle-class household, especially in towns' (Thomas 1984: 110). Of the many kinds of animals who were kept 'close to human society' (Thomas 1984: 100) – including horses, hawks, cats, monkeys, tortoises, otters, rabbits, squirrels and cage-birds (and on farms, lambs, hares, mice, hedgehogs, bats and toads) (Thomas 1984: 100–112) – dogs were 'the most favoured' (Thomas 1984: 101; Ritvo 1987: 20). By 1800, 'there were probably more than a million dogs in England, compared to a human population of about eight million, and the number of dogs grew steadily well into Darwin's youth' (Feller 2009: 267). The first dog show in 1859 and the foundation of the Kennel Club in 1873 institutionalised and further intensified what could be described as a national obsession with breeding (Ritvo 1987; Worboys et al. 2018), which, historian Harriet Ritvo writes, had long constituted both 'a metonymic attempt at [class] assimilation' (Ritvo 1987: 87) and an opportunity to police class boundaries (e.g. Ritvo 1987: 83–84).

Darwin, by his own admission, had a 'passion' for dogs (Darwin in Darwin 2009: 30), and he grew up in families – the Darwins and the Wedgwoods – who supported this passion. His correspondence indicates that the families took pride in and celebrated their animals (Townshend 2009: 19) and spent much time describing and reflecting on their dogs' characters, emotions and behaviours (Feller 2009: 267; Townshend 2009: 16–28). Shela, Spark, Czar, Sappho, Fan, Dash, Pincher, Nina, Bob, Bran, Quiz, Tartar, Pepper and Butterton: these were 'Darwin's dogs' (Townshend 2009), some owned, some purloined, some shared, some adopted. Also there was Polly, a Fox Terrier, who was Darwin's final dog, and his most beloved (Darwin 2009: 113). Unnamed here are the dogs whose hearts Darwin stole from others – 'I was an adept', he writes, 'in robbing their love from their masters' (Darwin in Darwin 2009: 30) – and the dogs who on lived on 'Barker Street', as Darwin dubbed it, of whom, as a child, he was afraid (Townshend 2009: 18). Unnamed finally is the puppy whom Darwin beat 'as a very little boy ... simply from enjoying the sense of power ... [T]his act lay heavily on my conscience' (Darwin in Darwin 2009: 30).

Despite Darwin's affection for dogs in general, it was arguably his contact with the dog culture of the Shropshire gentry in particular, with 'its lifelong passion for gundogs, show cattle, and fancy breeds' (Desmond and Moore 2009: 304), that enabled him to make the imaginative leap that would define one of his most significant contributions to science: inheritance by natural selection.³ Having 'question[ed] whether these very diverse forms [of domesticated animals] may have arisen from fewer ancestors … it was a logical step for Darwin to apply this reasoning to wild animals and to ask whether they too might share a common ancestor' (Van Grouw 2018: 23).⁴ In their proliferation of numerous different dog breeds, and in their cultivation of the technologies of artificial selection – in their discussions of breeding standards, bloodlines and 'perfect' breeds, and in the keeping of pedigree stock books (Townshend 2009: 31–32) – these dog fanciers provided Darwin with visible material evidence of a principle that, because of the relatively slow pace of evolutionary divergence in wild animals, would otherwise be invisible to the human eye (or invisible to the human imagination). 'Although the creation of new breeds of domesticated animal might seem superficial compared with the lofty science of speciation', Katrina van Grouw writes, 'it nevertheless shows how easily an animal lineage can be split into multiple isolated forms' (Van Grouw 2018: 49). Artificial selection, Desmond and Moore claim, was for Darwin 'the missing link between natural selection and the *beau idéal* mechanism'; '*artificial* selection in the kennel was the counterpart of *natural* selection in the wild' (Desmond and Moore 2009: 304, emphasis in the original).⁵ Artificial selection, in short, was a metaphor for natural selection.⁶

Van Grouw argues that Darwin's anecdotal accounts of dogs contributed to making the 'terrifying, godless abyss' (Van Grouw 2018: 56) that was the theory of evolution more palatable to the middle-class dog-owning amateur and expert scientists of the day (see also Knoll 1997). True to their name, *Canis familiaris* made the theory of evolution feel more 'familiar' and 'homely', in part because dogs were familiar, and in part because the familiarity of dogs served as a counterpoint to the unfamiliarity of apes, which a long history of racist classifications, given new potency by nineteenth-century colonialism and imperialism, ensured was inextricable from the unfamiliarity of other 'races'. I will address this history in Chapter 6. Here, my focus lies on the conceptual confusion that potentially follows from the artificial selection/natural selection metaphor. For it is perhaps *because* morphological and behavioural evidence of artificial selection can be witnessed in dogs within a compressed – i.e. a human – timescale that the metaphor encourages the mistaken idea that, just as a long-legged Corgi can 'morph' over several generations into a short-legged one, so too one species can morph into another.

The popular Facebook post that shows a dog lounging at a kitchen table and reads 'If dogs are descended from wolves, how come there are still wolves?' captures the common misconception that dogs 'rolled out' of wolves, i.e. that, over time, one form of species slowly transforms into another, perhaps even ultimately replacing that earlier form. This notion of gradual change unfolding over time – in effect, of gradation – animated some of the racist and imperialist politics of the nineteenth century, for it enabled 'races' and species to be conceived of in terms of an evolutionary scale or hierarchy (see Chapter 6). Yet Darwin himself was committed to an idea of evolution 'as an irregularly branching process producing marked discontinuities in forms of life that have survived to the present day' (Boakes 2008: 21). Contra the atemporality of fixed and static typologies, and contra also the concept of time as the medium of linear change, time can be conceived of as an element that introduces unpredictability to 'the encounter between individual variation and natural selection' (Grosz 2004: 7). Retrospectively traced lineages can be described as continuous, but the process of evolution, because it is temporal, is marked by discontinuity.

Discontinuity, or irregular branching, is relevant to how one understands the relations between different species. Different extant species have not evolved one from another. Rather, the principle of discontinuity invokes novel trajectories, which is why, on the 'tree of life', species are represented 'only [at] the very tips of these metaphorical branches' (Van Grouw 2018: 49). From these tips, species continue to 'evolve independently' (Van Grouw 2018: 49).[7] Nevertheless, Darwin's famous transmutation diagram – often called the 'Tree of Life' sketch (Figure 2.1) – which illustrates Darwin's thinking in branches, competes against his choice of words and metaphors, and his written descriptions of evolutionary change and variation as, for example, 'a series [that] impresses the mind with the idea of an actual passage' (Darwin 2008: 42). Indeed Darwin's choice of words 'impresses the mind' with a great number of problematic ideas. The very title *The Descent of Man* and the concept of a 'descendant' implies that lineages are continuous over time, while

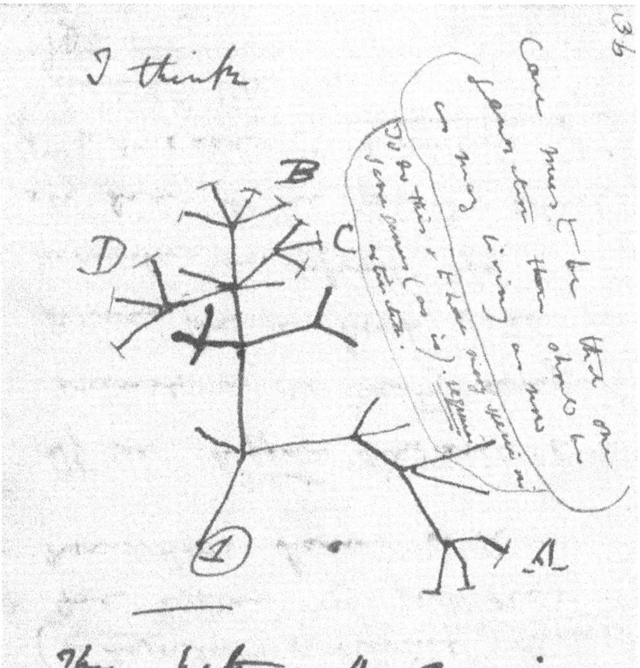

Figure 2.1 Darwin's transmutation diagram, 1837.

the term 'unity of descent' implies descent from an origin. Elizabeth Grosz seeks to rescue evolutionary theory from the conceptual, linguistic and political minefields that Darwin inadvertently laid for it, by arguing, for example, that Darwin 'analyzes only the *descent*, the genealogy, the historical movement (for we cannot even call it progress) of species, the movement from an earlier to a later form, a movement that presupposes an origin that it cannot explain, which perhaps is not an origin except in retrospect' (Grosz 2004: 21, emphasis in the original). Today, no scientist would dream of conceiving of evolution in terms of continuity and origins. And yet, the notion that there is some *point* at which, or after which, a dog is no longer a wolf, some *point* at which a dog becomes what it is, a dog, is difficult to dislodge.[8] Thus it is that much of the following discussion is obliged to engage with this very question.

How and when dogs became dogs

Like other living creatures, dogs have been categorised into a species, the species *Canis familiaris*. Unlike other species, the relationship between *Canis familiaris* and *Homo sapiens* is often said to be unique. This uniqueness is largely rooted in the perception of dogs as 'the first human companion species and the only large carnivore to ever be domesticated' (Freedman *et al.* 2014: 2). 'The early association of dogs and humans', the evolutionary geneticists Adam Freedman and Robert Wayne write, 'potentially allowed dogs to have a profound influence on the course of early human history and the development of civilization' (Freedman and Wayne 2017: 283). In other words, as the oldest domesticate, the dog's evolution, which preceded the agricultural revolution, is seen to be especially interesting not just for what it teaches scientists about dogs, but for what it teaches them about humans. This relationship, however, precisely because it is so 'ancient', is also especially obscure.

Crucially, in many, if not most, accounts of the evolutionary story of dogs, dog speciation *is* dog domestication. This is significant because it means that humans – whether by conscious design or not – become the pivot of the story of 'how dogs became dogs'. However, Darcy Morey, who is a canine palaeobiologist and archaeologist, proposes that wolf and dog genetic divergence, which is the main preoccupation of genetic scientists, and dog domestication, which is the central concern of archaeologists (among others), are two different things. If the findings of both, with their sometimes vastly differing timescales, are roughly correct, then 'the animals that were destined to become dogs must have made their living for some time essentially in the old-fashioned way, like wolves. It is entirely possible that the genomes became separated for reasons having nothing to do with domestication' (Morey 2006: 166–167). Although Morey himself seems hardly persuaded by this idea, I think it is an important one, because it opens the door to an entirely different species story – a door that, as it stands, is not only firmly bolted shut, but firmly bolts dogs in with humans. It also explains why it is so difficult to fit dogs' species story into some of the staples of conventional domestication paradigms, such as bottlenecks, reproductive isolation and strong selection (Frantz and Larsen 2020: 32), as I will illustrate below.[9] Rather than understand these difficulties to represent gaps in scientific knowledge, I take them to be indicative of the effort that the project of species-making demands.

It is now widely accepted in the animal sciences that 'the single progenitor of all domestic dogs, ancient and modern, was the grey wolf, *Canis lupus*' (Clutton-Brock 2017: 8). (I will return to the category *Canis lupus familiaris* below.) What this means is that, with the exception of the grey wolf, no other canid species is understood to have contributed to the 'genetic legacy' of domestic dogs (Freedman and Wayne 2017: 282). As I have already discussed, it is a mistake to jump from this ancestral relation to the idea that an extant grey wolf is the 'original' form of an extant domestic dog. Evolution takes place continuously *over* time, but the dog is a dog and the wolf is a wolf on account of the discontinuities/divergences between them, which are invoked by selection *in* time. This is why it is absurd to look to the wolf – and particularly to look to contemporary, living, wolves – for answers to dog behaviours. It is absurd not only because this is not how evolution works, but also because, some scientists argue, the relation between the ancestor grey wolf and the modern dog cannot, in fact, be directly established. One reason for this is because the processes through which the points of divergence between species are identified is far from straightforward.

It may be, for example, that the nearest common ancestor to dogs is extinct (Freedman and Wayne 2017: 282): that is, that the temporally closest relative of the dog does not walk on this planet today, which means that scientists have no way (or limited ways) of identifying who that ancestral creature was, from whom dogs departed. In the meantime, the assumption is that extant wolves are an out group for dogs. What is an 'out group'? An out group serves as a reference point for the investigation of evolutionary relationships. An out group is a lineage that is closely related to the 'in group' in the clade[10] – or branch of the evolutionary 'tree' – that is being investigated. Coyotes are an out group for wolves, on the assumption that between 1 and 2.5 million years ago, before wolves and coyotes began to evolve separately, they shared an ancestor (Miklósi 2017: 136). Genetic calculations regarding the date of the wolf–dog split are made on the basis of the coyote–wolf split. Both these calculations rest on the idea of a 'molecular clock' that, like all clocks, assumes continuous regularity of some kind of rate – in this case, of genetic mutation. Mutation rates, which occur at the molecular level, are believed to be constant. However, 'many mutations will not be detected if their carrier dies without offspring' (Miklósi 2017: 137). Scientists thus build into their calculations 'the chance of a mutation to transfer to the next generation of a population' (Miklósi 2017: 137). This is called the substitution rate. If the chances of transfer are 100 per cent, then the mutation and substitution rate will be the same.

Were a continuous regularity of genetic mutation to be assured, 'the number of mutations found in the descendants could offer some clues as to how much time has passed since the divergence' (Miklósi 2017: 136–137): i.e. time of coyote/wolf divergence to the present, divided by wolf/dog mutations, equals date of dog domestication. In 1997, in a 'benchmark' study (Freedman and Wayne 2017: 285; cf. Clutton-Brock 2017: 9), Carles Vilá and his colleagues calculated that dog mitochondrial DNA (mtDNA)[11] diverged from wolf mtDNA by a maximum of 12 substitutions and an average of 5.3 substitutions. Using fossil evidence that indicates that coyotes and wolves split 1 million years ago, the authors dated dog domestication to 135,000 years before the present (BP) (Vilá et al. 1997).

More recently however, the coyote/wolf split has been re-estimated at about 100,000 years BP (Freedman and Wayne 2017: 298), bringing forward wolf/dog divergence to 11,000–34,000 BP. This shift of timescale is striking, even bearing in mind that the calculation rates of mutations in humans are accurate to ±10,000 years. 'One should therefore not expect', the ethologist Ádám Miklósi writes, 'a more accurate dating for the domestication of dogs based on genetic data alone, especially because the realistic time frame for such an event to have taken place is much shorter' (Miklósi 2017: 139). The 'realistic time frame' to which Miklósi is referring is between 16,000 and 33,000 BP (Miklósi 2017: 138), which is consistent with archaeological evidence. Archaeological evidence is especially significant with regard to dogs' species story, because it is this evidence in particular that ties dog speciation to dog domestication (and therefore to humans).

So how secure is the archaeological evidence? Despite the frequent disputes between genomic scientists and archaeologists, 'genetic studies frequently rely on the fossil record to make temporal inferences', and they also rely on these records because 'data on ancient canids provide a line of evidence independent from genetics' (Freedman and Wayne 2017: 282). Research based on fossils, zoomorphic art, dog burials etc. (Morey 2010, 2006) has found evidence of dog-like canids, showing 'what are assumed to be the characteristics of incipient domestication' in their skulls and teeth, around 30,000 years ago in Europe, Ukraine and Siberia (Clutton-Brock 2017: 9; Freedman et al. 2014: 2). Skulls and teeth are used to distinguish between the archaeological remains of wolves and dogs because domestication is widely understood to affect morphology. Compared to wolves, domesticated dogs are said to show, for example, a diminution in the size of the body and head, a shortening of the muzzle and snout, changes in coat colour and so on (Clutton-Brock 2017: 11–12).[12] Alternative explanations for these characteristics, however, are available. It is possible, for example, that at least some of the morphological signs of domestication can be identified in wild canids who have been subject to 'ecological stress and inbreeding' (Clutton-Brock 2017: 10). Or it may be that dog remains are not an ancestor of the modern dog, but rather are evidence of a 'domestication process that eventually failed' (Freedman and Wayne 2017: 283). (This implies that domestication processes could have started at least more than once.) Or, as noted above, these putative dog remains may refer to 'a smaller, morphologically distinct lineage of wolves that is now extinct' (Freedman and Wayne 2017: 283), a lineage that may possibly, in place of grey wolves, be dogs' 'true' ancestor.

Wolves, dogs and other canids themselves confound these attempts at identification. In Freedman and Wayne's words: '[t]he canine genome is particularly porous with regard to admixture and contains signals of interbreeding on varying timescales across past and present geographic distributions' (Freedman and Wayne 2017: 299–300). Which means: whenever and wherever you find them, canids are given to mating. Because wolves and early dogs interbred, it is difficult to know whether an individual fossil finding – of possibly an individual dog – is representative, or not, of an emerging dog population, characterised by specific phenotypes. Not only did wolves and incipient dogs interbreed, but indigenous dogs bred with non-indigenous dogs, which complicates the mapping of the geographical origin/s of dogs. A further confounding characteristic of canids with regard to geographical mapping is that they move/migrate relatively fast. For example: although jackals became extinct in central Europe 100 years ago, Miklósi, writing in 2017, notes that since their return approximately fifteen–twenty years ago, they have been able to cover a 'range of a few thousand kilometres' (Miklósi 2017: 99). Given this rapidity of coverage, estimations regarding the migrations of species members of the *Canis* genus 10,000–20,000 years ago will be speculative indeed (Miklósi 2017: 101). Moreover, if dogs travelled with humans, they may have moved even faster than other members of their taxonomic family (the pace of human migration sped up during the Mesolithic period) (Miklósi 2017: 139). It is worth noting also, finally, that theories about human migration, which are considered to be crucial to the genetic and archaeological identification of human ancestry (to which dog domestication is seen to be connected), have been problematised in social science literature. As Joan H. Fujimura and Ramya Rajagopalan note, the accounts of human migration that scientists draw on, and which are often deployed as if they were facts, are 'constructed via histories written through archaeology, physical anthropology, linguistic anthropology, and social anthropology' (Fujimura and Rajagopalan 2011: 13). In these disciplines, these histories are often subject to reflexive and critical debate.

As one might anticipate in a hypothesis based on the biological species concept, which privileges sexual reproduction (see Chapter 6), the molecular clock is understood to ' "[tick]" by generations' (Miklósi 2017: 137). Wolves and dogs, however, 'generate' themselves differently. Wolves breed once a year. With the exception of Basenjis and some feral dogs, dogs, possibly as a consequence of domestication,[13] are able to breed twice a year, so doubling the wolves' rate of reproduction, and producing increased opportunities for variation (Miklósi 2017: 148). This difference complicates any calculation of divergence that is based on a 'simple linear relationship between genetic divergence and time' (Miklósi 2017: 137). This complicating factor may be a moot point, however, given that, in practice, extant wolf and dog populations (from whom genetic samples are mostly taken), for different reasons (for example the declining populations of wolves and the increasing genetic homogeneity of dogs on account of breeding), probably both show less variation than they have done in the past. 'The idea of a domestic bottleneck' – i.e. a reduction in genetic diversity on account of domestication – 'is so embedded in the genetic literature it is often taken to be prior knowledge' (Frantz and Larson 2020: 26). Yet in the case of dogs, the 'most drastic' (Frantz and Larson 2020: 26) example of a bottleneck is not the period of their domestication (whenever that was), or the periods of their multiple domestications (if there were more than one), but rather the Victorian era, which was characterised by intense breeding. Thus, as Miklósi points out, '[i]f the same data had been collected in antiquity, a smaller divergence between dogs and wolves might have indicated a more recent date for domestication' (Miklósi 2017: 137).

As well as questions pertaining to when and where dog speciation occurred, another key issue is *how* dogs became domesticated. Theories about the evolutionary mechanisms that led to dog speciation/domestication can refer to the individual level and/or to population level (Miklósi 2017: 125), and these map roughly onto theories of domestication by artificial and/or natural selection respectively. An example of an individual-level theory would be Konrad Lorenz's proposal that humans, perhaps especially women or 'little girl[s]' (Lorenz 2002b [1949]: 11), 'adopted' jackal pups as companions and in this way inadvertently alerted their human pack leaders, i.e. their fathers, to the usefulness of the human/half-wild jackal alliance, which the fathers then dominated, much to their daughters' dismay.[14] (Lorenz's theory reads as much like a human heteronormative patriarchal family psychodrama as it does an account of dog domestication.) Although this adoption thesis is often attributed to Lorenz, Stan Braude (a biologist) and Justin Gladman (a physical anthropologist) suggest that '[t]he popular acceptance of Lorenz's dog domestication scenario may actually result more from the popularity of Jack London's classic tale *White Fang*' (Braude and Gladman 2013: 1), which preceded it by some fifty years. This is why Braude and Gladman refer to it as the 'white fang model' (Braude and Gladman 2013: 5). In Miklósi's view, this theory of individual selection is indeed a fiction that, if anything, might have characterised the end, rather than the beginnings, of domestication (Miklósi 2017: 125).

The behavioural ecologists Raymond and Lorna Coppinger – to whom I will return in the following section – summarise the 'white fang model', which they call 'the Pinocchio hypothesis' (Coppinger and Coppinger 2001: 41), thus:

Capture a wolf.
Tame the wolf.
Train the wolf.
Breed the wolf to other tame, trained wolves.
And, presto! a domesticated dog.

(Coppinger and Coppinger 2001: 57)

Coppinger and Coppinger call this the Pinocchio hypothesis not because it is an untruth, but because '[c]hanging wolves into dogs by getting them to behave like dogs' has something of the same magical ring to it as does the idea of a puppet turning into a boy by way of his efforts to act like one (Coppinger and Coppinger 2001: 41). What the 'white fang' and the 'Pinocchio' models have in common is that they turn on artificial selection and, therefore, on human intentionality (whether conscious or inadvertent). Coppinger and Coppinger, like farmer and science writer Stephen Budiansky, are among those who believe that dog domestication is more likely to have occurred at least in part through the volition of animals 'taming themselves': '[t]he more one understands the motives behind coevolution in the wild', Budiansky writes, 'the less one feels the need to invoke the *deus ex machina* of human invention to explain domestication' (Budiansky 1992: 59). Wolves, Budiansky argues, appreciated the 'benefits' of parasitising human spaces (Budiansky 1992: 59–60; see also Budiansky 2001).[15]

Theories based on individual selection were largely replaced in the second half of the twentieth century by population-level theories of dog domestication, the most popularly known of which is probably the Coppingers' own 'village dog' scenario. According to Coppinger and Coppinger, the Pinocchio theory, which assumes that genetic transformation *follows from* adoption, socialising and training (Coppinger and Coppinger 2001: 57), has it all backwards. Their version goes:

> People create a new niche, the village.
>
> Some wolves invade the new niche and get access to a new food source.
>
> Those wolves that can use the new niche are genetically predisposed to show less 'flight distance' than those that don't.
>
> Those 'tamer' wolves gain selective advantage in the new niche over the wilder ones.
>
> (Coppinger and Coppinger 2001: 57)

In this version, which favours natural selection, those wolves who (for genetic reasons) were successfully able to exploit a novel food source ultimately became socialised to humans, and thus became trainable by them.

Yet, for every problem solved by a theory of dog speciation, a new one emerges. One of the problems with the village dog scenario is that it relies on the village – i.e. on human sedentism. Not only does this reinscribe the anthropocentrism that such theories seek to contest (wolves were attracted by something human); sedentism is an event which some argue postdates the beginning of dog domestication (e.g. Braude and Gladman 2013; Clutton-Brock 2017). The same theory – of wolves exploiting an anthropogenic niche – could be pushed back to human hunters (15,000–20,000 BP), but this in turn raises another set of issues, such as how and why an apex predator would 'help' *Homo sapiens* to hunt (Wynne 2020a: 166–169). Anthropogenic niche theories are also obliged to explain – especially in view of canid proclivity to mating – how one group of wolves could become reproductively separated from other groups within the same geographical area (as required by the biological species concept). Braude and Gladman argue that sympatric accounts, i.e. accounts that explain speciation among animals who share a geographical environment, are unconvincing when it comes to canids. The essence of their allopatric thesis is that groups of wolves became geographically isolated from each other approximately 15,000–20,000 BP, either because scavenger wolf populations followed humans moving south to a habitat that would have been unsuitable for the populations of hunter wolves, or because groups of humans and scavenger wolves became isolated by climate change (Braude and Gladman 2013: 3).

In his analysis of the 'closely woven' bond between dogs and humans (Paxton 2000: 6), the Australian veterinarian David Paxton addresses himself not only to the role of climate change, as Braude and Gladman do, but also to the roles of caves, olfaction, the specificity of Neanderthal social organisation, *Homo sapiens* social organisation, anatomy (especially the anatomy required for speech), migration, burials, 'brawn' and 'brains' in shaping early dog–human relationships (Paxton 2011). His argument in essence is that 'the human–canine complex evolved as an extended phenotype ... [P]art of what defines a human being is an association with dogs, and *vice versa*' (Paxton 2000: 7). 'We and dogs', Paxton writes, 'together make up a composite animal' (5). More specifically, Paxton describes dogs and humans as a 'composite conversationalist' (17), by which he means that this composite animal 'has the ability to speak' (5). What is significant about Paxton's argument is that it folds dogs into the speciation of humans in biological, as well as in social and symbolic, ways.

To explain: humans are by definition central to the anthropogenic niche accounts of dog speciation/domestication. Nevertheless, in most of these accounts, humans and wolves/dogs constitute two separate units of biological analysis. Partly, this is because the timeline in these narratives starts much more recently, approximately 30,000–15,000 years ago, when *Homo sapiens* was already established as the dominant Homo species. Partly, it is because the many uses to which humans put dogs – for example 'to transport goods and people, work as hunting aids, serve as bed-warmers, warn people of potential danger, ward off predators, and act as sources of food and fur' (Perri *et al.* 2019) – appear to have no bearing on the transformation of human biology *per se*. Even similar biological transformations in dogs and humans, transformations that might have been evoked by events that dogs and humans experienced simultaneously, are usually held apart analytically. This, the anthropologist Helen Leach argues, is typical of many conventional domestication accounts in which there exist, for example, 'one set of explanations for cranio-facial and tooth-size reduction in early Epipalaeolithic and Neolithic dogs and another for humans' (Leach 2003: 359).[16]

Paxton's argument, that dogs and humans are an 'extended phenotype', is not metaphorical. Nor does it refer centrally to the effectiveness of dog–human communication (although this certainly follows from his thesis). In his 'speculative' (Paxton 2000: 7) account of dog–human associations, Paxton proposes that the physical anatomy that makes speech and enunciation possible in humans could only have developed through a close association with an animal who retained fully developed senses, and particularly the sense of olfaction. The animal with whom humans associated, in his view, was the emerging dog, who passed through an evolutionary bottleneck 135,000 years ago, at approximately the same time that humans were emerging as ecological niches (7). The 'short blunt piston' tongue and the 'dropped face' (6), for example, which characterise *Homo sapiens*, gave humans a competitive edge over Neanderthals, 'whose sense of smell was as good as dogs' (108). As Haraway summarises it: 'the hypertrophied human biological capacity for speech emerged in consequence of associated dogs' taking on scent and sound alert jobs and so freeing the human face, throat, and brain for chat' (Haraway 2003: 31). By pushing back the association between emerging dogs and humans to 135,000 years BP, before *Homo sapiens* was fully established within the Homo genus, Paxton is enabled to argue that 'people and dogs ... have co-evolved in a complex and subjective association that includes a dimension of biological interdependency' (Paxton 2000: 6). Dogs and humans, Paxton argues, 'are aspects of each other' (6), which accounts, in his view, for the 'deep need' that humans have of dogs (7).

Paxton's hypothesis, which is somewhat outlandish, is rarely cited in the scientific literature on dog speciation. Part of the reason I mention it here, though, is that it seems to me to be not very much closer to 'the truth', nor very much further from it, than is any other account of dog becoming that I explore in this chapter. Trying to establish the empirical veracity of theories of dog speciation/domestication on the basis of extant animals and extant animal–human relations is challenging in the extreme. It is a bit like trying to identify who is an individual's extended 'family', whom they have been mixing with, and where they have travelled – over the course of tens of thousands of years no less – on the basis of a few blurry pictures of their (possibly) very distant relatives, and a few natural or artefactual remains that might (possibly) have been connected to them. Yet, new 'breakthroughs' regarding the date of wolf/dog divergence, or what kind of dog was the premodern dog, are greeted every time with breathless enthusiasm – I cite an example of this in the epigraph to this chapter. It is not as if scientists do not appreciate the difficulty – they do (e.g. Freedman and Wayne 2017: 300–303; Coppinger and Coppinger 2016: Chapter 1; Miklósi 2017: 146). Nevertheless, the will to species-making is strong.

Dog racialisation

Many scholars have fruitfully examined the ways in which dog breeds are cross-cut with class (Dayan 2016; Kete 1994; McCarthy 2016; Ritvo 1987) and also how they are racialised (Boisseron 2018; Guenther 2019, 2020; Kim 2015; Rosenberg 2011; Weaver 2013, 2021). An implicit assumption usually undergirds this approach, which is that dogs, like humans, constitute a single homogeneous species that is internally differentiated by classism and racism. In the case of dogs, that differentiation often maps onto breed. This identification of the classed and raced aspects of breeds is not, in my view, problematic. There are, however, other ways in which dogs are racialised, one example of which I will be exploring in this section. In the work of Coppinger and Coppinger, the question of racialisation is bound up not with breed, but with species. Although the Coppingers' analysis does not exclude breed, breed is not the fulcrum for racialisation. Rather, that fulcrum is the ecological niche.

In 1758, Carolus Linnaeus classified the domestic dog *Canis familiaris*, so distinguishing it as a species from *Canis lupus*. In 1993, dogs were reclassified by the Smithsonian Institute and the American Society of Mammologists as *Canis lupus familiaris*. This new name was intended to reflect scientific confidence that there is 'minimal genetic difference between dogs and wolves' (Morey 2006: 166), that 'the dog is not only a *descendant* of the wolf, but really *is* a wolf' (Coppinger and Coppinger 2016: 13; my emphasis). Today, the transformation of *Canis familiaris* from an independent species into 'a mere variety of the wolf' (Morey 2006: 166) remains a matter of debate among scientists (Bekoff 2018: 213). Or rather, it is a matter of debate among *some* scientists, while others ignore it entirely. In James Serpell's (2017) widely read collection *The Domestic Dog: Its Evolution, Behavior and Interactions with People*, for example, the issue of reclassification is discussed just once, and this once is the sole occasion (out of the 128 that refer to the taxonomic classification of dogs) on which this new nomenclature is mentioned. Miklósi has a geocultural explanation for what he describes as this 'unfortunate and confusing situation', which is that 'European zoologists, behavioural scientists, and geneticists over the world still refer to the dog as a separate species, while in many papers written mainly by North American authors, dogs are categorized as subspecies of wolves (*C. l. familiaris*)' (Miklósi 2017: 99). Nevertheless, this reclassification cannot be dismissed, for as the Coppingers note in the context of Konrad Lorenz's mistaken views about dogs' descent from jackals, and as I indicated in the introduction to this chapter with regard to the dog-is-wolf thesis, 'once an idea gets into print, it stays in people's perceptions for years' (Coppinger and Coppinger 2016: 171).

One might imagine that the Coppingers, being North Americans, would be in broad agreement with the idea that dogs are a variety of wolf. They are, however, also behavioural ecologists, and it is as behavioural ecologists that they strongly object, in *What Is a Dog?*, to the reclassification of dogs on the basis of genetic ancestry.[17] For Coppinger and Coppinger, the dog-is-wolf classification marks dogs out from all other domesticates, and they impute this 'exceptionalism' not, as one might imagine, to the 'appeal for a dog to be part wolf' (Coppinger and Coppinger 2016: 12),[18] but rather, more subtly, to dog speciation theories that connect the dog–human 'special relationship' (127) to human domestication of wolves and, from there, to the 'euphori[c]' 'mythology' that 'dogs were domesticated by humans to do something useful' (224). In other words, they impute this exceptional classification to a wishful story about humans, in which humans somehow conquer wolves and transform them into useful employees – i.e. dogs.

The 'when, where and how questions' that I addressed in the previous section are described by Coppinger and Coppinger as 'entertaining' (Coppinger and Coppinger 2016: 65). According to the Coppingers, they are based on two mistaken beliefs: that the symbiotic relationship between dogs and humans is mutual, and that evidence for such mutualism can be identified in human domestication of wolves. For sure, Coppinger and Coppinger write, dogs and humans have a symbiotic relationship, which is to say that they live in close proximity to and interact with each other. But that relationship is one of commensalism, which means that dogs and humans '[eat] at the same table' (Coppinger and Coppinger 2016: 133), a practice – or rather, an evolutionary strategy – that is obligatory for dogs and without which they would become extinct (cf. Pierce and Bekoff 2021). The argument for commensalism rather than mutualism is that, were dogs to become extinct, human reproduction would be unaffected (Coppinger and Coppinger 2016: 133). Not only is human reproductive success/survival independent of dogs *today*, it has *always*, the Coppingers argue, been independent of dogs, regardless of the 'imaginative' (Coppinger and Coppinger 2016: 132) accounts of the origins of dogs that relate how wolves/dogs were the first human companion species, or how they were an aid to humans on account of their sense of olfaction, or as hunters, herders, guarders, bed-warmers etc. It is noticeable that Coppinger and Coppinger are careful to report on the costs to humans of the global dog population in terms of bites, rabies and other diseases, livestock harassment and deaths, and negative effects on wildlife (Coppinger and Coppinger 2016: 140). Their purpose in doing so, it appears, is to provide evidence for their claim that dogs are not necessarily 'good' for humans.

So if not the wolf, who is the ancestor of the dog? Coppinger and Coppinger argue that there are two different kinds of dogs in the world, and it is the group that is in the numerical minority – 'Western breeds' (Coppinger and Coppinger 2016: 20) – that define, wrongly, what is a dog.[19] The ancestors of these 'fancy hobby pet' dogs are the 'real dogs' who are everywhere visible in nearly every part of the globe today, with the possible exception of 'the West' (which is the location of the densest production of scientific knowledge about dogs). They write:

> Man's best friends live ubiquitously in the United States, Europe, and other developed countries and, in these countries, are by and large household pets ... We need to add our professional opinion, however, to display a little squeamishness toward the fancy hobby pet group about the few hundred Western breeds that set the standard for what dogs are supposed to be. Could it be that breeds represented as working, or hunting, or pet groups don't represent real dogs? Could it be that the so-called stray dogs, street dogs, neighbourhood dogs, village dogs, and even feral dogs of the world are the real, naturally evolved, self-selected dogs? We will argue that those street dogs are not mongrels or strays. We will argue that they are the real dogs, the ancestral type of our modern breeds ... They are much more ancient than any 'ancient' breed.
> (Coppinger and Coppinger 2016: 21)

The relevant ancestor of the 'Kennel Club creations' (Coppinger and Coppinger 2016: 20), in short, is not some misty species of grey wolf, but rather that population of dogs which all 'look alike' (Coppinger and Coppinger 2016: 39),[20] that has evolved, over approximately 7,000 years, 'on [its] own', and that is 'adapted to the [human] niche in which it makes its living' (Coppinger and Coppinger 2016: 42). 'The dog is its own, individual species. A lot of us think it is a beautiful species. And not because it looks or acts like a wolf but just the opposite: it doesn't look or act life a wolf – it looks and acts like a dog' (Coppinger and Coppinger 2016: 21). The significant difference pertaining to dogs lies not in the difference between dogs and wolves, or among dog breeds, but rather between *dogs with a history of breeding* and *dogs without a history of breeding*. Street dogs (dogs without a history of breeding) are not derived from once-wolf modern breeds; rather, modern breeds (dogs with a history of breeding) are derived from the street.

To suggest otherwise would be racist. Although Coppinger and Coppinger do not mention the word racism specifically, they note that it would be 'politically incorrect' (by which I assume they mean that it would be racist) to ask whether 'white people evolved from black people or was it the other way around, and did they both evolve from Asian types?' (Coppinger and Coppinger 2016: 9). They continue: '[i]f we asked the same question for the members of the genus *Canis* isn't it equally absurd?' (9). The point here is unusually difficult to grasp because the terminology 'white people', 'black people' and 'Asian types' is generally associated with 'races', whereas members grouped under the genus *Canis* are generally identified as species. Are they saying that it would be racist to identify human 'races' as species? Or that it is racist to identify dog species as 'races'? The Coppingers' critique is buried deep within the confusion that follows from their rhetoric. As I understand it, it is this: to imagine that any one group evolved from another, be it a 'race' or a species, is racist. One response to such a claim would be to confirm that it is indeed racist to imagine such a thing, because only racism could make such a contention intelligible. And in fact racism *did* make such a contention intelligible, in the nineteenth century, by insisting on evolution as a continuous, gradual process of change over time, a conception that can be effortlessly bent to the service of an ideology of human and animal hierarchies (see Chapter 6 of this book).

This is not, however, the Coppingers' response. 'Races', for the Coppingers, do in truth exist. They refer, for example, to '*Canis* (races) ... jackals, wolves, dingoes, coyotes, and dogs' (Coppinger and Coppinger 2016: 9), and to 'landraces', which means 'a geographically based population within a species that contains a non-random distribution of alleles (forms of a gene)' (19). What is the difference between the Coppingers' ostensibly non-racist identification of *Canis* races and the racist identification of – or question with regard to – the evolution of some groups of humans or animals from other groups of humans or animals? The difference is that the *Canis* races are defined not by lineage, but by niche-based adaptation: 'wolves, coyotes, and jackals were ever-changing adaptations to a niche. The niches were constantly changing, and the species were constantly readapting to those changing niches' (Coppinger and Coppinger 2016: 207). Note how easily here (and above) Coppinger and Coppinger slip between 'race' and species. In the end, this slippage returns the Coppingers to where they began. It leads them to ask a second 'politically incorrect' question, a question that is too 'politically incorrect to talk about at the moment', which is whether humans who are adapted to different niches (e.g. the arctic tundra or the African semidesert scrubland) are different species (216).

It seems that for Coppinger and Coppinger, as for Darwin, 'race' and species ' "come back" to the same thing' (Darwin in Desmond and Moore 2009: 265). I will return to what this meant, for Darwin, in Chapter 6. For Coppinger and Coppinger, 'race' and species come back to the same thing because all identities are derived from, and defined by, the niche. Thus, one can call a dog a 'race' or one can call a dog a 'species', but it does not ultimately matter which it is, because the identity of a dog is not defined by either category. A dog is a dog because, for 7,000 years, according to the Coppingers, they have been exploiting a human niche. The fact that niches are 'constantly changing', and that species are 'constantly readapting' to such changes, might do away with the essentialism of species and 'race' in theory, but the timescale – thousands of years – ensures that it does not do away with them in practice. By way of the niche, Coppinger and Coppinger place 'race' firmly within the long timescales of evolutionary biology. The implications of this equivalence between the identities and temporalities of 'race' and of species are grave. Trapped in 'niche time', 'race' becomes resistant to 'political time', that is, to the times of *specific* forms of historical and contemporary racisms, and to the kinds of anti-racist analyses that this temporality allows (see also Chapter 6).

Coppinger and Coppinger enact what they themselves are trying to illustrate and critique, which is that speciation theories are tied up with 'race' and racism. I don't think this enactment can be explained solely by their superficial understanding of 'race'. I think it is also a consequence of their efforts to replace one theory of speciation with another. Coppinger and Coppinger are at liberty to criticise 'race' (in which they are evidently not especially interested), but are not at liberty at all, it seems, to criticise, or even to think reflexively about, the concept of species. Yet this is precisely the Coppingers' agenda: to expose the implications, especially for street dogs, of the dog-is-wolf speciation thesis, and the 'special relationship' that goes with it. The issue for them is not merely that the 'fancy dog', ostensibly 'a mere variety of the wolf', defines 'what is a dog'; it is that the relations that humans have with fancy dogs – relations of governance, domination and control, that are rooted in the fantasy that it was by such relations that humans turned wolves into dogs – are naturalised as *the* model for all dog–human relations. Street dogs pay the price for this, in the form of sterilisation, adoption and killing.

In a strange twist of analysis, Coppinger and Coppinger themselves offer an explanation for the powerful lure of the dog speciation theories they condemn. In the course of their niche account of dogs' evolution, they argue that dogs developed a wide range of physiological, behavioural and social capacities that ensure they will be successful when *they* initiate the 'special relationship' on which their lives depend (Coppinger and Coppinger 2016: 155). Included among their examples are: the early abandonment of dog pups by their mothers, such that their best hope of survival is to find a human companion; the 'cuteness' of pups at the moment of abandonment; the social bonding abilities of dogs that enable them to build lifelong relationships, especially with species to which they are exposed during the socialisation period; and the ease with which they can be adopted (they can eat almost anything, starve relatively easily, and can tolerate high levels of abuse and handling) (Coppinger and Coppinger 2016: Chapters 11 and 12). Reading between the lines, one is almost led to believe that the invitation to write the story that the Coppingers oppose – that dogs, to quote again, were 'domesticated by humans to do something useful' (Coppinger and Coppinger 2016: 224) – was sent out by dogs themselves.

Conclusion

If one must speak of origins, as it seems one must, then perhaps the origins of dogs and of humans, of *Canis familiaris* and *Homo sapiens*, are best dated, give or take a few decades or centuries, to 2,300 years ago, to Aristotle – or perhaps to 500 years ago, to the sixteenth century, if it was Christian theology and not Aristotelian logic, as John Wilkins argues, that gave birth to the concept of species. 'I have become convinced', Wilkins writes, 'that the reason for the introduction of species in the first place was the attempts by theologians in the sixteenth century to determine how many kinds of animals were included on the Ark' (Wilkins 2017: xxiii). Like the evolution of dogs themselves, theories of dog speciation do not reveal themselves easily; they are based upon numerous competing methodologies, conjectures and assumptions regarding events that could have happened anywhere between 10,000 years ago (if not less) and 135,000 years ago (if not more). In this chapter,

I have drawn attention to the great effort that is required to create a coherent narrative of dog speciation in order to begin to denaturalise the stories that are told about dogs and their behaviours. There are other ways to pursue this project. In his book *Animal Biographies: Towards a History of Individuals*, the historian Éric Baratay offers an incisive critique of the contemporary ethological conception of 'the universal, timeless, "natural" dog (Baratay 2015: 9) by illustrating how the behaviours of dogs and, importantly, their relations with humans, change over generations: 'not biological generations … but social generations, having to do with the communities of one period, occurring after communities of other periods' (Baratay 2022: 121).[21]

To understand species as a story, as I am doing here, is not to suggest that it could be easily changed or dismissed. Dogs' species story has acquired a substantive reality, not because it explains what dogs 'really are', but because biology, genetics, archaeology, zooarchaeology, anthropology (etc., etc.) bear witness (Stengers 2000: 98), in their differently tenuous ways, to it. Tenuous though they are, they together constitute a powerful and influential 'order' (see Chapter 7) that defines a particular relation between dogs and humans today. It is on account of this order that dogs' species story cannot simply be extracted from dogs, and on account of it also that contesting its implications is so urgent, for this is not a narrative that necessarily shapes the lives of dogs for the better. In Chapter 4, I will address how expectations regarding dogs' behaviours are articulated and justified with reference to their species story. Before doing so, it is important to address how species and behaviour come to be connected at all. For it seems almost to go without saying, today, that behaviour, as Thom van Dooren notes, 'is a key part of the identity of [a] species' (Van Dooren 2016: 33).

Notes

1 And, indeed, by the owner's total surrender to the trainer, as Woodhouse's 1954 book, *Dog Training My Way* (Woodhouse 1997 [1954]), indicates.
2 Of course there are exceptions. See for example my discussion, below, of the veterinarian David Paxton, whose account of the speciation

of dogs and of humans could be understood in terms of a biological co-becoming. Paxton, however, is something of an outlier.

3 On whose contribution, precisely, this was, see Grosz (2004: 20).

4 The connection that Darwin identified between artificial and natural selection was not in fact 'a logical step' for everyone. Worboys, Strange and Pemberton observe that while race and breed were used synonymously for dogs, breed was 'rarely, if ever, applied to human grouping' (Worboys *et al.* 2018: 164). This, they continue, was because races of humans were understood – especially by the racist polygenists (see Chapter 6 of this book) – to be fixed, while breeds of domesticated animals were considered mutable (Worboys *et al.* 2018: 164). In other words, it was possible to believe that one rule of inheritance did not apply to all species.

5 Although Darwin also went on to argue that natural selection 'is a power incessantly ready for action, and is as immeasurably superior to man's feeble efforts, as the works of Nature are to those of Art' (Darwin 2008: 50).

6 A metaphor is quite distinct from a blueprint. Darwin's relationship with breeders was 'superficial', Van Grouw argues, because Darwin wanted to use selective breeding and the creation of diversity *only* as a metaphor for evolution, and not 'as an evolutionary process in its own right' (Van Grouw 2018: 60). Darwin's eugenicist cousin Francis Galton, by contrast, was deeply interested in the real implications of breeding not only for animals, but also for humans. Not surprisingly, he was also the only biologist of the period, Worboys, Strange and Pemberton argue, to be genuinely involved with breeders (Worboys *et al.* 2018: 182).

7 Although see Chapter 7 on biological theories suggesting that all evolution is co-evolution.

8 For some scientists, as I will illustrate in Chapter 4, that point arrives when the eyes of a dog, unlike the eyes of a wolf, swivel to look at what a human is pointing to.

9 Although as Frantz and Larson note, the trend in genomic science now is to view domestication pathways as species- and region-specific (Frantz and Larson 2020: 32) (rather than generic).

10 From the Greek word *klados*, meaning branch. A clade is a monophyletic group, and it includes 'an ancestral species and *all* of its descendent species' (Wilkins 2017: 242, emphasis in the original). As John Wilkins explains: 'a clade is understood to be uniquely isolated from the rest of the tree by a single stem or "cut" ' (Wilkins 2017: 291).

11 Mitochondrial DNA – is used in the investigation of gene flow (geographic distribution, migrations etc.). Unlike nuclear DNA, which

is inherited from both parents, mtDNA is inherited from the maternal line.
12. For a critical analysis of the significance of these changes in domesticated animals more broadly, and especially of paedomorphism in companion animals, see Tuan (2004 [1984]).
13. Some evidence for this claim is found in Dimitry Belyaev's famous Silver Fox Study, which suggested that the reproductive cycles of silver foxes changed after forty years of selection for tameness (Trut 1999: 167).
14. In 1975, in the foreword to M. K. Fox's edited collection *The Wild Canids*, Lorenz rescinded his view that jackals are the ancestors of one type of dog (see the introduction to this book on Lorenz's distinction between types of dogs). As he explains it: 'I am guilty of writing a popular book on domestic dogs and also of having propounded an erroneous hypothesis: I had inherited, from my teacher Oskar Heinroth, the assumption that the bulk of domestic dog races are descended from the golden jackal, *Canis aureus*' (Lorenz in Morey 2010: 14).
15. Social scientists have similarly moved away from understanding of domestication as something that humans do *to* animals (e.g. Tuan 2004 [1984]) toward analyses of domestication as the product of accident and chance, leading possibly to a kind of symbiosis or mutualism (see for example Cassidy and Mullin 2007; Swanson et al 2018; Weil 2012). One key difference between the sciences and social sciences, however, is that social scientists only rarely perceive or assume the relationship between domesticated animals and humans to have been, or now to be, advantageous to animals. This may be because reproductive success ('species survival') is not necessarily, for them, a criterion of advantage. As Yuval Harari (a historian, not a social scientist) says in relation to cattle: '[i]n evolutionary terms, cattle represent one of the most successful animal species ever to exist. At the same time, they are some of the most miserable animals on the planet' (Harari 2011: 108).
16. Leach's argument, which describes parallel domestication, is that physical transformations resulting from domestication – defined by her as 'acclimatization to life in a household' (Leach 2003: 359) – were first seen in *both* dogs *and* humans. 'Though it would be unreasonable to expect one overarching explanation for these [biological] phenomena', she writes, 'at the very least we should ask why one explanation should not be tested for closely similar changes in two symbiotic animals' (Leach 2003: 359). Leach's use of the word 'acclimatization' in her definition of domestication is significant. Her point

is that the 'culturally modified, artificial environment' (359) of the household could have exerted selection pressures as strong as those brought about by climate change.

17 *What Is a Dog?* was the final book that Raymond Coppinger co-authored with his wife, Lorna (Coppinger and Coppinger 2016). He died in 2017, at the age of eighty.

18 Which social scientists would surely recognise as a valorisation of the wild over the tame (see for example Deleuze and Guattari (1987: 240), or Berger (2009) on animals; for critiques of the wild/domestic dualism in general, see the references in note 15 above, and, in relation to dogs specifically, see Lescureux (2020)).

19 Although I very much appreciate the Coppingers' critique here, which is that 'western breeds' cannot define 'what is a dog', their division of all dogs into just two categories – in essence, street dogs and captive dogs – is problematic: first, because dogs live together or alongside humans in many different ways (see for example Natasha Fijn's (2018) ethnographic account of how dogs live with herding communities in the Khangai Mountains of Mongolia and how dingoes live with the Yolngu in Aboriginal Australia), and second, because there exists huge diversity *within* the categories of street dog and captive dog (as indicated, for instance, by Gris *et al.*'s (2021) scientific study of the patterns and levels of the activities of village dogs, v. owned dogs who roam freely, v. family and farm dogs).

20 This physical similarity is important to Coppinger and Coppinger because '[f]or a biologist, that kind of uniformity implies the process of natural selection' (Coppinger and Coppinger 2016: 42). The dogs' particular size and shape 'fit' a niche that has only so much 'carrying' capacity.

21 For a more detailed account of Baratay's book, see Motamedi Fraser (2023).

3

Vanishing animals: How to turn an individual dog into a species ambassador

I pause for a moment, with this chapter, to address some of the ways that the idea of a species and actual animals' behaviours come to be connected. For dogs' species story would not necessarily, in itself, bear so very heavily on dogs, were it not that this story often shapes contemporary scientific understandings of what dogs need and want, and how they do and should behave (see especially Chapter 4). This is one of the reasons why species stories matter: if species is the lens through which behaviours are framed, then how a species is characterised assumes real, material significance. Chapter 3 is also important, with regard to the argument in this book, in a second sense, for it is here that I begin to introduce the process by which 'species thinking' erases the significance of particularity, and especially the particular individual.

Where the previous chapter attended largely to scientific theories, this chapter addresses itself to scientific methods: specifically, to the methods of Konrad Lorenz, Conwy Lloyd Morgan, George Romanes and Charles Darwin, all of which, in their different ways, serve to tie species and behaviours together, such that one is illustrative of and reinforces the other. I choose these scientists because they were at the forefront of three major disciplinary approaches to animals in the late nineteenth and the twentieth century: classical ethology; that branch of comparative psychology that would become behaviourism; and what might loosely be called Darwinian 'anecdotalism'. Anecdotalism continues, today, to shape critiques of contemporary ethology.

I begin with Lorenz's work, which yokes together species and behaviours in a most transparent fashion. Lorenz's concept of instincts (innate 'fixed action patterns') is now associated with a limited understanding of animals driven, as Marga Vicedo concisely summarises it, by 'species-specific, stereotyped, "machine-like", behaviors that are "immutable in the face of experience"' (Vicedo 2009: 267). Nevertheless, what will be of special interest here is not so much Lorenz's conception of animals – brilliantly analysed by Eileen Crist (2000) – as his method of 'keeping animals'. 'Keeping animals', I will argue, was an exercise in species manipulation, that is, an exercise in the manipulation of individual animals in order to identify and confirm, through the disintegration and reassemblage of their behaviours, species identity and genealogy. Contra Vinciane Despret, who argues that the image of Lorenz as 'a scientist who adopts his animals, swims with his geese and ducks, and speaks with his jackdaws ... is faithful to his practice but less so to his theoretical work' (Despret 2016: 39), my argument will be that Lorenz's romantic image is betrayed by both, by his theory *and* his practice/method, which were deeply bound up with, and lent validity to, each other.

Even during his own lifetime, Lorenz's work was subject to considerable, if not devastating, criticism. Among the best known of these critiques was Daniel S. Lehrman's 1953 paper, published in the *Quarterly Review of Biology*, in which Lehrman argued that (among other things)[1] Lorenz's model of behaviour was not able to distinguish between instinctual and learned elements of behaviour, and that it neglected almost entirely the impact and implications of ontogenetic development. 'Four decades on' (the title of his article), Aubrey Manning – who was a student of Nikolaas Tinbergen and one of the early 'hard core' members of Tinbergen's research group at Oxford (Manning 2005: 287)[2] – recalls Lorenz's antipathy, particularly in conferences, to any analysis of the way that behaviour '*develops*' (Manning 2005: 288, emphasis in the original).

The psychologist Richard Held was witness to that antipathy when it was displayed at a conference in Ithaca, New York, in September 1954. As Held describes it, the event was dominated by tense exchanges between the representatives of European ethology, who were perceived to be insisting upon a rigid biological hereditarianism, and the North American comparative psychologists, who 'continually raise[ed] the question of the role of experience' in the development of behaviour (Held 1956: 691).[3] Although the psychologists were certainly critical of behaviourism, especially insofar as it had 'become little more than a science of "rat learning"' (Burkhardt 2005: 362), they nevertheless remained the inheritors of that legacy which had historically been 'concerned about the ways in which the individual acts upon and transforms his environment' and which, as such (Held drily added), took 'the upwardly-mobile American male as the touchstone for psychological theory'. The vision of a potentially perfectible society, made possible by the postulate of the malleability of individual behaviour, was one that the New York psychologists were loath to give up (Held 1956: 692).

It may seem surprising that there is any place at all for behaviourism in this chapter, given that behaviourism is usually associated with the very opposite of species-typical behaviours, that is, with the transformation of individual behaviour through learning. The 1954 conference staged that contrast, and was especially interesting for it (see Burkhardt (2005: 398–403) for an extensive and nuanced discussion). Yet, when it comes to species identities, the difference between behaviourism and other scientific schools of thought may not be as stark as it first appears. This is why I turn, in the second part of the chapter, to Conwy Lloyd Morgan. Although the origin of behaviourism is usually credited to John Watson – who coined the term in 1913 – B. F. Skinner argues that its central principles were first conceived of in the minds of Morgan and his student Edward L. Thorndike (to whom Watson acknowledged his debt) (Skinner 1959). It was Morgan's claim that an instinctive behaviour pattern, acquired through adaptation, may be modified by learning and therefore, through experience, transformed into 'intelligent' behaviour. Nevertheless, not only were Morgan's theories of behaviour informed by species thinking, as I will demonstrate; so too his methods operated *like* a species theory insofar as they had the effect of erasing the significance of the particular, singular, individual animal – the animal who, in this case, was Morgan's own dog, Tony.

This brings me finally to the third section of this chapter, which is concerned, largely, with the relationship between the 'anecdotal tradition' – best exemplified, perhaps, by Darwin's protégé, George Romanes – and species thinking. Both Morgan and Thorndike were critical of Darwin's and Romanes's anecdotalism, in keeping with the burgeoning professionalisation of science that characterised their (and especially Thorndike's) time. Yet two centuries of professionalism have not expunged anecdotes from science. On the contrary, contemporary cognitive ethology is sometimes described, in derogatory terms, as 'anecdotal cognitivism' (Allen and Bekoff 1999: Chapter 2). Although the anecdotal method is often associated with individual animals (one reason for its supporters to support it, and its critics to criticise it), as I will show in this final section the use of anecdotes – from Darwin through to cognitive ethology today – may nevertheless confirm rather than subvert species thinking, and so transform the individual animal into a species ambassador.

Unlike other chapters in this book, the 'species-making' methods and methodologies that I address here could apply – indeed, they are usually expressly designed to apply – to nearly all animals. Thus, although I try to use scientists' examples of dogs wherever possible, and although these techniques certainly have implications for dogs, they are not specific to dogs. Tony the Fox Terrier played an important part in the elaboration of Morgan's Canon (on which see below, pp. 104–109), but the point of the Canon is that it is as relevant to the study of the behaviours of ducks as it is to the study of dogs. Such general techniques are nevertheless worthy of attention for precisely this reason: they are illustrative of the ways that species thinking sweeps up multitudes – multitudes of individual animals within a species category (Lorenz), and multitudes of individual animals regardless of their species categories (Morgan) – in its non-discriminatory wake. There is another reason, however, why dogs serve mainly as examples in this chapter. As I will discuss in Chapters 4 and 5, dogs did not become the subjects of systematic scientific research 'in and of themselves' until the late 1990s.

Keeping animal species (the ethological tradition)

Lorenz's first scientific paper was on Tschock, a female jackdaw whom he had bought in a pet shop, and who proved so attracted to him that he did not have to keep her in an aviary. Tschock's relationship with Lorenz gave him particular observational advantages: he was in 'possession' of a wild animal who was neither afraid nor confined to a cage and who therefore 'performed many of its natural behavior patterns in Lorenz's presence' (Burkhardt 2005: 134). While this relation clearly suited Lorenz's circumstances and his temperament – 'the animal that could escape and yet remains with me affords me undefinable pleasure, especially when it is affection for myself that has prompted it to stay' (Lorenz 2002b [1949]: 5) – in time 'keeping tame individuals of wild species under free-ranging conditions' came to be recognised, as Tinbergen wrote in a draft of his obituary for Lorenz, 'as one of the basic methods of behavior research' (Tinbergen in Burkhardt 2005: 480).

Lorenz often likened himself to 'the farmer' and Tinbergen to 'the hunter'. Historian Richard Burkhardt explains the difference: 'Lorenz liked raising and breeding animals, nurturing them when they were ill,[4] and having them as companions. Tinbergen preferred stalking animals in the field, matching wits with them, and discovering how the details of their behavior contributed to their survival' (Burkhardt 2005: 11). Tinbergen's practice – which is described with humour by Burkhardt as 'crouching in a hide and spying on a creature' (Burkhardt 2005: 132) – had been shaped partly by the widespread social activity of nature study in the Netherlands during his youth, and partly by the British field tradition, which included Charles Darwin and Julian Huxley, that influenced Tinbergen during his career at Oxford. As Burkhardt notes, these different methods and practices ultimately led Tinbergen and Lorenz to make different contributions to ethology. Tinbergen's focus was on the ways animals adapt to the ecological demands of their environments, the survival value of behaviour patterns in natural settings, behavioural evolution and evolutionary convergence. Unlike this 'ecological-evolutionary outlook' (Tinbergen in Burkhardt 2005: 475), Lorenz was more concerned with behaviour patterns as '*historical* arrangements' of survival value (Burkhardt 2005: 419, emphasis in the original). That is, he understood behaviour patterns to be a key – if not *the* key – to species: to the identification of the evolutionary history of a species and of the distinctions between species, and to the confirmation of species identities.

This notion that behaviour patterns might offer a kind of 'evolutionary genealogy' of a species can be traced in part to two important influences on Lorenz: the North American zoologist Charles Otis Whitman, and the German zoologist Oskar Heinroth (Tinbergen 2005 [1963]: 298). In Lorenz's view, 'C. O. Whitman and O. Heinroth were phylogenists and not physiologists. Their chief interest in innate behaviour patterns was of a systemic and taxonomic nature' (Lorenz 1950: 246). 'Instinct and organs', Whitman wrote, 'are to be studied from the common standpoint of phyletic descent' (Whitman in Lorenz 1950: 238). Having first learned how to study evolution through comparative anatomy (which at that time was concerned less with the mechanisms of evolution and more with homologous structures), Lorenz too believed that behaviour patterns could be used 'to determine common ancestries and reconstruct phylogenies' (Burkhardt 2005: 134). As he put it:

> behaviour patterns are not something which animals may do or not do, or do in different ways, according to the requirements of the occasion, but something which animals of a given species 'have got', exactly in the same manner as they 'have got' claws or teeth of a definite morphological structure.
>
> (Lorenz 1950: 238)[5]

One of the analytical implications of this conception of behaviour patterns is that it makes it possible 'to *isolate* a very distinct physiological process as an independent constituent of behaviour and to study it separately' (Lorenz 1950: 238, emphasis in the original). These distinct processes, Lorenz wrote, are *'particulate elements'* of behaviour (Lorenz 1950: 238, emphasis in the original). And they are unchanging in a species. Lorenz argued that the most an animal's experience can do is to determine 'the intensity with which the instinctive response is performed', and perhaps also *'which* response is elicited by a particular stimulus' (Lorenz 1970 [1937]: 268, emphasis in the original). For instance: even though the 'escape response' may diminish as an animal becomes increasingly tame, it could *'at any time* be elicited by a specific frightening stimulus of a particular strength, without any preceding experience' (Lorenz 1970 [1937]: 268, emphasis in the original).

Although Eileen Crist insists that 'neither Tinbergen nor Lorenz wanted to "desubjectify" animals' (Crist 2000: 89), as she illustrates, Lorenz's analysis of instinctive behaviour patterns in terms of particulate elements, and as inherited and unchanging in a species, had the effect of bracketing off animal behaviours from the subjectivity of the animal who 'has' them. In Lorenz's view, for instance, it is not the *animal* who responds to a stimulus; rather, it is the 'innate releasing mechanism' that 'chooses' and reacts to it, and this reaction *itself* initiates a pattern of behaviour (Crist 2000: 100). Moreover, according to Lorenz's 'hydraulic reservoir' model of motivation, 'energies' that are specific to a single behaviour pattern 'can be dammed up, accumulated, diverted or used up' (Beer 2020: 263). If a specific behaviour activity becomes 'dammed up', for example (perhaps in the absence of 'eliciting stimuli'), the threshold for releasing it will become very lowered until finally, as Lorenz explains, 'the activity in question will … go off *in vacuo*, with an effect somewhat suggestive of the explosion of a boiler whose safety valve fails to function' (Lorenz 1950: 247).

Although Lorenz was no less critical of the 'mosaic' approach of mechanists than he was of the summative approach of vitalists (Lorenz 1950), it is interesting to note – indeed I think it is something of a giveaway – that he believed that mechanists were likely to be 'less wrong' in their analysis of behaviour than were vitalists: 'the atomistic investigator is not guilty of any methodological error, as long as he really is examining a comparatively independent constituent part. It is just because they may legitimately be isolated theoretically and experimentally that the discovery of independent constituents always is such a tremendous step forward in analytical research' (Lorenz 1950: 227). Or as he put it rather defensively elsewhere: 'the existence of the wood as a "holistic" living community is [not] somehow threatened by recognition of the fact that wood just happens to consist of trees as well as other components' (Lorenz 1970 [1942]: 355).

On the one hand, given what Lorenz says about the holistic living community not being threatened by the components of which it consists, it could be a mistake to contrast too strongly the romantic Lorenz who talks to his animals – some editions of his popular book *King Solomon's Ring* include the subtitle 'He Spoke with the Beasts, the Birds, and the Fish' (Vicedo 2009: 279) – with the scientific Lorenz whose analytic method disaggregates behaviour from subjectivity and experience and divides it into particulates. On the other hand, however, Lorenz deployed and honed his somewhat Dr Dolittle practices precisely because he considered 'keeping animals' to be ideally suited both to the reconstructive phyletic task in the zoological system, and to the identification of instinctive behaviour patterns in the biological system. Keeping animals was a powerful and effective method in both these regards, Lorenz believed, because captivity induces what he called 'miscarrying behaviours', that is, behaviours that are performed 'wrongly', or in an inappropriate context, or in the absence of eliciting stimuli, or with a substitute object. This is why the 'completely-satiated domestic dog' will nevertheless '[shake] his master's slippers "to death"' (Lorenz 1970 [1942]: 360): because '[a Dachshund or terrier] retains an unaltered, irrepressible appetite' for the performance of the motor pattern of shaking prey (Lorenz 1970 [1942]: 360; see also Lorenz 2002c [1963]: 84–87).

With respect to the reconstructive phyletic task, for example: keeping animals compels the observer to deduce from miscarrying behaviour patterns what were the environmental conditions that gave those patterns their 'normal' adaptive value. 'Just as he would deduce from the morphological characters of a mole's forepaws that this species needs earth to dig in', Lorenz wrote, 'so he must, from slight "hints" of miscarrying behaviour patterns, be able to deduce the corresponding environmental exigencies of the species' (Lorenz 1950: 237). With respect to the identification of instinctive behaviour patterns: under conditions of captivity, particularly if the keeper is not familiar with the 'needs' of a species, instinctive behaviour patterns often disintegrate into 'a jumble ... of parts' (Lorenz 1950: 236). When the species' needs are restored by the keeper, so too will be the behaviour patterns. 'I hardly know a more *instructive* object of observation than just this type of disintegration and reassembling of the system of actions in animals kept in captivity. It is, in fact, an actualized example of analysis and resynthesis of behaviour!' (Lorenz 1950: 237, emphasis in the original).

Regardless of Lorenz's enthusiastic conviction here, I would argue that even though the purpose of the method appears to be the observation of behaviour, in fact is it the observation of species; or more strongly, it is a method of species-making. 'Keeping animals' offered Lorenz three things: a retrospective insight into the becoming of species ('this species needs earth to dig in'); a means to identify fragments of species behaviours by way of their undoing (into a 'jumble ... of parts'); and a confirmation of the integrity of species behaviours/species identities in their redoing (in the 'reassembling the system of actions'). Animal behaviours, which could potentially lead anywhere or mean anything – a Deleuzian 'line of flight', to go to the other extreme – lead only to, and reveal only, species. Not only are behaviours *theorised* by Lorenz as mechanistic, therefore; the *observation* of behaviours under these particular conditions becomes, in Lorenz's hands, a powerful way of keeping an animal captive in the cage of species.

Thom van Dooren's discussion of the ethics of Lorenz's imprinting is relevant here. For van Dooren, Lorenz's relationships with the birds on whom he imprinted himself represent not so much novel 'possibilities for connection and care' as they do a '*captive* form of life' (Van Dooren 2014: 103, emphasis in the original). This form of life is captive because the relationships, rather than being constituted 'between two subjects, who – however unequally positioned – already have a significantly well-formed way of life, a way of being in the world' (101–102), were 'knowingly manipulated' by Lorenz, at an early stage of development, with the specific intention of creating 'a lifelong attachment' (103). Although imprinting is a very particular mode of biological, social and subjective manipulation, I think it is an apt metaphor for Lorenz's method (keeping animals) more broadly. I say this not because to be a kept animal is to live a life in captivity (although it is, in a general kind of way), but rather because Lorenz himself considered keeping, as he considered imprinting, to be scientifically valuable *because* it is a manipulation, *because* it is an interference, *because* it induces miscarrying behaviours. Because, in short, it creates a distortion of or deviation from 'species-typicality' that enables species and species norms to be identified, 'confirmed' and consolidated. In *On Aggression*, Lorenz stated that '[p]hysiology, the science concerned with the normal life processes and how they fulfil their species-preserving function, forms the essential foundation for pathology, the science investigating abnormalities' (Lorenz 2002c [1963]: 27). One might argue that the relation between physiology and pathology is inverted by Lorenz's method: now, keeping animals is the essential pathology-inducing foundation, designed to enable the investigation of the species-preserving physiological norm. The fact that Lorenz may have diligently cared for his birds,[6] or that he believed that the attachment of his animals to him was freely given and, as I cited earlier, based on 'affection for myself' (Lorenz 2002b [1949]: 5), does not preclude this method from being coercive, especially insofar as miscarrying behaviours are produced '*at the expense* of a whole set of other ways of being' (Van Dooren 2014: 103, emphasis in the original) – and at the expense, I would add, of a whole set of other ways of *understanding* being.

This chapter, as I noted in the introduction, is concerned not only with species-making, but also with one of its most important consequences, the transformation of particular individual animals, singular animals, into generic species representatives. One way of achieving this, as I have been demonstrating, is to deploy species identity and species-typicality as the lens through which all behaviours are viewed. This erasure of particularity is, ironically, especially well dramatised in Lorenz's popular books – ironically, because in these books Lorenz refers to named animals, whom he describes through personalised stories and anecdotes. Yet it is this very individualisation that draws the reader's attention to the vanishing of the animals into instinctive behaviour patterns. Lorenz's popular books, such as *Man Meets Dog* (2002b [1949]) and *King Solomon's Ring* (2000a [1949]), cannot be lightly dismissed, not only because they convey, in an accessible form, some of the themes and ideas that Lorenz developed in his scientific work, but also because they created a powerful and enduring image of what it was to be, to live and to think as an ethologist. Indeed the style and significance of these books arguably secured for Lorenz, and perhaps for ethology as well, considerable public acclaim. It also helped to fund his research at Altenberg, Austria, where Lorenz had built a research station on his father's estate (Burkhardt 2005: 11).

At the time of writing *Man Meets Dog* in 1949, Lorenz was engaged in debates over whether the dingo was 'a true wild dog' or a domesticated dog turned wild, as Lorenz thought (Lorenz 2002b [1949]: 116).[7] In part in order to answer this question, Lorenz devised an experiment to test whether and how a domestic dog would rear a dingo, and how the dingo would behave in response. As I noted in the introduction to this book, he did this by presenting a dingo pup to his own dog, Senta, who had whelped at approximately the same time as a dingo in Schönbrunn Zoo. I recount Lorenz's description of this episode because it illustrates, again, but here in a most visceral way, the uses he made of interference and manipulation in his work. It illustrates his interference with Senta, and with the dingo puppy, whose life – if Lorenz's analysis of the 'brood defence' is to be believed – he put at great risk. I also recount this anecdote because, as it turns out, it is not about the particular individual, Senta, at all.

The story begins with a portrayal of Lorenz at his '[e]bullient and egocentric' (Burkhardt 2005: 5) best, rushing between the zoo and a funeral with the dingo pup in his dispatch case. It also illustrates him at his narrative best, moving from humorous self-portrayal to sober pedagogy to dramatic suspense. Lorenz teaches his reader that the best way to encourage 'a mammal mother to adopt a strange baby' is to elicit the 'brood-tending instinct', which can be done by presenting the infant to the mother 'outside her nest and in as helpless a form as possible' (Lorenz 2002b [1949]: 119). He then notches up the tension by advising that stimulation neither of the brood-tending instinct nor of 'the carrying reaction' (carrying the pup back to the nest) is a guarantee that, once in the nest, the infant will not anyway be 'recognised as an intruder and remorselessly devoured' (Lorenz 2002b [1949]: 120). Lorenz describes this devouring in some detail, underscoring that, if it is going to happen, it will begin at the infant's abdomen, since it is a 'defect' in the process by which a mother removes the foetal membrane and placenta from the newborn and severs the navel-cord. If the process does not stop at that point, 'the abdomen of the young is also opened at the umbilicus' (Lorenz 2002b [1949]: 122). The scene is thus set, and the reader understands the stakes. The 'action' that follows, however, turns not so much on Senta and the dingo puppy as it does on the battle between two instinctive drives, elicited by two different stimuli: the dingo pup's helplessness (which elicits the brood-tending instinct in Senta) and his strange smell (which elicits the 'brood defence' instinct and the devouring impulse).

First, Senta licks the dingo's belly carefully. But then she begins to nip the skin with her teeth. When the dingo cries out and whimpers,

> Senta jumped back horrified as though she suddenly realized, 'I am hurting the wee thing.' It was clear that the brood-tending reaction, the 'pity' elicited by the cry of pain, had once more gained ascendency. She made a decided movement towards the puppy's head as though she wished to carry him to her bed; but as she opened her mouth to seize him, she encountered once more the strange, unknown scent, and the hasty licking began anew, increasing in fervour until she started once more tweaking the skin of the pup's abdomen; then came the cry of pain and again the bitch recoiled in horror. Now

she approached him again and this time her movements became more hurried, her licking more frantic and the exchange of opposing drives more rapid as she was swayed between carrying the orphan or devouring the unwanted 'wrong-smelling' changeling.

(Lorenz 2002b [1949]: 123–124)

This passage – for all its chummy vernacular – exemplifies how, by breaking down behaviour into physiological 'particulates' (single behaviour activities), by attaching these particulates to specific stimuli and by transferring the initiation of behavioural activity from the animal to innate releasing mechanisms, Lorenz simultaneously breaks down the animal's – in this case Senta's – world such that it appears to possess neither 'experiential unity' nor 'continuity' (Crist 2000: 100). Lorenz is not narrating a *sequence* of events here, a joined-up, temporally continuous sequence in which, for example, Senta hears an infant, responds to his cry, and then realises she has misrecognised him as one of her own, etc. Instead, her reactions are understood by him to take place *serially*: they are released by two different stimuli (Lorenz would argue that the pup, from Senta's perspective, is two different objects), and they occur 'in discontinuous – even if contiguous – pockets of time' (Crist 2000: 105). Not merely, then, does Senta have no experience, she has no experience of experience either. As Crist notes in her analysis of Lorenz's account of a mallard duck who rescues a musk duckling, from which I have taken this valuable distinction between sequence and serial, the awareness of the animal of her own situation is not in fact required 'for the contact between subject and object' (Crist 2000: 104). The reason for this is that 'the object gathers all the necessary and sufficient features for the elicitation of the proper behaviors; it need not be known, assessed, understood, recognized, misrecognized, or witnessed by the subject of action' (Crist 2000: 104). The implication – which Lorenz does not spell out in *Man Meets Dog* but which any engaged reader can deduce – is that, even in a 'normal' situation, in which a mother retrieves a pup of her own, 'it only *appears* that her actions manifest an understanding of objects, events, and their connections' (Crist 2000: 105, emphasis in the original).

Lorenz's interference with, and manipulation of, both Senta and the dingo puppy melts away in the heat of the dramatic narrative. The desubjectifying implications of Lorenz's conception of instinctive behaviour, by contrast, are exaggerated by the narrative, partly because the story is intentionally told with heightened suspense to appeal to a general public, and partly because the stimuli and mechanisms that are driving Senta's actions (or reactions, rather) are in conflict with each other, which renders their 'independence' from her subjectivity all the more stark. As Despret says, Lorenz's concept of instinct offered him 'the perfect cause: it escapes from all subjective explanations, and it is at once a biological cause and motive (a motive, moreover, that completely escapes the knowledge of the subject himself)' (Despret 2016: 40). The reader cannot help but identify with Senta's anguished cry, which brings Lorenz's anecdote to a close. Senta, Lorenz writes, 'sat back on her haunches in front of the Dingo, raised her nose to the sky, and gave vent to her distress in a long, wolf-like howl' (Lorenz 2002b [1949]: 124).

Senta's howl – her 'inward torment', her 'suffering' (Lorenz 2002b [1949]: 124) – represents for Lorenz the suffering of a canid being torn apart by two opposing specifies-specific instinctive behaviour patterns, behaviour patterns that Senta, *because* she is a canid, 'has got' – or which, more accurately, might be said to 'have got' Senta. Alternative interpretations are not available to Lorenz because that would require 'one [to] see that if the animal responds by using his own way to arrive at articulating the problem, he no longer responds to the question "in general." Which means that his response has nothing generalizable about it' (Despret 2016: 93). Senta may, for example, already be familiar with Lorenz's experiments (even if she does not understand them as such). Or she may be exhausted from feeding her newly born infants and frustrated by being obliged to address the question of this new puppy stranger. Or both. Or perhaps it is something else altogether. The howl could even be the sign of a resolution, a resolution *neither* to devour the dingo, *nor* to take him in contentedly. There is some evidence for this in Lorenz's account of the conclusion of the episode: he notes that even though Senta 'suckled [the pup] with her own, one day she bit him so severely in the ear that it never properly recovered its shape and ever after drooped to one side' (Lorenz 2002b [1949]: 124). Whatever the reasons, these would be the reasons of the individual Senta, which, if given space for consideration, would interfere with the story that Lorenz is telling about the instincts that drive the behaviour of a female member of the species *Canis familiaris*. The howl would be *Senta's* response, a howl that another dog might not sound.

Species scales (the behaviourist tradition)

In the introduction to this chapter, I referred to a conference, held in 1954, that brought together, in great tension, European ethologists and North American psychologists. The tension lay in the perceived contrast between the ethologists' emphasis on the fixity of heredity in determining behaviour, and the psychologists' emphasis on the pliability of experience and learning in shaping behaviour. In his review of that event, the psychologist Richard Held was nevertheless led to wonder about the opposition. 'After all', he wrote, 'we know that American psychology has been enormously influenced by ideas of biological evolution' (Held 1956: 691). And indeed, this is where this section of the chapter begins, with the fact that comparative psychologists in (what was to become) the behaviourist school also, as the philosopher Bernard Rollin writes, have 'their own version of Darwinism':

> namely, the belief that the key concept for psychology was learning, and that learning was pretty much the same all along the evolutionary scale, differing only in degree or complexity. Thus principles of learning arrived at by studying one sort of organism gave conclusions which were believed to have universal validity.
>
> (Rollin 1998: 207)

This, for Rollin, explains why behaviourists are 'extremely interested in animals' and why so much of behaviourism relies on animal experimentation (Rollin 1998: 207). The implications of this behaviourist 'version' of Darwinism, for species-making through method, is especially well demonstrated by Conwy Lloyd Morgan's Canon, which is the specific focus of the following discussion.

Morgan's Canon is 'possibly the most important single sentence in the history of the study of animal behavior' (Bennett Galef in Steward 2018: 293). As the philosopher Helen Steward summarises it:

> The influence the principle [Morgan's Canon] has had on the conduct and methods of comparative psychology over the succeeding 120 years,

cannot be overestimated … It was certainly implicated in the widespread adoption of radical psychological behaviorism during the middle decades of the twentieth century, but its impact has outlasted the demise of that doctrine. The Canon is still regularly explicitly invoked by scientists working on animal behavior and is perhaps even more often silently applied as part of an implicit orthodoxy concerning the appropriate methodology for a sober psychological science.

(Steward 2018: 293–294)

The Canon states: '[i]n no case may we interpret an action as the outcome of the exercise of a higher physical faculty, if it can be interpreted as the outcome of an exercise of one which stands lower in the psychological scale' (Morgan 1903: 53; emphasis omitted). Today, as Steward indicates, Morgan's Canon is often used to chastise and curb any interpretation of an animal's behaviour that is deemed to be too generous, that is, which gives too much 'credit' (usually 'intelligence') to the animal. It is, in short, understood 'as simply the application of the general law of parsimony to explanations of behaviour' (Boakes 2008: 40).

Yet Morgan, the psychologist Robert Boakes argues, justified his Canon neither in terms of animal intelligence nor in terms of parsimony. Rather, he justified it 'on the grounds of evolutionary theory':

If a particular process is sufficient to allow the development in a given species of appropriately adaptive behaviour, then there is no selective pressure for the evolution of a more complex process. In cases where there was firm evidence from one situation that a species possessed some complex process, Morgan was prepared to be generous in some other situation where the behaviour of this species could be interpreted either in terms of the same process or in terms of a simpler one.

(Boakes 2008: 40)

In other words, why would the response of a species be characterised by more complexity than is needed to adapt to the selective pressures that shaped its evolution? The 'psychological scale' to which the Canon refers is an evolutionary scale. Species and scales of species complexity are integral to the Canon. This is why '[t]he major theme of the *Introduction to Comparative Psychology* … discuss[es] in turn processes of increasing psychological complexity' (Boakes 2008: 41). To this end, Morgan begins with an analysis of 'simple associations' (all animals are capable of this), and then moves to 'perceptions of relations'. Finding no evidence of such perceptions in any animal, the remainder of the book is dedicated to human psychology.

Morgan famously considered anecdotes to throw 'a misleading glamour over what were not more than special tricks' (Boakes 2008: 35). Yet it was the special (or not so special) tricks of his Fox Terrier, Tony, recounted by Morgan in the form of two anecdotes, that furnished evidence for Morgan's claim that animals do not perceive relations. Although contemporary canine scientist Brian Hare (see Chapter 4 of this book) describes Morgan's anecdotal accounts of Tony's antics as 'a classic example of how complex behaviour can be explained by simple forms of cognition' (Hare and Woods 2020a: 168), they might also be understood as a classic example of how species thinking can transform an individual animal into a representative of their species. In what follows, therefore, I address the implications of the anecdotes not for what they tell about the Canon, which is Hare's interest, but for what they tell about the individual dog, Tony, who lies – or rather, who bolts out of gates and fetches sticks enthusiastically – at their heart.

Where George Romanes's correspondents were particularly impressed by their dogs' understanding of mechanical appliances – believing them to be examples of canine reasoning – Morgan asks, in a chapter entitled 'Do animals reason?', 'whether Tony's behaviour can be fairly explained without his forming any conception of the relation between the means employed and the ends attained', and answers: 'It appears to me that it can' (Morgan 1903: 292). The behaviour to which Morgan is referring is Tony's ability to raise the latch on Morgan's gate. Tony was able to do this, Morgan explains, not because he understood how the latch works (which would constitute evidence of reasoning), but because, one day, when Tony was standing with his head beneath the latch and between the bars of the gate – 'looking restlessly and wistfully at the familiar road' (293), 'where there was often much to interest him; cats to be worried, other dogs with whom to establish a sniffing acquaintance, and so forth' (292) – he by chance raised his head. The latch lifted, but Tony was looking elsewhere. It was only when Tony noticed the gate swinging open that 'out he bolted' (293). After this event, Morgan, instead of raising the latch himself, waited for Tony to do it until Tony was able to go 'at once and without hesitation to the right place and put his head without any ineffectual fumbling at the right place under the latch' (293).

In their discussion of anecdotes in the animal sciences, Paul Morris, Margaret Fidler and Alan Costall write that '[s]ome may object that Morgan made repeated and careful observations of his dog and should not be deemed anecdotal; however, the same may be said of many observations of animal trainers, farmers, and pet owners in general' (Morris *et al.* 2000: 152). It was against the 'somewhat rough and ready interpretation[s]' of 'the man who has to deal with animals for practical purposes' (Morgan 1903: 52), however, that Morgan distinguished his own observations, and the science of psychology. Such men include '[t]he farmer, the keeper of a kennel, the cattle-breeder, the gamekeeper, the breaker-in of horses, all the practical men who are employed in the breeding, rearing, and training of animals, and the great number of people who keep animals as pets in domestic service' (Morgan 1903: 51–52).[8] The problem with 'rough and ready interpretations', Morgan thought, is that they fail to recognise, and therefore fail to redress, their subjective dimension. This subjective dimension, which applies to the study of both humans and animals, therefore requires what Morgan calls the 'doubly inductive' method. The doubly inductive method has not only an objective aspect – induction of the kind witnessed in chemistry, physics, astronomy, geology etc. – but also, necessarily, a subjective one. Necessarily, because 'the psychologist has to reach, through induction, the laws of mind as revealed to him in his own conscious experience' (Morgan 1903: 47). Morgan is speaking here to any person who imagines that, when it comes to the 'psychical faculties of animals' (50), the subjective dimension of the method that applies to the study of humans can be either bypassed or ignored. Better, Morgan argues, to be fully cognisant of the role that the doubly inductive process plays in analysing the psychology of animals, than to be ignorantly given to common-sense explanations: to the kinds of explanations of animals that, for example, one would use to account for the actions of one's 'human neighbours and acquaintances' (50).

With regard to Tony, one can surmise that Morgan would probably distinguish his interpretation of his vignette from any other interpretation of it, because not only does he '*know the whole history of it*' (Morgan 1903: 293, emphasis in the original) – as animal trainers, farmers and pet owners usually know the history that informs an individual animal's behaviour – he also understands the significance of that history, which in this case is that it took Tony 'nearly three weeks' (293) to perfect the trick. The reason it took 'so long', Morgan writes, was that 'there was so little connection between gazing out into the road and getting out into the road' (293). The time it took to learn the trick, in other words, *is* the evidence that Tony has no perception of the relations between 'means and end' (293). *Had* Tony such a perception, not only would he have learned the trick sooner, it would in fact not be a trick at all. If this hardly seems ground-breaking, Morgan spells out its implications more clearly in another anecdote, which is in addition intended to support his case against anecdotal evidence. The incident once again involved Tony and his tricks.

During the course of a series of 'experimental investigation[s]' (Morgan 1903: 255) involving Tony and some sticks, Morgan 'prepared a short yew stick with a crook at one end' (Morgan 1903: 157), which he threw over a fence for Tony. When Tony attempted to return it to Morgan, the knotted end would inevitably catch on the fence, which left Tony 'tugg[ing] at it in the most ridiculously energetic fashion' (257). After several failed attempts, Tony seized the crook and wrenched it off, which enabled him to get through the fence with the stick. He did so just as a passer-by 'paused for a couple of minutes to watch the proceedings'. The passer-by then turned to Morgan and said 'Clever dog that, sir; he knows where the hitch do lie' (258). Which remark, Morgan writes,

> was the characteristic outcome of two minutes' chance observation. During the half-hour or more that I watched the dog he had tried nearly every possible way of holding and tugging at the stick. And such is the method of sense-experience – continued trial and error until a happy effect is reached ... In other words the facts observed can be completely explained on the hypothesis that there is sense-experience only. The perception of relations as such is not necessary to the performances, and is therefore by our Canon of interpretation to be excluded.
>
> (258–259)

The power and persuasiveness of Morgan's case for his Canon rest here on the very evidence (anecdotal evidence) that Morgan wishes to dispute: it enables him to illustrate that although one *could* impute 'cleverness' to Tony on the basis of his behaviour, as did the person who conveniently happened to pass by (so conveniently as to be almost suspicious),[9] Tony's performance could equally – and, Morgan believes, correctly – be explained not by the successful strategy of wrenching the crook off the stick, but by the numerous imperceptive efforts and failures that preceded it. Indeed it is the very numerousness, as well as the perceived arbitrariness, of these efforts that demonstrate to Morgan that, even after Tony wrenched the crook off the stick, he remained ignorant of the mechanics of the size of the stick, the size of the gaps between the vertical rails and the obstructiveness of the crook. Morgan relies here on a classic anecdotal trope, which is an observer watching, by chance, as unexpected events unfold. The difference is that, in Morgan's anecdote, there are two observers: the passer-by who watches the dog, and Morgan, who watches both the dog and the passer-by. It is in this position, of the meta-observer in the meta-anecdote, that Morgan is enabled to pass judgement on anecdotal evidence and to 'prove' that the simplest explanation is more likely to be the correct one.

As I noted earlier, contemporary scholars and scientists continue to debate what Morgan intended by his Canon, how it should be interpreted and whether it is of value. These discussions add nuance to the Canon and to Morgan's own conception of it. Nevertheless, broadly speaking, the Canon has become crudely associated with the general law of parsimony, and with the banishment of understanding, intention, motive and feeling from the science of behaviour.[10] One might say that Morgan's Canon marked the moment when animals lost their minds (Bekoff and Jamieson 1992) or, perhaps, when animal scientists did (Rollin 1998). There is another vanishing point here, however, which is Tony himself. For what truly marks the difference between Morgan's anecdote and the anecdotes of 'animal trainers, farmers, and pet owners in general' is that it is, in the end, not *about* a specific dog at all. In Morgan's vignette, Tony is a cipher for *all* dogs, and for all dogs' limited problem-solving abilities. As significant, then, as Morgan's dispute with the passer-by's misguided interpretation – 'clever dog' – is his objection to the passer-by's attention to Tony – 'clever dog *that*, sir'. In this regard, the Tony anecdotes bear one of the key hallmarks of species thinking: they turn Tony the individual into an ambassador for his species.

Despite the 'opposition' between classical ethology and psychology, psychologists also often took their cue from Darwin's theory of evolution. The origins of Morgan's 'trial-and-error learning by accident', for example, lie in his studies of ducklings and chicks, in which Morgan showed how arbitrary associations – akin to the arbitrary associations that he thought explained how Tony came to open the latch – 'might work in a natural environment to produce adaptive behaviour' (Boakes 2008: 35). By changing the environments of ducklings and chicks, and watching them either repeat a behaviour to no purpose or develop a taste aversion for no explicable reason, Morgan concluded that 'behaviour is modified by its immediate consequences' (Boakes 2008: 35). Such consequences could apply as well to an ecological niche as they could to an artificially manipulated environment. Eighty or so years later, in an article entitled 'Selection by consequences', Skinner would draw a parallel between natural selection by consequences and ontogenetic behavioural selection by consequences (Skinner 1981). Gone was the conquering individualism of the 1954 conference. Instead, Skinner argued that just as living creatures are not the agents of evolution, so they are not the agents of their own actions: 'so long as we cling to the view that the person is an initiating doer, actor, of causer of behavior, we shall probably continue to neglect the conditions which must be changed if we are to solve our problems' (Skinner 1981: 504). Perhaps the difference between the ethologists and behaviourists lies in the *uses* they made of evolutionary theory. For the classical ethologists, processes of evolutionary adaptation explain the mechanical behaviours of a species. For the behaviourists, adaptation is to be explained by mechanics.

'I once had a dog ...' (the anecdotal tradition)

Morgan, Skinner wrote, distinguished himself in the history of the scientific study of behaviour by showing how 'evidences [*sic*] of mental processes could be explained in other [than anecdotal] ways' (Skinner 1959: 197). Yet his student Edward Thorndike criticised Morgan – as Morgan had criticised George Romanes – for belonging to the 'anecdote school' (Thorndike 1911), and for conducting only a handful of informal studies on birds and a dog.

Despite this, Thorndike was much influenced by both Romanes's and Morgan's anecdotes, and especially by their descriptions of the mechanical abilities of animals. 'Thorndike', Boakes writes, 'took the kind of situation described by Romanes' correspondents and also by Morgan in the latter's account of how the fox terrier learned to operate the latch of a gate, and turned it into an experimental method' (Boakes 2008: 69).

The most famous of Thorndike's experimental methods is probably the 'puzzle box', precursor to 'the Skinner box', which Thorndike devised by cutting doors into wooden crates. By way of various devices, these doors could be opened by the cats and dogs whom Thorndike put into the boxes. Ultimately, the puzzle boxes led Thorndike to his 'law of effect', which, at its most basic, states that satisfaction leads to reinforcement: i.e. if a response to a stimulus 'works' for an animal, then they will do it again (and again, and again). 'What had started as an explanation for the manner in which animals learned to escape from his puzzle boxes', Boakes writes, became 'a general law of behaviour' (Boakes 2008: 75). If Morgan's Canon struck the death knell for Tony as an individual, Thorndike's puzzle box would be his tomb. Gone is the rich particularity of the latch that *Tony* opens, of the gate that *Tony* bolts through, of the dogs that *Tony* sniffs, and of the cats that *Tony* worries. Instead, the individual dog is relevant only as a point on 'a curve representative of learning' (Cladland 1993: 245).

There is no room for anecdote here, not only because anecdotes do not (usually) 'represent what happens on average' (Crist 2000: 43) but also, more fundamentally, because Thorndike was interested in how individual animals of the same species act in similar ways (which tells something about the species), and not in how individual animals differ (which tells something about these individuals). This was the gist of the critique of T. Wesley Mills – who was, Douglas Cladland writes, one of Thorndike's most thoughtful contemporaries – when he asked what Thorndike's representative curves tell 'about *this* animal, or *that* one?' (Cladland 1993: 245, emphasis in the original). The answer is that they tell nothing, because they are not intended to. Thorndike was speaking to species, and would ultimately make the 'nonsense' claim, as Boakes puts it, that one species can be judged more intelligent than another 'simply because it learns how to solve some particular problem more rapidly' (Boakes 2008: 71).

My contrast between Morgan and Thorndike (and Thorndike's view of Morgan) implicitly establishes a number of dualisms: storytelling v. science; particular v. generalisable; concrete v. abstract; spontaneous event v. planned experiment; individual v. species. These are some of the dualisms that subtend debates about the value or not of anecdotes in science. My purpose in this final section – in which I explore the anecdotal tradition as it is found in the work of Romanes, Darwin and (briefly) at the birth of contemporary ethology – is not to question these dualisms but, rather, to bring some nuance to them. As I will illustrate, 'even' anecdotes – which often stage the spectacular behaviours of an individual animal – can support species thinking.

Contemporary literature on anecdotes in both the sciences and social sciences usually understands their contested status to derive from their association with the concrete, the particular, the specific, the local, as well as from their association with novel and/or rare situations and events (Bates and Byrne 2007; Byrne 1997; Crist 2000; Philo and Wilbert 2000; Lestel 2011). But anecdotes are also nearly always about the actions of an individual animal, or a small group of individuals, and this too, as George Romanes knew only too well, makes them an awkward method through which to formulate and justify general scientific claims. Part of the reason that George Romanes's successors would see him 'only as the archetypal purveyor of anecdotes about animals' (Boakes 2008: 25), Boakes argues, is that Romanes made the fateful decision to divide his research into two, and to publish, first, evidence of 'animal intelligence' – evidence that mostly takes the form of stories about individual animals' feelings and behaviours – and, second, 'his general principles for the theory of mental evolution' (Boakes 2008: 25). This division, and its implications for Romanes's reputation as a scientist, now looks like a portent of the bifurcation of knowledges of animals (a bifurcation that was hardening during Romanes's lifetime) into the 'scientific' on the one hand, and everything else on the other.

Romanes himself knew that his work, and especially the first volume of his book *Animal Intelligence*, 'may well seem but a small improvement upon the works of the anecdote-mongers' (Romanes

2012 [1884]: 20). One of the sources of anecdote-mongering that Romanes undoubtedly had in mind was the flourishing nineteenth-century publishing industry that was transforming 'a long anecdotal tradition' into sentimental books about animals, and especially about dogs (Thomas 1984: 108). 'Whereas earlier dog literature', Harriet Ritvo writes, 'seemed simply a specialized branch of natural history, the new books included not only descriptions of the dogs' physical and moral characteristics, but a selection of heartwarming and enlightening anecdotes' (Ritvo 1987: 87). And to be sure, the first volume of *Animal Intelligence*, and in particular the chapter on dogs, reads – as Romanes anticipated it would – as a series of anecdotes about individual dogs, unsupported by any 'general principles'. Indeed, the chapter on 'the dog' is composed almost exclusively of cosy vignettes, many of which begin with 'I had a dog …', or 'I have a setter …'. While this is to be expected, given that all the dogs described in this book either lived with or were known to Romanes or lived with and were known to his correspondents, it nonetheless represents a serious methodological flaw.

A flaw, not because these are descriptions of individual dogs, but because, Boakes argues, Romanes and his correspondents were members of the same class, and the authority of the descriptions often seems to derive less from the narrators' powers of observation and analysis, and more from their social status (Boakes 2008: 26). Romanes extended this social status to dogs, whom he often classified as either 'low-life' or 'high-life' (Romanes 2012 [1884]: 1072). This had Morgan bristling, in a lecture published in the journal *Mind*, in which he recounts an anecdote narrated by Romanes, in which Romanes describes how Mr St John's retriever cut off his relations with his 'humble friends' – 'a rat-catcher and his cur' – on sight of his 'master' approaching (Morgan 1886: 180). Such 'caste' interpretations of dog behaviours cannot suffice as scientific evidence, Morgan argued, because they attribute 'motives and underlying states' to dogs (Morgan 1886: 180). Although a more sparing use of such attributions, Morgan continued, would unquestionably exclude as scientific evidence 'a vast amount of carefully collected anecdote', science would not ultimately be 'the loser' for it (Morgan 1886: 180).

Romanes's anxieties about the anecdotal status of his work – confirmed as justifiable by Morgan's and others' criticisms – indicates that, by the time of his writing, the value of anecdotes as a legitimate source of knowledge about animals had already begun to be depreciated. In *Man and the Natural World*, the historian Keith Thomas describes how 'the scientific study of animals, birds and vegetation' (Thomas 1984: 51) in the early modern period had a 'traumatic' effect on 'ordinary people' (Thomas 1984: 70). Systematisers, such as the naturalist John Ray in the seventeenth century and Comte de Buffon and Carolus Linneaus in the eighteenth century, began to classify animals and plants on the basis of their 'intrinsic qualities' (Thomas 1984: 52) or 'structural affinities' (Ritvo 1987: 13) rather than their relationships to humans, and especially their relationships of use and value as food, medicine, or signs and symbols. New technologies, such as the microscope; new 'content'; and in particular a new, Latin, nomenclature, displaced the copious and varied vocabulary that once described plants and animals. Together, these developments constituted a 'revolution in perception' (Thomas 1984: 70), Thomas writes, that entrenched the growing (and classed) division between the knowledges of 'ordinary people' who lived and worked with animals, and modern scientific knowledges of animals. Along the way, anecdotes became associated with sentimentality, amateurism and 'rustics' (Thomas 1984: 86).

But 'science', in the nineteenth century, was hardly consolidated as such. When contrasting the anecdotalism of Darwin and Romanes – and the anecdotalism of Morgan too, according to Thorndike – to Thorndike's experimental methods, it is impossible not to acknowledge how different were their research contexts, and how significant in shaping Thorndike's work were the professionalisation of psychology and the rapid expansion and reform of the North American university system during his career, from his undergraduate degree onwards (see Arnet 2019; Boakes 2008: Chapter 3). Darwin, Romanes and, to a lesser degree, Morgan conducted their research during a period in England when natural science was largely 'a hobby' confined only to those who could afford it, or who were prepared to face financial penury (Boakes 2008: 54). The kinds of men to whom these men 'paid attention' – attention with regard to what they 'had to say about the behaviour of animals' – Boakes notes, were 'the country parson, whose hobby was watching birds, or the colonial officer with time to take an interest in local fauna' (Boakes 2008: 57). Such folk would also have been publishing in scientific journals such as *Nature*, whose contributors were not 'limited to scientific professionals' (Arnet 2019: 437). Thorndike, by contrast, developed his experimental methods while working as a doctoral research student at Harvard, under the tutelage of the esteemed William James.[11]

The epistemological tensions that characterised Darwin's and Romanes's period, a period of scientific transformation, and of science on the brink of professionalisation, are captured in the difference between the two answers that Thomas Huxley gave to the rhetorical question he posed to his audience at the start of one of a series of talks on dogs that he delivered to the Royal Institution in 1879 and 1880. 'What', Huxley asked, 'is a dog?' First, '[a] dog is a hairy, four-footed, tailed animal ... which barks and howls and is often singularly intelligent and affectionate' (Huxley in Worboys *et al.* 2018: 163). Second – and this is the answer, Huxley said, that a 'scientific zoologist' would give (Huxley in Worboys *et al.* 2018: 163) – a dog is described in terms of its class, Mammalia, and species, *Canis familiaris*. Although Huxley is known as 'Darwin's bulldog', as Darwin's 'foremost champion' (Boakes 2008: 5), he nonetheless cast doubt on Darwin's approach to animals during Darwin's lifetime, and this doubt was symptomatic of less generous ways of conceiving of both animals and humans. Darwin's continuity of animal and human physiology, cognition, and emotions did not, for Huxley, point to the richness of animals' lives. On the contrary, it suggested to him that humans, like animals, are 'conscious automata' (Huxley in Boakes 2008: 20). Where Huxley described himself as a 'doubting Thomas', Darwin nearly always gave animals the benefit of the doubt. Huxley was a sceptic, willing to suspend belief in the service of science, while for Darwin, scepticism is a 'frame of mind which I believe to be injurious to the progress of science' (Darwin in Boakes 2008: 26). In the end, Huxley's scepticism became his student Morgan's Canon. The step from understanding dogs in terms of the species *Canis familiaris*, to understanding dog behaviours as uniform and species-typical, would be a short one.

But the contrast between Huxley's and Darwin's/Romanes's lineages is not quite straightforward. Certainly, Darwin and Romanes are associated with more generous and expansive ways of thinking about animals than the comparative psychologists, behaviourists and, indeed, classical ethologists who were to follow. Rollins argues, for example, that 'Darwinian science gave new vitality to ordinary commonsense notions that attributed mental states to animals' (Rollin 1998: 33), while Crist proposes that Darwin's rich and detailed anecdotes were a reflection of 'his perception of subjectivity in the animal world; his premise … that living is experientially meaningful for animals and that their actions are authored' (Crist 2000: 12). But Romanes, for one, never intended his anecdotal first volume to be 'read without reference to its ultimate object of supplying facts for the subsequent deduction of principles' (Romanes 2012 [1884]: 20). Which is to say that, while these anecdotes were in one respect about individual animals, in another respect they were the 'stuff' out of which a more generalisable knowledge about *the* animal was to be hewn. Even though Darwin and Romanes took it upon themselves to serve 'as hubs for sprawling networks of observers, collating and clarifying the contributions of hundreds of casual animal watchers' (Arnet 2019: 443), they did not accept these contributions uncritically. When these stories and anecdotes appeared 'suspect, surprising, or open to scepticism', Romanes in particular designed and performed experiments to test their veracity (Rollin 1998: 48). 'Virtually every [anecdotal] instance [Romanes] cites', writes Rollin, 'is subject to experimental replication and verification' (Rollin 1998: 48).

With regard to Darwin, it is worth noting that anecdotes offered two kinds of support for his theory of evolution: they offered scientific support, because anecdotes attest to a wide range of individual variability, with all the evolutionary implications that follow;[12] and, as I discussed in the previous chapter, they offered political support, softening the otherwise 'terrifying' (Van Grouw 2018: 56) proposal that humans and animals are 'a community of descent' (Darwin 1981: 32). In both capacities, Darwin used anecdotes to illustrate not so much the 'singularly intelligent and affectionate' (as Huxley puts it) individual dog, but rather the individual dog as offering scientific insight into speciation and the species as a whole (as well as its evolutionary relations to other species). Darwin did not dismiss 'extraordinary stories about animals' – anecdotes, in other words – out of hand because, Crist writes, he appreciated 'without reservation' that 'the dog's show of sympathy for the cat … [was] sound evidence of the capacity of sympathy in dogs' (Crist 2000: 43). In short, although anecdotes were unquestionably of genuine interest, in and of themselves, to both Darwin and Romanes, this does not mean that they were not also a means to more generalisable species-making ends.

It was not until the mid-1970s, the ethologist Gordon Burghardt argues, that science would once again consider legitimate 'the study of animals' subjective states' (Burghardt 1985: 909). One of the contributing factors to this sea change, says Burghardt, was the publication in 1976 of Donald Griffin's (1994b) book *The Question of Animal Awareness: Evolutionary Continuity of Mental Experience* (Burghardt 1985: 905). *Animal Awareness* may have come as something of a surprise at the time, given that Griffin, who had been best known for his discovery, with Robert Galambos, of echolocation in bats, was renowned for his empiricism and scepticism. A student anecdote, for instance, tells that when Griffin and a companion were travelling in a car and passed a flock of sheep, Griffin's reply to his companion's observation that two of the sheep were black was: 'black on the side facing us anyway' (Griffin in Gross 2005: 200). One of the distinctive features of *Animal Awareness*, in which Griffin 'advocated a new field called "cognitive ethology"' (Burghardt 1985: 905), was the foregrounding of the methodological value of paying scientific attention to the 'rare event' (Bekoff 2003: 83). The reason the rare event is important – as Griffin laid out explicitly in a later book, *Animal Minds* (1994a) (published in 1992) – is that it demonstrates animal versatility. Specifically, it demonstrates what an animal is capable of, when '[n]either evolutionary selection [n]or learning from previous experience could provide a specific prescription for what the animal should do' (Griffin 1994a: 233). Once the limits of evolutionary or learned scripts are reached, there will lie evidence of conscious thinking and decision-making (Griffin 1994a: 233–234).[13]

Given Griffin's focus on animals' 'ability to handle unpredictable, or barely predictable, situations' (Griffin 1994a: 233), their creative problem-solving in the face of 'novel ... challenges' (Griffin 1994a: 27), it was perhaps always a foregone conclusion that he would be charged with anecdotalism – indeed he is often accused of revivifying 'anecdotal cognitivism', as Darwin's and Romanes's work is sometimes described (Allen and Bekoff 1999: Chapter 2). This is because the narration of 'unpredictable, or barely predictable, situations' is more than likely to sound (and perhaps very often *is*) anecdotal. Despite demonstrating the *scientific* necessity of investigating the rare event, Griffin's work – and especially his book *Animal Minds* (1994a) – is described by even the most sympathetic of writers as full of '[g]ee-whiz stories' (Allen and Bekoff 1999: 34).

When anecdotes describe versatile, unexpected and novel behaviours in an individual animal or small group of individual animals, they raise a number of questions, including the question as to whether the behaviour of that particular animal is generalisable. Generalisable, here, is often code for 'species-typical' or 'species-representative'. Are *all* animals in this species category similarly capable? One of the ways that a long tradition of animal investigators, from Romanes to contemporary ethologists, have sought to answer this question, and in the process to recoup anecdotes and to recoup species, is by using, as the primatologist Richard Byrne puts it, 'the descriptive record of one of these unanticipated events ... to inspire ideas to test with systematic, controlled observations or experiments' (Byrne 1997: 134; Bekoff 2007: 121). What I understand Byrne to be saying, here, is that an anecdote can become a kind of animal 'pedagogy', which encourages a scientist to ask the right questions (Despret 2016) of an (individual) animal, and then ask them again in the laboratory to check that they gave the right (species-specific) answers. It is in the laboratory, Vinciane Despret argues, that the 'miraculous transformation of anecdotes into scientific facts' occurs (Despret 2016: 106). And in the laboratory, too, that individual animals are miraculously transformed back into species ambassadors.

Conclusion

My efforts in this chapter have been to illustrate how the connections between species and behaviours are established through scientific method, and some of the consequences that follow for individual animals. Conceptually, theoretically and methodologically, they vanish (almost). This exercise has also demonstrated, I hope, how species thinking informs and shapes scientific understandings of animals, even when the subject of species is ostensibly not being directly addressed. Too often, classical ethology and comparative psychology are pitted against each other, both politically (one is rigid, the other flexible; one authoritarian, the other individualistic), and methodologically (one is of the field, the other of the laboratory; one is naturalistic, the other experimental). One of the limitations of this focus on their differences, however, is that it disguises what they have in common, which is their thinking behaviour through species. For as long as species remains a key mode of scientific generalisation, anecdotes that recount the non-typical behaviours of an individual animal will continue to trouble science, despite the many ways that exist of dismissing their significance.

One way of dismissing 'controversial' animal behaviour is by the practice of pooling data to achieve statistically analysable results. As the philosopher Colin Allen and ethologist Marc Bekoff explain:

> Many studies establish a statistically reliable connection between a given stimulus condition and a response, in the sense that (for example) subjects produce the response in 90 percent of stimulus presentations. The 10 percent of cases where the stimulus fails to produce the response tend to be ignored in the analysis. (Labelling observations as 'anecdotes' and then dismissing them is also symptomatic of this concern with statistical reliability.) Yet, for really understanding the causal complexity underlying the production of behaviour, we argue ... that it is a mistake to dismiss these data as noise.
>
> (Allen and Bekoff 1999: 61)

Allen and Bekoff's point here – which is certainly indebted to Griffin – is that a 'stimulus-free' response *also* has scientific value. Two things are unspoken here: first, that anecdotes, in a context such as this, are themselves scientific; and indeed, elsewhere, Bekoff, quoting the political scientist Raymond Wolfinger, argues that 'the plural of anecdote is data' (Bekoff 2007: 121). Second, those individuals who 'fail' to respond as predicted challenge the idea of typicality, and perhaps even the value of typicality as an explanatory tool.

Rather than understand Allen and Bekoff's argument as 'merely' a contribution to debates about what scientists should be paying attention to (the statistical average or the noisy exception), one might see it as an argument in favour of a shift in attention away from behaviours that are identified as species-typical on the basis of their statistical 'significance', to behaviours that, in their departure from that *particular* kind of significance, point to something else of importance. To the importance, say, of what Dominique Lestel calls 'the singular animal'. Lestel writes: '[t]he singular animal embodies an extra plasticity which allows innovation within the species. Indeed such singular animals destabilize our conceptions of the term species, while inverting the relation between the species and individuality which we spontaneously establish in ethology' (Lestel 2011: 93).

I introduce Lestel's work here because it brings clarity to Allen and Bekoff's: it says what they could have/should have said, but didn't. But I also introduce it because Lestel and Allen and Bekoff are problematic in similar ways. Like Allen and Bekoff, Lestel gives a different, potentially 'destabilising', weighting to the relation between individual variation and species-typical behaviour. Nevertheless, his definition of the singular animal – like Allen and Bekoff's 10 per cent of animals who fail to respond as predicted to a stimulus – arguably ties that animal back into the concept of species, insofar as both singularity and failure acquire their intelligibility only by way of their departure from species-typicality. In view of this, it is not surprising that Lestel's singular animal should also be a *special* animal, as he explains:

> A singular animal is represented by an individual that is able to establish a different relation with the world: it is able to form the world in its own, distinctive way. Singular animals have the capabilities of learning and 'personal development'. Such capabilities evolve through their individual lives, and differ from one to another.
>
> (Lestel 2011: 93)

Although I welcome this emphasis on the singular individual (see Chapters 5 and 7 especially), the risk is that, in this context, the descriptor, singular, outshines a somewhat more prosaic individuality, an individuality that matters *regardless* of species, and not on account of any extraordinary relationship to the category species. In Chapter 5, I return to this rather more banal individual, to illustrate just one example of how they can come to matter in science – can come to matter, even, dramatically. Before doing so, in Chapter 4, I will demonstrate again how the theoretical and methodological entanglement of species and animal behaviours strengthen and reinforce each other – not in the abstract, but in practice; not in relation to any and all animals, but in relation to dogs. As will be evident, the organising principles and preoccupations of late-nineteenth- and early-twentieth-century animal science, which I have been addressing here, persist as obdurately as ever.

Notes

1 Among those 'other things' was Lorenz's despicable war record (see the introduction to this book). In the draft version of his critique of Lorenz, Lehrman argued that Lorenz's 'endorsement of Nazi ideas', especially with regard to racial purity, was the inevitable consequence of his scientific theorising (Burkhardt 2005: 385). The published version gestured less explicitly to this point (Lehrman 1953: 354).
2 Tinbergen was appointed at Oxford in 1949.
3 So heated was the debate between Lorenz and Theodore Christian Schneirla that a psychiatrist in the room by the name of Spiegel was prompted to admit that, 'really, a large amount of the emotional force of the difference in view is passing me by' (quoted in Held 1956: 691). One might conjecture, as Held did, that 'the vehemence of these oblique criticisms and rejoinders' (Held 1956: 691) was in part inspired by recent political history, and by the 'distaste resulting from a tendency in America to identify hereditarianism with anti-democratic views' (692).
4 Lorenz's first – reluctant – degree was in medicine.
5 Although contemporary ethologists are often critical of classical ethology, and especially its attention to instincts, the 'organ' metaphor lingers on. See for example Frans de Waal's *Mama's Last Hug*, in which he argues that '[e]motions are like organs' (de Waal 2019: 165).
6 Lorenz's care for birds is well documented. So too, however, is his carelessness with them. For example: during a three-month lecture tour in the United States, Lorenz appeared on the American Museum of Natural History's television show *Adventure*, 'where he was able to charm a large viewing audience by displaying five baby ducklings from the Bronx zoo that he had imprinted on himself only a day earlier' (Burkhardt 2005: 403). It is difficult to imagine how Lorenz would have been able to take responsibility for these ducklings under these road show conditions.
7 Current scientific opinion suggests that dingoes are not feral dogs who rewilded (Bradley Smith in Pierce and Bekoff 2021: 35; Brad Purcell in Pierce and Bekoff 2021: 35).
8 As for the '[t]he skilled naturalist or biologist', Morgan writes, 'we cannot help feeling that their psychological conclusions are hardly

on the same level as that reached by their conclusions in the purely biological field' (Morgan 1903: 52–53).

9 As Morris, Fidler and Costall note: 'the available evidence, supposedly demonstrating the unreliability of the psychological description of animal behavior, is itself suspect and often anecdotal' (Morris *et al.* 2000: 152).

10 There is a sad irony in this, for as Caroline Hovenac notes, even though Morgan 'devoted most of his career to comparative psychology … late in life he began to express more serious doubts about scientific method as a tool for understanding animals' (Hovenac 2018: 167). This is not quite as startling as it first appears because, while Morgan objected to 'mind-story' phrases (Morgan in Burkhardt 2005: 97), an animal's behaviour was for him always an indicator of 'what its subjective experience is like' (Boakes 2008: 136).

11 Among other structural transformations, doctorates were a recent and important addition to the North American university system, particularly because they created the opportunity to establish, institutionalise and transmit disciplinary traditions and methods.

12 See Chapter 6 of this book on Darwin's 'essentialism of individuals' (Grosz 2004: 42).

13 This is why Crist considers 'local and concrete evidence [to be] the best (if not the only) evidence for the global and abstract claim that thinking and reasoning do exist in the animal world' (Crist 2000: 46).

4

Do dogs work? The labour of 'the bond'

> [F]or labour to become a site of interspecies justice, animals must also have the right to enter and exit the labour relationship, to freely choose their work, and not be subject to forced labour. Animals are harmed by unfreedoms to a far greater extent than we currently acknowledge.
> (Blattner 2020: 109)
>
> *Our Dogs, Ourselves: The Story of a Unique Bond*
> (title, Horowitz 2019)

This chapter is organised around two connected parts. The first analyses two popular scientific books about dogs, in which the authors seek to explain to their readers what dogs are. The second part explores some of the implications of those explanations, for dogs. I use Jocelyn Porcher's theory of animal labour to do this. My argument in essence will be that dogs' species story – exemplified in these two books – actively militates against an understanding of dogs as labouring subjects. And because dogs are not perceived to be labouring subjects, it is difficult to identify, let alone challenge, the on-going exploitation of companion and working dogs, or to recognise their forms of 'resistance'. As for the creative potentiality that Porcher claims exists in labour: dogs' species story allows no leverage for this at all. In making this argument, this chapter shows how helpful Porcher's theory, and other theories of animal labour, are with regard to the task I have set myself, which is to illuminate the political implications of dogs' species story. It should be noted at the outset, however, that I am not myself an advocate of labour as the *only* or even the best lens through which to refract animal–human relations. The debates about animal labour are complex, and I will touch on them briefly in conclusion.

The two popular scientific books that I analyse in this chapter are *The Genius of Dogs: Discovering the Unique Intelligence of Man's Best Friend*, by Brian Hare and Vanessa Woods (2020a), and *Dog Is Love: The Science of Why and How Your Dog Loves You*, by Clive Wynne (2020a). These books do more than rehearse the evolutionary theories of dog speciation/domestication that I discussed in Chapter 2. In addition, by providing further 'proof' for and embellishment of such theories through their interpretations of contemporary behavioural and biological research, the authors are enabled to draw out, to a greater degree than in their scientific papers, how the dominant dog species story 'should' be materially expressed in actual individual dogs. Although they do address the 'origins' of dogs as a species, their purpose is more fully to create, for a broad readership, an enduring conception of what a dog is today, how a dog should be understood, and what people who live and/or work with dogs can legitimately – that is, scientifically, objectively – expect from them. While recognising the individuality of dogs, they ultimately seek to account for all aspects (emotional, affective, cognitive, physiological etc.) of all dogs over all time. For these several reasons they are, in my view, exemplary contributors to what Gregory Hollin *et al.* describe as the 'vast sociotechnical networks' that instantiate irreversible realities (Hollin *et al.* 2017: 935). Like the theories of dog speciation that I explored in Chapter 2, these books actively mitigate against 'other ways of being' a dog (Van Dooren in Giraud and Hollin 2017: 173).

In rereading these versions of dogs' species story through the analytic framework of labour, my aim is to bring some clarity to the political implications that follow from them. If these implications are largely disguised, then that is in part because the research cited in these books is mostly conducted on dogs who are well-regarded and well-rewarded 'family' members and/or work colleagues, whose every need is often the top priority of the people with whom they live and work. This should not be surprising: for the most part, contemporary canine science focuses on companion and working dogs.[1] I will return to the methodological implications of this focus in Chapter 5. Suffice it to note here that, of the estimated 1 billion dogs on the planet, only around 150–180 million live and/or work intimately with humans. Yet, as Raymond and Lorna Coppinger note, this small minority population has come to stand, in science, as representative of the species as a whole (Coppinger and Coppinger 2016: 21). In science, what *they* are is what *all* dogs are (see Chapter 2).

What dogs are

The two books that I will (mainly) be addressing in this section are representative of the genre of popular science writing about dogs. Like other books in this genre, *The Genius of Dogs* (Hare and Woods 2020a) and *Dog is Love* (Wynne 2020a) read like scientific adventure stories, stories that are characterised by trials and tribulations, wrong turns, revelatory moments, and ultimately satisfactory closure (which in this case means the satisfaction of firm scientific knowledge). The cultural references and normative expectations with regard to dog–human relations in these books indicate that they were written for audiences in the Global North, most probably for people who live with dogs and who at least know about working dogs, if not have some experience of them.

With regard to their authors: Hare trained originally as an evolutionary anthropologist, Wynne as a behaviourist. Hare is now Professor in the Center for Cognitive Neuroscience and in the Department of Evolutionary Anthropology at Duke University, where he founded and co-directs the Duke Canine Cognition Center and where he also plays an important public-facing role in the commercially funded 'citizen science' data collection platform Dognition.com. Wynne is Professor of Psychology at Arizona State University, and director of the Canine Science Collaboratory. Both emphasise the dog–human 'bond' over and above any other aspect of what a dog 'is', and both consider that bond to have been a key part of dog speciation.

Vanessa Woods, who has a background in research with bonobos and chimpanzees, is a science writer and author of children's books. She also handles the media side of Hare's Canine Cognition Centre. This is probably a substantive job, given that Hare, like Woods herself, is a high-profile figure, one of a handful of canine scientists who have acquired some celebrity status. Hare and Woods have recently co-authored a second book together, entitled *Survival of the Friendliest: Understanding Our Origins and Rediscovering Our*

Common Humanity (2020b), which expands on and extends some of the themes of *The Genius of Dogs*. It is worth noting, with regard to commentaries on *The Genius of Dogs*, that Hare is often considered to be the principal – if not the only – author. This is probably because the book takes the form of a first-person narrative, with Hare being the first person. I too find myself obliged on occasion to discuss this book as if it was written solely by Brian Hare.

I have chosen to focus on Hare and Woods's *The Genius of Dogs* because Hare is one of two researchers who are understood by many scientists working in the field of canine research to have kickstarted the interest in dog cognition in the late 1990s.[2] For Hare and Woods, the most interesting thing about dogs is their 'genius' cognitive abilities, the parameters of which, as I will illustrate, are strictly defined by their evolutionary and on-going relationships with humans. Wynne, very much by contrast – and this is the reason why I have chosen *Dog Is Love* as my second text – focuses on dog emotions, specifically dog 'love'. Unlike Hare, with whose work Wynne engages at length in his book, Wynne's argument is that dogs are not especially 'genius' at all. Instead, dogs' evolutionary distinction lies in their ability to form affective bonds with humans and other species. In keeping with the genre, Hare and Wynne trace the origins of their insights into dogs as a species to 'enlightening' experiences they had with dogs of their own. I begin with their accounts 'of how it all started', since these 'new destiny' stories (Despret 2015a: 97) encapsulate the authors' arguments in a nutshell, which they subsequently go on to illustrate through scientific experiments. (The subsection that follows the recounting of Hare's 'destiny story' is titled 'The importance of experiments' (Hare and Woods 2020a: 41).)

Hare's story is as follows: in his second year at university, he was working with the comparative psychologist Michael Tomasello, who was studying infant psychology. Specifically, Tomasello was investigating human infants' ability to understand communicative intentions. Since '[i]ntention reading provides a cognitive foundation for all human forms of culture and communication' (Hare and Woods 2020a: 37), one of Tomasello's aims was to establish whether this skill developed before or after the Pan–Homo split, some 5–7 million years ago (the answer to this question was to be deduced from whether chimpanzees share this skill, or not). During a session of signalling games with chimpanzees, and in the light of the chimpanzees' difficulty in understanding the experimenters' intentions, Tomasello suggested to Hare that humans *uniquely* 'spontaneously and flexibly use gestures, such as pointing':

> I blurted out, 'I think my dog [Oreo] can do it.'
> 'Sure'. Mike was amused. 'Everybody's dog can do calculus.'
> ...
> 'No, really. I bet he could pass the tests.'
> Seeing I was serious, Mike leaned back in his chair.
> 'Okay', he said. 'Why don't you pilot an experiment?'
> (Hare and Woods 2020a: 40–41)

And the rest, as reported on the Dognition.com website, is history. By 'challenging him to prove it', Tomasello sent Hare 'on a 15-year odyssey to unlock the cognitive and evolutionary mysteries of our four-legged friends'.[3]

Where Hare and Woods insist on Oreo's 'genius' – I will discuss their understanding of 'genius' in a moment – Wynne is intent on underscoring, in *Dog Is Love* and elsewhere (e.g. Wynne 2020b), that his 'lovable little mutt wasn't very smart' (Wynne 2020a: 56). Xephos was adopted from a shelter in north Florida in 2012 as a birthday surprise for Wynne from his family (Wynne 2020a: 13). Once she arrived at the house, Wynne describes how Xephos had trouble with stairs, trouble with the dog flap, trouble with the leash (Wynne 2020a: 56–57). She did, however, have a 'superpower', and 'that superpower, naturally, we called love' (Wynne 2020b). What Xephos 'worked very hard to make sure I grasped', writes Wynne, was 'that there was indeed something unique about dogs' (Wynne 2020a: 58):

> I could spend all day at the office reading and writing scientific papers about dog behaviour, poking holes in the scientific literature about dogs' supposedly unique cognitive abilities, yet when I came home to Xephos, her wild enthusiasm on seeing me again … made it impossible for me not to recognize that there was something quite extraordinary about these animals, something that set them apart from all other creatures.
> (Wynne 2020a: 58)

Xephos's affection led Wynne, he writes, 'to question some of my most basic convictions as a behavioural scientist' (Wynne 2020b): first, that emotion is not relevant to the scientific study of animals; second, that 'the simplest explanation for a phenomenon is always to be preferred over others' (Wynne 2020a: 59; for more on these and other behaviourist convictions, see Chapter 3 of this book).[4] Again, the rest is history: Xephos 'left a behaviourist ... in a bit of a bind. So I did the only thing I could do: I kept digging' (Wynne 2020a: 90).

For the sake of brevity, I will concentrate on only the core aspects of Hare and Woods's and Wynne's arguments. These are Hare and Woods's claim that dogs have evolved a particular 'genius', and Wynne's claim that dogs are hard-wired for 'love'.

Genius

I begin, somewhat counterintuitively, with the only chapter in *The Genius of Dogs* that argues that dogs are not geniuses. The essence of this seventh chapter, entitled 'Lost dogs', is that dogs are lost without humans – literally lost. In it, the authors refer to a number of experiments that are intended to illustrate that dogs are not as skilled as wolves at navigating barriers and detours, nor as skilled as rats at using and remembering landmarks (Hare and Woods 2020a: 149–154). Dogs also have a poor understanding of 'physics', by which Hare and Woods mean the 'principle of connectivity' (155) and the 'principle of solidity' (158). With regard to the former, and in an echo of C. Lloyd Morgan's disparaging view of his terrier Tony's inability to 'perceive relations' (see Chapter 3 of this book), the authors show how dogs apparently struggle to identify how things are connected to each other (e.g. that if a rope is pulled, a dish containing food will slide forward within reach (Hare and Woods 2020a: 155–157)). Although dogs have some understanding of 'the principle of solidity' (e.g. the sound of rattling indicates there is kibble in the tin), this is not especially profound. A dog can infer that food falling down a straight tube will land in the box below it, but not which of the boxes will receive food that falls down an angled tube (Hare and Woods 2020a: 158–160). Dogs fail the mirror self-recognition (MSR) test (although see Horowitz's (2017) dispute of this claim),[5] and are not as good at associative learning as are chimpanzees and wolves (Hare and Woods 2020a: 163–164). As Hare and Woods later summarise: 'The most important lesson about dognition is that when dogs are left to their own devices, they are completely unremarkable' (Hare and Woods 2020a: 164).

Hare and Woods's 'Lost dogs' chapter, which addresses the ways in which dogs are unremarkable, serves two important purposes in the book as a whole. First, it supports their argument that 'intelligence' or 'genius' are not concepts that can be applied in the abstract. Thus: '[a]sking if a dolphin is cleverer than a crow is like asking if a hammer is better than a saw. Which is the better tool depends on the task at hand or, in the case of animals, which challenges they must regularly confront to survive and reproduce' (Hare and Woods 2020a: 233; see also Miklósi 2017: 29). 'Genius', in other words, is species-specific. Indeed, tracing the genealogies of different kinds of geniuses, in Hare and Woods's book, looks suspiciously like identifying histories of speciation. When explaining why scientists test the cognitive abilities of a species against an out group, for example, Hare and Woods write: 'if one species has a special ability that a close relative does not, we can not only identify their genius but also, more interestingly, ask how and why that genius exists' (Hare and Woods 2020a: 8). This was the purpose of Tomasello's research on intention reading in chimpanzees, which I mentioned earlier: to distinguish the genius of humans from chimpanzees, to use the distinction to date that genius, and to use the date to try to identify an evolutionary reason for it.

The relation between 'genius' and 'species' is so tight here that they could almost be substituted for each other. 'Wolves', Hare and Woods write, 'have their own kinds of genius' (Hare and Woods 2020a: 59). Since '[d]ogs are not meant to be lone wolves' (Hare and Woods 2020a: 165), they have not acquired, over the course of their evolution, the cognitive skills to solve problems in social isolation. Or more accurately – and this is the second reason why the chapter 'Lost dogs' is important – they have not acquired the cognitive skills to function independently of humans, when humans are available to them. Hare and Woods illustrate this point with reference to an experiment in which some hand-raised wolves showed themselves easily able to find a toy whose position had been changed by a human, in full view of the wolves, from one spot to another. So too could the dogs in this study, but only when the toy was transported by transparent strings. If the toy was moved by a human, the dogs returned to the toy's original spot to find it. The reason? 'The error is caused by the social context [the presence of humans], not a lack of memory … [The experiment] shows how relying on humans too heavily can get dogs confused in some situations' (Hare and Woods 2020a: 165).

Such confusion, however, is also dogs' 'genius', for theirs is 'a basic understanding of human communicative intentions' (Hare and Woods 2020a: 60). This means, among other things, that dogs are able to understand human pointing and gestures, distinguish between communicative and non-communicative cues, draw inferences from human behaviours, and pay attention to what humans are paying attention to – all of which developed through evolutionary domestication (Hare and Woods 2020a: 60).[6] From as young as six weeks of age, with relatively little exposure to humans, puppies 'are already so good with human gestures that there is little room for improvement' (Hare and Woods 2020a: 55). In keeping with some of the speciation/domestication theories that I discussed in Chapter 2, Hare and Woods consider these skills to be especially interesting because they are the very skills that may have secured the evolutionary success of humans too. The ability and willingness to 'co-operate and communicate [that is witnessed] in foxes, dogs, and bonobos ... may also have catalysed [in humans] an evolutionary chain reaction leading to the evolution of completely new cognitive abilities – not just the expression of old cognitive skills in new contexts' (Hare and Woods 2020a: 114; see also Hare and Woods 2020b). As other canine scientists have argued, Hare and Woods too propose that '[d]ogs may have civilised us' (Hare and Woods 2020a: 121).

The veracity of these contested claims is not my concern here. What is significant is that Hare and Woods are telling a story that illustrates not merely that dogs have acquired the cognitive skills to understand some forms of human communication, but that dogs are inconceivable, *as dogs*, without humans. Returning to Morgan's experiments with Tony and the latch, the mechanics of which, Morgan argued, Tony never understood (see Chapter 3), Hare and Woods write:

> Morgan would be pleased to learn that while Tony did not understand how the latch worked on the gate, scientists have discovered that dogs do not solve this type of problem only by means of trial and error. A recent experiment has shown that dogs can solve the latch problem immediately if they see someone else [a human someone] solve it first. Tony's case demonstrates how experiments can reveal where animals are geniuses and where they are not.
>
> (Hare and Woods 2020a: 44)

In other words, there is more than one way of solving a problem, and the genius of dogs – of *all* dogs, Hare and Woods argue – is to solve it by turning to humans. Probably, Hare and Woods chose the concept of 'genius' to make their work accessible to a public audience. Nevertheless, the scientific take-home message is clear. Specific skills ('genius') are largely definitive of a species. Because dogs are *not* geniuses without humans, the species 'dog' must be understood in relation to humans. There are no dogs *qua* dogs without humans.

Love

I will leave aside Clive Wynne's point-by-point (or rather, method-by-method, experiment-by-experiment) objections to Hare and Woods's thesis that dogs have evolved unique cognitive skills. It is enough to record here that much of this refutal turns on experiments, Wynne's own and others', that demonstrate that wolves and other animals can also read human intentions (so dogs are not cognitively unique in this regard), and that an individual dog's life experiences play a significant role in shaping their cognitive skills (so 'dognition' is not given solely by evolutionary adaptation). Dogs do indeed have an 'essence' that marks them out as special, Wynne argues, but this specialness pertains not so much to cognition as to their affective capacities. Dogs have 'an emotional engagement with our species', Wynne writes, which is written into 'their bodies' (Wynne 2020a: 118). 'Scientists are digging deeper and deeper into the biological essence of the dog, finding more and more evidence that their bodies are programmed for emotional connections' (Wynne 2020a: 114). This 'programming' can be identified in 'a range of neurological, hormonal, cardiac and other physiological markers' (Wynne 2020a: 118).

Wynne draws on a number of studies to support this argument, including Gregory Berns *et al.*'s well-publicised functional magnetic resonance imaging (fMRI) research, which first illustrated that the 'reward system' in two dogs' brains became activated when the dogs anticipated a food reward (Berns *et al.* 2012) and then, later, that the caudate activity in thirteen out of fifteen dogs was more intense in anticipation of social praise than in anticipation of food (Cook *et al.* 2016; Wynne 2020a: 121–130).[7] Having also outlined cardiac studies, which seem to show that the hearts of dogs and humans will synchronise when the human is stroking the dog (Wynne 2020a: 119–121), and chemical studies, which focus on the role of neurochemistry and especially oxytocin in developing and maintaining social bonds (Wynne 2020a: 130–138), Wynne turns finally to genetics, 'to the most basic building blocks of their (and our) biology – their genetic code' (Wynne 2020a: 139). Here Wynne draws on the work of three scientists: Mia Persson and Anna Kis, both of whom investigated genes that code for oxytocin receptors and, in Kis's case, their possible relations to dog breed; and Bridgett vonHoldt, whose controversial argument is that the significant difference between wolves and dogs is not cognitive but social, and that this sociability – in fact, this 'exaggerated gregariousness, referred to as hypersociability' (vonHoldt *et al.* 2017: 1) – is connected to the 'orthologous [chromosomal] region that has been mapped to human WBS [Williams-Beuren syndrome]' (vonHoldt *et al.* 2017: 2).

Williams-Beuren syndrome (WBS), or Williams syndrome (WS), is a rare, non-hereditary, congenital disease affecting 1 in 18,000 people in the UK. The Williams Syndrome Foundation UK writes that it 'causes distinct facial characteristics and a wide range of learning difficulties … WS people tend to be talkative and excessively friendly towards adults' (Williams Syndrome Foundation 2023: para. 1). Wynne reports that when he first learned of vonHoldt's results, he became somewhat concerned about the implications of the alleged genetic connection between dogs and people with WS: 'for all that I was thrilled to be involved with such an exciting scientific breakthrough, I was anxious that parents of children with Williams syndrome might be offended by our discovery that there are genetic similarities between their offspring and dogs' (Wynne 2020a: 153). Apparently, he 'needn't have worried' – a board member of the United States Williams Syndrome Association, when commenting on vonHoldt's study, told a journalist that 'the connection made immediate intuitive sense … "If they [children with WS] had tails, they would wag them"' (Wynne 2020a: 153).

In her discussion of the gestures and expressions of sign language, disability scholar and activist Sunaura Taylor argues that sign has been both racialised and animalised through its association with the 'primitive' and 'rudimentary', such that 'the gestural language could no more be called a language than expressive animal movements like the wag of a dog's tail' (Taylor 2017: 51). The racialised history of ableism goes some way to explaining why the claim about children with WS – '[i]f they had tails, they would wag them' – might make one feel not less but *more* uneasy about the WS–dog association. Nevertheless, the parallels between dogs and disability – not only in his discussion of the genes associated with WS in humans, but also throughout the book – is the prompt that enables Wynne to organise his argument in terms of ethics.

Wynne makes clear, for example, at the start of *Dog Is Love*, that his objection to Hare and Woods's canine research is not solely scientific. Hare and Woods's claim that dogs' cognitive skills are independent of their life experiences (hence the importance of their emphasis on the already-established skills of puppies in recognising human gestures) implies, Wynne fears, that dogs who do *not* exhibit an 'innate capacity' to understand human intentions have 'some sort of deep cognitive deficits' (Wynne 2020a: 36). The significance of this for potential companion dogs who are waiting to be rehomed in shelters is serious: '[a]ny qualities that might help to determine whether a dog stays in a shelter or goes home with an adoptive family could literally be the difference between life and death' (36). This is why Wynne conceives of his and Monique Udell's research on shelter dogs to be partly an ethical project. Wynne and Udell sought to understand 'what the implications of their [shelter dogs'] handicap were' (37), with the intention of ensuring that the dogs 'could find fulfilling lives in human homes' (36). Having trained these dogs to understand human pointing in under half an hour – i.e. having ostensibly illustrated that this skill is 'learned, not inherent', and that these dogs were not 'handicapped' after all – Wynne writes: '[t]his was such a thrilling result: these dogs obviously were not beyond saving!' (39). As for his own position on dogs – this too has an ethical dimension. For if '[t]he essence of dog is love' (155), Wynne writes, then to ignore this '*need* [for love] ... is as unethical as denying them their need for food and exercise' (9, emphasis in the original).

Wynne is not the only canine scientist to craft an ethical position on dogs that derives from dogs' perceived relations with humans. Berns *et al.* also suggest that dogs' orientation toward humans renders them 'particularly vulnerable to exploitation' (Berns *et al.* 2012: 3), which is why the authors include in their first article on dogs and fMRIs some ethical guidelines for future research in this area (Berns *et al.* 2012: 3–4; see also Berns *et al.* 2017: 2–3). Because dogs are likely to do what they are asked, scientists must place 'the dogs' welfare above all else' (Berns *et al.* 2012: 3–4). There are points of resonance here with Eva Giraud and Gregory Hollin's analysis of research Beagles at University of California, Davis, who, as they note, were bred to be 'amenable' (Giraud and Hollin 2017: 170). In addition to this breeding, Giraud and Hollin also show how the care practices at Davis were intentionally designed to manipulate the Beagles, to mould them into ' "experimental dogs" ', and to pacify their 'objections and desires' (Giraud and Hollin 2016: 36). The common argument here is that, when it comes to their affective relations with humans (however those relations come about), the agency of dogs, and especially their ability to object, is compromised. It is only ethical, therefore, to account for this. But where Giraud and Hollin confine their concerns to the breeding of research dogs, and where Berns confines his to his experiments,[8] the ethical implications of Wynne's claim that 'dog is love' necessarily extends to the entire membership of *Canis familiaris*, for *all* dogs are 'love'. This is why Wynne is obliged to find evidence for his argument in research conducted not only on companion dogs, but also on the 'un-owned dogs' (Wynne 2020a: 75) that he finds living in Moscow and in and around Kolkata (Wynne 2020a: 75–83).

The implicit argument of *Dog Is Love* is that the 'genius' of dogs *is* disability. In the opening pages of the book, Wynne writes that dogs 'have an exaggerated, ebullient, perhaps even excessive capacity to form affectionate relationships with members of other species. This capacity is so great that, if we saw it in one of our own kind, we would consider it quite strange – pathological, even' (Wynne 2020a: 8). It is no accident, in a book devoted to pathological love, that Wynne should be preoccupied with 'disorders' of affectivity. In addition to his identification of dogs' 'pathology' as genetically akin to Williams syndrome, Wynne reports on genomic and behavioural research that suggests dogs more oriented toward humans have genetic markers that are associated in humans with autism (Wynne 2020a: 153). Although he does not say it in the book, the genetic research that he cites here was conducted on highly bred laboratory Beagles (Persson *et al.* 2016).

One reason why the connections Wynne makes between the subjects of disability, animals and ethics might be read as controversial is on account of the influence of Peter Singer's work, which has done relations between the disability and animal liberation movements no favours (Taylor 2017; Chapter 12; Salomon 2010). In his anti-speciesist ethics, Singer argues that the criterion for moral consideration should rest not on any ostensibly human species-specific capacity (such as 'reason'), but rather on the capacity for suffering, which is shared by all sentient creatures, human or animal. Although this argument has enabled Singer to dispute the moral value attributed to humans solely on the basis of a prejudice in favour of that species, his own prejudices, and especially the normative value that he ascribes to autonomy, self-governance, agency and activity, have intensified discrimination *between* humans. Using suffering as ethical leverage, Singer has argued that '[m]ental capacities' make a 'difference' to suffering and therefore to the moral worth of a life and indeed the moral significance of a death. 'Some deaths', he writes, 'are more tragic than others' (Singer 2006: 6).

As many critics have argued, Singer's calculations of tragedy (the greater tragedy of the death of a 'full person', the conception of disability as 'tragic', the 'tragedy' of suffering) are underpinned by an ableism that defines for Singer not only quality of life, but also what is a good life, a life worth living. Although Gary Francione often takes issue with Singer (e.g. Francione and Charlton 2015; Francione 2010), his abolitionist approach arguably represents the logical, if extreme, conclusion of their shared ableism. Francione and Anna Charlton argue that domesticated species are so vulnerable to human exploitation and abuse that the only ethical response available is the forced sterilisation of all extant animals, with the ultimate goal of extinction (Francione and Charlton 2015: 23–28). As Taylor argues in her critique of Francione, the 'pitiability' of domesticated animals is intelligible only to the extent that dependency/codependency is seen to be diminishing. 'In a parallel to the "better off dead" narrative of disability', Taylor writes, 'domesticated animals are viewed as "better off extinct"' (Taylor 2017: 215). In response to both Singer and Francione, Taylor argues that '[t]he challenge is to understand dependency not simply as negative, and certainly not as unnatural, but rather as an integral part of our world and our relationships' (Taylor 2017: 210).

It is not the case that Wynne's argument reveals or exposes relational co-dependency, however, for the direction of (biological) 'need' flows principally and most powerfully from dogs to humans. (Herein lies the ethical obligation, in the affective asymmetry.) Nor does Wynne's understanding of dogs as pathologically sociable – pathologically relational, one might say – challenge the 'able' human subject. On the contrary, his ethics takes that subject for granted. This is the normatively capable, and now also normatively caring, human who, *because* they are capable and caring, should look out for dogs, because dogs, so devoted are they to humans, cannot look out for themselves. Such is the vulnerable underbelly of Wynne's paternalistic ethics, which relies on a benevolent perception of 'disability' and on 'good will' toward dogs' dependence on humans. Rather than deploy dependency to challenge the relations between ability and disability, as Taylor seeks to do, in Wynne's analysis 'disability' serves only to intensify the otherness of dogs. Not only are dogs other to humans because they are animals; not only are dogs aligned with humans who, on account of their 'disabilities', are themselves perceived to be other; dogs are in addition other *among* animals, for as a species they are uniquely 'disabled' by their affective dependence on humans. In Wynne's account of what dogs are, dogs are deeply disadvantaged by that affectivity, and also inescapably tied to it, for it is definitive of their species.

So, what does the reader learn from Hare and Woods, and from Wynne, about dogs? First, the degree of interspecies relationality that is evident between dogs and humans, be it cognitive (Hare and Woods) or affective (Wynne), is unique. Second, they learn from Hare and Woods that it is natural – literally, that it is given by natural selection – for dogs as a species to be able to engage in sophisticated communication with humans. From Wynne, the reader learns that it is given by genetics (and neurochemistry, and hormones, and …) that dogs, regardless of whether they can or cannot communicate successfully across species (which is anyway something that can be taught), can and do love humans: that dogs, in fact, cannot *help* but love humans, given the opportunity.

What is the immediate implication of these stories, for dogs? It is that dogs are *not* unique, special or genius without humans, for one reason or another. For one reason or another: this is an aspect of Wynne's argument that he himself omits to address – the straight substitution of one definitive feature of dogs, their 'genius' for communication with humans, with another definitive feature, their unparalleled capacity for 'love'. Such is the mark of a species story. What these two versions of dogs' species story have in common is that they both perceive dogs to be, inherently, creatures of 'the bond'. Whether they tell of a bond that is communicative, or of a bond that is affective, these stories bind dogs to humans. I am returned to my discussion of Stanley Coren's intelligence ranking, in which dogs bred to work independently were listed least 'intelligent' (see Chapter 1), and to the story of Beth, as it is described by Harlan Weaver, who was euthanised for her 'disinterest in humans' (see introduction). Both can be explained by Hare and Woods's and Wynne's versions of the species story. For who is an unintelligent dog? They are a dog without the genius to look to humans. And who is a 'problem' dog? They are a dog without the love to show to humans.

In the next part of this chapter, I want to consider some of the more profound implications of dogs' species story.

What dogs are not

In this second section, I use Jocelyn Porcher's analysis of animal labour to understand and explore the implications, for dogs, of these scientific stories about them. The question as to whether animals can or should be described as workers (is such a description possible? Is it desirable?) is complex, and Porcher's contribution to this debate is somewhat controversial. I will return to both these topics in the conclusion. First, I zoom in on the nuts and bolts of Porcher's theory – specifically 'the link', the 'interface' between worlds and species – to illustrate how she understands animal labour to operate in practice, and from where, in her view, it accrues its value. Second, I demonstrate how dogs' species story dismantles the relations between these nuts and bolts, and how this leads inexorably to the conclusion that dogs, while certainly doing things for/with humans, are not truly working. Interestingly, this exercise highlights not only how deeply bound up with the concept of species is dogs' perceived non-labour (as one would anticipate), but also how bound up in species is Porcher's theory itself, which would not be intelligible without it.

Porcher's conception of labour, and especially the link between humans and animals that is built through it, promises much to domesticated animals. Among those promises is the opportunity to transcend what Karl Marx called their 'species life', their 'mere doing', as one might put it. Numerous critics have illustrated, however, how unlikely this promise was to be realised in practice historically (for example Delon 2020: 166), and how unlikely it is to be realised today (for example Eisen 2020). To these empirical critiques I would add a theoretical one, which is that labour's promise does not bear identically upon all domesticated animals, because these animals are made into species differently. Most obvious, in the context of *Dog Politics*, is the difference between the significance of 'the link' for cows, as Porcher understands it, compared to its significance for dogs, as it is understood in dogs' species story. Herein lies the usefulness of Porcher's theory for my own analysis, and the problem: while her concept of 'the link', established through 'living together', enables me to expose the limitations that dogs' species story imposes on dogs, her valorisation of it prevents me from identifying, in her work, a way for dogs to escape those limitations. Like the link or 'the bond' itself, therefore, the limitations on dogs are binding.

Living together

In her article with Sophie Nicod, Porcher argues that frameworks that seek to dominate and instrumentalise domesticated animals give rise to generic conceptions of them: 'bovine *for* tractive power, sheep *for* wool, cow *for* milk, pig *for* meat and fat' (Porcher and Nicod 2020: 251, emphasis in the original). Across her work, Porcher deploys her understanding of labour to challenge this idea that domesticated animals are reducible to their roles in production (or to their roles as products). Animal labour, and the labour of humans who work with animals, are not primarily about production, she says. Instead, they are about relations. '[P]roduction is not its [labour's] first and sole purpose … Working is production, but it is mainly living together' (Porcher and Nicod 2020: 252).

'Living together' with humans – or, more specifically, 'the link' (which is sometimes translated as the tie, the connection or the bond) – is a key element in Porcher's theory. Labour, as Nicolas Delon explains, 'on this view, implies a dyadic or collective relation between human and non-human co-workers. Its value is inherently relational. Indeed, it's "the link" that Porcher considers worth preserving for its own sake' (Delon 2020: 164). Porcher's position, Delon continues, is cleaved from both history and anthropology: 'in a nutshell: we are happier together and have always lived together … The empirical premise implies an axiological one: work uniquely embodies the intrinsic value of living together' (Delon 2020: 165). The link between animals and humans is forged through work, the link is the reward for animals when they work and the link is the main criterion by which animals judge their work. 'The judgment on the link', Vinciane Despret explains, 'or judgment on the conditions of living together – makes the difference between work that alienates and work that creates, even in situations that are radically asymmetric between farmers and their animals' (Despret 2016: 183). In work that creates, animals 'collaborate intentionally' (Porcher in Delon 2020: 163). In work that alienates, '[a]nimals do not say thank you; they can even sabotage the work' (Porcher in Delon 2020: 163). This is why industrial-scale food production is not an example of 'living together', for either human or animal workers. Rather, it represents 'the breakdown of relations' (Delon 2020: 163).

Porcher's definition of domestication – 'the insertion of animals into human work' (Porcher and Schmitt 2012: 40) – is of consequence for this book because it displaces species as a mode of classification. As I understand it, for Porcher domestication is a way of organising animals' lives and experiences and, therefore, domesticated animals of different species may have more in common with each other than domesticated and non-domesticated animals of the same species.[9] Yet, even though it is not immediately obvious, species plays an important role in Porcher's analysis of the link. For it is in the 'interface between their own world and the human world built by labour activities', Porcher and Nicod write, 'that domesticated animals find purpose in their existence and enjoy a richer, more interesting, surprising and challenging life compared to a life outside of the human' (Porcher and Nicod 2020: 256).[10] What are these 'worlds'? In an article written with Tiphaine Schmitt on cows, Porcher argues that farm animals inhabit three worlds: 'the "natural" world'; 'their own world – that of their species'; and 'our human world', in which they 'live, from birth to death' (Porcher and Schmitt 2012: 40). The intersection among these worlds is important, because it is here that the richer, more interesting, surprising and challenging life is engendered. For example: cows 'have a need that is not entirely natural, a need for recognition. It is with speech and petting that the farmers recognize their animals, and it is with trust and proximity that animals recognize their farmers' (Porcher 2014: 7). The cows' need is not entirely natural, because it is located not in the natural world or in the cows' species world, but in the human world of work.

Can this understanding of animal labour be transposed to dogs? In my view, there are two characteristics of domesticated dogs, ascribed to them by dogs' species story, that disrupt the operations of Porcher's model. First, dogs are not bred primarily for production-related traits, but for behavioural traits. Second, dogs' species story collapses the distinction between worlds (in this case, the dog world and the human world) that subtends the power of the link, as Porcher conceives of it. With regard to the former: insofar as these behavioural traits support 'an extraordinary variety of working and social roles' (Serpell and Duffy 2014: 32), one might argue that the on-going process that is 'living together' *is* the dog product. Sheep *for* wool, cow *for* milk, dogs *for* living together. Consider again Beth, touchstone for this book, who could not live together 'well' with humans and who did not bond with them successfully (from the perspective of humans). This 'failure' brought an end to Beth's life, precisely because, at least in the Global North, domesticated dogs supply no other purpose or product than living together with humans.

With regard to the latter: true, dogs inhabit a world that is sense specific. But dogs' species story comes dangerously close to suggesting – and Clive Wynne's version of the story is exemplary here – that the near totality of the biological, genetic, neurological, physiological, cognitive, communicative and affective processes that give rise to that dog *Umwelt* have evolved in relation to/are organised around humans. Unlike domesticated cows' need for recognition from farmers, therefore, which Porcher describes as 'not entirely natural', dogs' species story, by strong contrast, insists that nothing could be more natural than dogs' need for recognition from humans. Indeed, Wynne goes so far as to suggest that dogs would die without it (recall his claim, which I quoted above, that a dog's need for human love is equivalent to their need for food and exercise).

How might these challenges to the conceptual architecture of Porcher's theory of animal labour transform its direction and implications? Oddly, I want to answer this question by reflecting on an article written by Porcher and Élisabeth Lécrivain, in which the authors criticise the belief of French shepherds that Patou dogs do not work, while sheep dogs do.[11] This is odd, because it means I will be deploying an analysis of dogs to demonstrate why dogs, ultimately, are an exception to that analysis (!). So let me remind the reader that, in the first instance, I am comparing Porcher's analysis of the shepherds' conception of Patous' work with my analysis of the conception of dog labour that emerges, albeit implicitly, in dogs' species story. Although they have much in common, dogs' species story goes much further. Not only does it claim to account for all dogs, it also transforms the characteristic of 'doing but not working' into an existential and political limitation for dogs.

Doing but not working

Patou, originally known as the Pyrenean Mountain dog, is the generic term for the large white dogs who are now almost entirely responsible (they constitute 85 per cent of the dogs responsible) for protecting herds of sheep against wolves in France (Porcher and Lécrivain 2019: 116–117). Although Porcher and Lécrivain consider the work of the Patou to be on a par with that of police or military dogs, the shepherds conceive of their protective activities as 'not work'. One reason for this is that these dogs have for generations, from a young age, been raised with sheep. Their activities, therefore, are considered by the shepherds to be genetic and instinctive (Porcher and Lécrivain 2019: 119). This means that not only do the shepherds have nothing to do with it – '[n]ous, on n'y est pour rien' (Porcher and Lécrivain 2017: 71) – neither, apparently, do Patous. In the eyes of the shepherds, because this work is 'innate', it is 'work without a subject': '[l]e travail de la chienne patou est un travail sans sujet puisqu'il est renvoyé à des caractéristiques innées' (Porcher and Lécrivain 2017: 74).

If the work of the Patou is opaque to the shepherds, Porcher and Lécrivain argue, then this is because the shepherds consider the activities involved in protection to be proper to the species world of the dog, which is distinct from the human world of work (Porcher and Lécrivain 2019: 122). In other words, wherever a dog appears to be doing something that belongs to their species world – i.e. something that, as a member of their species, they would be doing 'naturally'/ anyway – then those activities cannot be considered to be work. If the activities belong to the world of human work, however – indicated by the fact that for such activities, dogs require training (because they would *not* do them naturally/anyway) – then work they are. This is the difference between Patous and sheep dogs, according to the shepherds. The sheep dogs' work, by contrast with the Patou dogs', is only partly genetic and instinctive (and therefore not work), and partly trained (and therefore work) (Porcher and Lécrivain 2019: 122).

There are recognisable echoes of the shepherds' schema, as Porcher and Lécrivain describe it, in dogs' species story. The shepherds consider 'innate' activities to be not work. Similarly, if 'living together' with humans, or the 'link', is 'innate' to dogs – as Hare and Woods and Wynne propose – then any dog activity that involves humans cannot ultimately be considered to be work. Since there is no work as such being done by dogs (they are doing but not working), the analytical consequence is perhaps better described not in terms of 'work without a subject', which is how the shepherds see Patous' work, but rather in terms of a subject without work. Of course, scientists will protest that dogs do work, as evidenced for instance by the fact that dogs need to be socialised and trained to work. This is, after all, one of the reasons that so much funding is invested in research on the socialisation process, as I indicated in Chapter 1 of this book: to ensure that dogs can be trained to work, whether as companions or workers, as economically, efficiently and 'successfully' as possible. Moreover, neither Hare and Woods, nor Wynne, nor Berns, ever describe, or even imply, that the things dogs do are 'natural' in and of themselves (in the way that the shepherds imagine that Patous' protective activities are 'natural'). What they do assume, however, is that *it is natural for dogs to do for/with humans things that humans often call work, but which a dog would call 'being a dog'*.[12] This is everywhere evident in the assumptions that underlie these scientists' understandings of dogs.

Berns, for instance, is concerned with the ethics of putting dogs into an fMRI machine (it is not natural, nor is it work). He has no ethical qualms at all, however, about using fMRI technologies to identify dogs who are more likely to succeed at service work: at work, that is, that supports humans. Yet '[m]ost dogs', as Berns and his colleagues themselves confess – up to 70 per cent of dogs in fact – 'are not suited to be service dogs' (Berns *et al*. 2017: 1). This statistic – like the statistic I quoted in Chapter 1 of this book, which suggested that, in a study of over 4,000 dogs, 85 per cent of them had behavioural 'problems' – might be the cue to ask whether dogs really are as accomplished at their 'non-work' (which is living with humans) as they are said to be, and what the experiential consequences of that might be, for dogs. The cue passes unnoticed, however. Because for Berns *et al*., the statistic is relevant not to dogs, who of course do things for/with humans, but to the economics of service-dog programmes, which can cost up $50,000 per dog (Berns *et al*. 2017: 1).

The assumption that it is natural for dogs to engage with humans in activities that humans might call work is the *de facto* position of Hare and Woods's book, and indeed provides much of the rationale for the Duke Canine Cognition Center. In an interview with Maggie Spini, Hare describes the aims of the Duke Canine Cognition Center thus:

> What we'd really, really love to see is some of the things that we learn here at the Duke Canine Cognition Center be applicable to real-world problems. Either helping people teach dogs to be better at finding bombs, or to be better companion animals to, say, children with autism or helping people with disabilities. The medical community is also getting more and more excited about using dogs in different ways to help people. There's a huge supply problem – there are not many dogs available, and it's very labor-intensive to train these dogs to help people. So, if we could understand dog psychology, we might make the whole process easier and there would be more dogs that are better at helping people.
>
> (Hare in Spini 2010: para. 1)

This, then, is what a centre dedicated to dogs' psychology is for. It is not for helping dogs *per se*; it is for helping dogs to help humans.

How is it possible, once again, for the politics of this to pass unremarked and perhaps, even, unnoticed? Arguably, because dogs' species story renders the politics invisible by naturalising dogs' 'living together' with humans. This is probably why the name of a centre dedicated to enabling dogs better to help humans need only refer to dogs. At the end of the day, dogs helping humans *is* all about dogs; or, it is what dogs are all about. 'What's in it for the dogs?', asks Lisa Rabanal (personal communication), following Lynda Birke (2009). What's in it for dogs is humans. To the extent that this is reassuring for humans, dogs' species story can be understood to be a pseudo-ethical balm, applied to a political wound.

A further consequence follows from the naturalisation of dogs' 'living together' with humans, and therefore of their labour: it is that labour does not and cannot offer dogs – as Porcher argues it potentially offers other domesticated animals – the opportunity of a 'second nature'.

Labour as a route (or not) to a 'second nature': species life and species being

In the *Economic and Political Manuscripts of 1844*, Marx (1988) argues that species life means a life determined by the dictates of the species, without – and this is the important part – any consciousness of being a species. According to Marx, this is how animals live: '[t]he animal is immediately identical with its life-activity. It does not distinguish itself from it' (Marx 1988: 76). Socialised humans, by contrast, are capable of species being, which means they are capable of making species life 'the object of [human] will and of [human] consciousness' (76). As Tim Ingold explains:

> They are aware of what they are doing, and they are aware that it is they who are doing it. As agents, they can separate themselves out from their activity and, by the same token, they can imagine themselves doing all kinds of different things, including even the things that other animals do.
>
> (Ingold 2013: 17)

The shepherds' view of the Patou bears a striking resemblance to Marx's conception of species life. According to the shepherds, the Patou do what is typical of/natural to their species, without recognising that this 'doing' is something that they, as a species, do. For this reason, the Patou's protective activities count as work to the shepherds, but as being a dog to the Patou. This is how, in the minds of the shepherds, there can be a Patou form of work without a Patou working subject.

Porcher and Lécrivain raise a formidable objection to the shepherds' conception of the Patou, and in doing so pose a challenge to Marx's assumption that animal life is species life. They argue that Patous' work could not be carried out successfully if the dogs were not able to distinguish between different species, and to adopt appropriate relations toward each of them. In other words, the Patou do *not* form things only 'in accordance with the standard and the need of the species to which it belongs' (Marx in Porcher and Lécrivain 2019: 124). Patous know that to the shepherd they should show obedience and trust; to sheep, protection and respect; to herding dogs, respect and trust; to wolves and stray dogs, aggression; to tourists, passive observation; and to tourists' dogs, distance without aggression (120). Every one of these differing relations presupposes that Patous understand their work, and what it entails. In order to be respectful to and confident about the sheep dogs, for instance, Patous must recognise what is the sheep dogs' job with regard to the flock, and how it differs from their own (120). 'A dog's activity', Porcher and Lécrivain conclude, 'goes beyond the needs of the species they belong to, and they know how to produce according to the standards of other species, whether they be human, sheep or cattle' (124).

If the shepherds recognised the Patou's labour, then labour could become for them, Porcher and Lécrivain argue, a way to acquire a second nature: '[w]hen the animals engage with us at work, as animals and as individuals, they also transform nature, and their natures … [D]omestication gives them a second nature' (Porcher and Lécrivain 2019: 123). Not only, then, are Porcher and Lécrivain using Patous' work to dispute Marx's distinction between human species being and animal species life, they are also arguing that labour beyond capitalist alienation could be for animals, as Marx argues it can be for humans, a privileged site for the realisation of potentialities (Porcher and Lécrivain 2017: 76).

The conflation of the dog world with the human world in dogs' species story arguably presents an obstacle to this optimistic vision.

To recall: for Porcher, it is the movement between worlds, and especially the movement out of their species world and into the human world of work, that enables animals to enjoy larger, more expansive, lives. This is why Porcher describes the need that domesticated cows have for recognition of and from humans as 'not entirely natural' – because it is not a need that is natural to their species world. The very fact that 'living together' is not natural to cows' species world, however, is what enables domesticated cows to secure for themselves a 'second nature'. Compare to dogs' species story. The long and short of Hare and Woods's argument is that, for evolutionary reasons that remain singularly relevant today, dogs can only 'find their way', both literally and metaphorically, with humans; the long and short of Wynne's is that dogs' 'withness' with humans is so basic it is biological. The 'link' between dogs and humans, as it is cast in dogs' species story, is perhaps thus best described not as a relational need for recognition on the parts of both animals and humans, but as the possessive inscription of dogs *into* humans. It is the mechanism by which dogs' undoubtedly multiple worlds are absorbed into the human world, such that barely a whisker of a difference can be identified between them. *Canis familiaris*. Of the household, defined by the household.

It follows that, in dogs' species story, dogs' need for living together, for human recognition, for the link, *is* entirely natural. The 'link' with humans is not acquired through labour; rather, it is constitutive *of* dogs' 'nature'. It is not the vehicle through which dogs can transcend their species life; rather, it is *definitive* of dogs' species life (of what dogs are and do, as a species). Since the Patou dogs, for similar but not entirely identical reasons, are denied their way into a second nature by the shepherds, I look to them, again, to learn what are the consequences. 'The most acute consequence' of the misrecognition of Patous' labour as not labour – of the conception of their activities as 'natural' to their species world – Porcher and Lécrivain argue, is that it is a denial 'of the dogs' agency, intelligence and capacity to make decisions, which results in a lack of recognition of the work by the shepherd and, potentially, in the Patous becoming demotivated about their work' (Porcher and Lécrivain 2019: 119).

I would argue that dogs' species story similarly diminishes domesticated dogs' agency, their 'intelligence' beyond humans, and their capacity to make decisions. I realise that my claim here goes against the grain of much popular and scientific thinking about dogs. Dogs receive considerable 'recognition' from humans, both for their work and for their companionship, and this recognition usually includes all the things the Patous are denied by the shepherds (the enrichment that follows from interspecies ties, intraspecies play, petting, rewards etc.). As I write this chapter, Kaiser, a German Shepherd police dog, is being hailed across the UK press and on social media for his 'immense bravery' (Superintendent Emma Richards in Davis 2021: para. 12). Kaiser held on to ('subdued', 'detained') an intruder in the back garden of a house in south London, while simultaneously being violently attacked. When I say that dogs' species story diminishes dogs, I do not mean to deny how agential, 'intelligent' and capable dogs are *with* humans. My point is that this kind of agency, this kind of 'intelligence' and capability, does not, and should not, represent the limits of what dogs 'are' and what they could become.

For sure, some domesticated dogs may sometimes benefit from what the biologist Heini Hediger described as the 'catalytic effect', 'whereby contact with human beings potentialises and augments animal capabilities' (Chrulew 2018: 492). Equally, however, their contact with humans may erode such capabilities. Consider, for example, the tightening behavioural and physical constraints on dogs' lives, the ongoing deployment of basic stimulus/response models of learning and training, conditioning and counter-conditioning, all those eternal repetitions, or the myriad ways in which companion dogs, in particular, are infantilised. Alexandra Horowitz's book title *Our Dogs, Ourselves: The Story of a Unique Bond* (one of the epigraphs to this chapter) bears testimony, in its appeal to a general audience, to the widespread belief in the dog–human 'bond'. But her account of dogs' lives, as she describes it herself in this book, is 'humorless' (2019: 251). 'The dog sleeps all day', she writes elsewhere, in an eviscerating summary of domesticated dogs' lives in captivity, 'because we give them nothing to be awake for' (Horowitz 2014a: 18). Dogs' capabilities may or may not be augmented by their relations with humans. Either way, I think it remains important to ask whether Kaiser's actions were exemplary of species being, or whether they point to a deep unfreedom. It is important to ask because the key achievement of dogs' species story, i.e. the achievement of claims such as those found in Hare and Woods's and Wynne's books, is, as I have been arguing, the obliteration of any conceptual, biological, affective and/or political 'outside' for dogs. This renders this most fundamental question, this question as to whether dogs would or could live a flourishing life if they were not living their lives with humans, not only *unnecessary* to ask, but also, even, *unintelligible*. And so it must be asked.

What compelled Kaiser to hold on to that intruder, while being stabbed five times in the face and head with a kitchen knife? It is not my aim to unpack what for Kaiser was dog world or human world; what was determination, loyalty or fear; what was breed; what was training; what was work; or what about Kaiser's behaviour was natural or unnatural. Because in the end, there is no need. For whatever reason, Kaiser did what dogs are believed to do, which is to do for humans, which is what dogs are. Porcher argues that 'when the working relation collapses, so does the domestic relationship with the animals' (Porcher and Nicod 2020: 252). One has to wonder, though, whether and how such a collapse could come about where dogs are concerned. For without the link (or the bond), so most dog species stories tell, a dog simply would not be a dog. It is this tautological bind that explains why Kaiser was in no position to refuse 'the link', even if he had wanted to. For to refuse the link or the bond would be to refuse to be a dog, with all the deathly consequences that follow. To call this heroism is to tighten the false legitimacy of 'the bond' still further. This profound unfreedom is the price dogs pay for 'living together'.

It is the naturalisation of this unfreedom, I think, that accounts for the strong human resistance to recognising dogs' judgement on the link/bond that is said to define them. For judge it they surely do. Marc Bekoff and Jessica Pierce, to whom I will return in the following chapter, find in the 'high demand' for 'dog trainers and veterinary behaviorists' evidence of dogs' resistance to living with humans on human terms (Bekoff and Pierce 2019: 7–8). The high percentage rate of dogs who fail to qualify as service dogs (the 70 per cent of them, according to Gregory Berns *et al.*, whom I cited earlier), who fail 'even' to qualify as 'problem-free' companion dogs (a startling 85 per cent, as I discussed in Chapter 1), also suggests that dogs may not be as keen to go along with 'being a dog' as their species story implies they should. It must have been easier, or more convenient, to euthanise Beth than to accommodate her judgement on the bond, which was that she would prefer not to be bound by it. But Beth is hardly the exception (see for example Guenther (2020), especially chapter seven). Today, dog 'resistance' is often misrecognised as a problem of the individual dog, as a problem with *that* dog, rather than as a problem with the story that proposes to define all dogs.[13]

Conclusion

The choice of how to frame work and workers is always political (Besky and Blanchette 2019: 14). In particular, the idea that human beings work on the world in order to transform it according to their designs has served many ideological causes. Sarah Besky and Alex Blanchette show how it 'formed and [gave] flesh' to the 'aspirational European category of "Man"' during the Enlightenment; how the 'improvement of "nature"' justified in John Locke's mind individual property; and how it provided a rationale for colonialism and the '[t]he displacement and murder of Native peoples deemed incapable of durable and transformative work' (Besky and Blanchette 2019: 2). Also, there is the cause of human exceptionalism, as demonstrated by Marx's distinction between species being and species life, which Besky and Blanchette neatly summarise as: 'human beings plan their laboring endeavors, creatures such as honeybees or spiders do not' (Beksy and Blanchette 2019: 2). Marx's distinction is undoubtedly informed by a long tradition of western thinking – inaugurated, Cary Wolfe argues, by Aristotle – that conceives of 'the difference between human and nonhuman animals in terms of the human's ability to properly "respond" to its world rather than merely "react" to it, an ability made possible (so the story goes) by language' (Wolfe 2010: 63).

Today, the idea that animal behaviour is confined to reactions is too reductive to be persuasive. Yet, as both Porcher's analysis of the shepherds' view of the Patou and my analysis of dogs' species story illustrate, the role ascribed to species in conceptions of animal labour – and especially the role ascribed to species-typical behaviours and species-typical environments – continues to contribute to the idea that animals do not *really* work; rather, they do what they do instinctively, or programmatically (because they have been trained), and sometimes that doing is co-opted, for better or for worse, by humans. Herein lies a reason for identifying animal activity as labour: not only does it move beyond 'the language of rights and welfare that has largely dominated animal ethics', it also, as Dinesh Wadiwel notes, 'offers the opportunity to understand the specific roles of animals as active forces within various productive circuits, and as forms of value creation' (Wadiwel 2020: 183–184). Cows, Porcher argues, actively participate in work, and invest their affectivity, intelligence and subjectivity in it.

Yet one instinctively recoils from some of Porcher's claims here, in view of the relations of domination that characterise much animal labour, especially in the agricultural industry, and the conditions that support such relations, which include the deaths of animals (see Delon (2020) for a discussion). It may be, for example, that so deep is the instrumentalisation of animals, and so oppressive the conditions under which they 'work', that the labour model is at best 'inappropriate' (Eisen 2020: 141) and at worst normalises, legitimises and/or whitewashes the extreme exploitation of animals (Eisen 2020: 139–140, 146). The history 'of factory farms, labs, and circuses describing animals as willing partners and workers' (Blattner *et al.* 2020: 9) is long, and assumes ever new forms. In the conclusion of their important analysis of dog welfare in the conservation sector, for instance, Renée D'Souza, Alice Hovorka and Lee Neil note that the idea that the dogs ' "seem happy" doing conservation work means that welfare measures of enjoyment and suffering may reproduce the use of dogs as conservation labourers' (D'Souza *et al.* 2020: 82; see also Chapters 1 and 7 in this book on the welfare of companion dogs).

And then there is the broader question of to whom labour actually matters. On the grounds that labour and labour relations matter primarily to humans, Jessica Eisen suggests developing alternative, richer versions of 'the link' that are based on 'social categories that focus on the social relationships that animals value themselves' (Eisen 2020: 154). Her own research, for example, reveals 'ample evidence that cows care deeply about their friends and offspring', and that the social relationships of most significance to cows, and the priorities currently most devastatingly frustrated by the conditions of industrial agriculture under which they work, are those of parent and friend (Eisen 2020: 153). As for dogs, Eisen writes:

> While there is certainly evidence that many dogs, in particular, enjoy aspects of their work for people, I am sceptical that work for people is a *core priority* for dogs – and even more sceptical that this would be so absent the systems of reproductive control and intra-species isolation that characterize contemporary human uses of dogs.
>
> (Eisen 2020: 152, emphasis in the original)

I share this scepticism and would emphasise that 'work for people' includes being the 'best friend' of a human, and/or a member of their family. I am not advocating a 'species apartheid' (Acampora in Blattner *et al.* 2020: 4), only anticipating how difficult it will be to conceive of dogs differently, and to conceive of dogs' lives 'free from human imagination and domination' (D'Souza *et al.* 2020: 82).[14] 'The standpoint that matters', Nicolas Delon writes, 'is that of animals themselves' (Delon 2020: 167). Yet, in part on account of the power of dogs' species story, it is possible that humans in fact know relatively little about what the core priorities of their 'best friends' might be.

In my view, no single kind of a 'link' can or should account for all animal–human relations. But as my use of Porcher's theory has hopefully illustrated, labour does potentially offer some valuable analytic tools with which better to understand the reality of animals' lives and 'work-lives', as Kendra Coulter puts it. Coulter develops this term, 'work-lives', in order to encourage attention not only to the quality of an animal's life while they are working, but also to 'their physical, intellectual, and emotional well-being before and after formal work' (Coulter 2020: 41). These basic temporal distinctions are important and helpful, so how do they apply to dogs' lives? *Do* they apply to dogs' lives? Drawing on Wadiwel's analysis of time 'as a productive focus for thinking about animal labour, and developing strategies for change' (Wadiwel 2020: 183), I ask: how long is a companion dog's working day? When, if ever, do working and companion dogs get 'time away from their duties' (Wadiwel 2020: 191)? Are domesticated dogs managed episodically, or is their management continuous (Wadiwel 2020: 190–191)?[15] And: at what *point* in their life does a dog start working? Should the socialisation process, which may begin the very moment a dog is born (see Chapter 1), count as time dedicated to labour? Should socialisation be seen as 'training' for employment? 'Enrichment' as on-going training?

Contra Porcher, Wadiwel asks whether labour really is 'a positive activity that contributes to flourishing', or whether, alternatively, labour should be understood 'as something that stands in the way of our capacity to flourish' (Wadiwel 2020: 186). Flourishing, Wadiwel argues, occurs mainly in 'free time' (186), and yet, he writes,

> it is as if humans regard animals as lacking interest in free time, in time outside of the time we require from them as part of their utilization. Indeed, in this context, one may assert that the nature of our anthropocentric violence is marked by the fact that it is almost without limits or regulation when it comes to time: there is no apparent social limit on the time we demand from animals.
>
> (Wadiwel 2020: 193)

One of the reasons this matters is that the lives of individual animals are finite. As Wadiwel notes, 'as organic subjects our time as living subjects has a definite end, and this means the question of how much time we labour, versus how much time we spend doing other things, is important for us, for our flourishing' (Wadiwel 2020: 189). In asking about the free time of working animals, Wadiwel is not seeking to contribute to a debate about how much time off animals 'deserve'. Instead, he is using time as a way to make the domination of animals more clearly visible, and as an opportunity to imagine what a flourishing life for animals might look like (Wadiwel 2020: 197). This seems especially important to me, in view of how dogs' species story – as I have illustrated in this chapter – renders invisible the labour of the bond, and therefore also the time, the *life time*, that dogs are obliged to dedicate to it.

Charlotte Blattner argues that 'we typically see and encounter animals only in highly restrictive environments, and this, in turn, influences our judgement of their agential capacities' (Blattner 2021: 69). In this chapter, I have argued that we typically see and encounter dogs in highly restrictive *relations*. In the following chapter, I explore how these restrictive relations do indeed shape our conceptions, as Blattner argues, of dogs' agency.

Notes

1 A large number of these studies are conducted on dogs in shelters, which I assume is in part because shelters provide a ready and available source of research subjects. I include these shelter dogs under

the categories of companion and working dogs because this is ultimately their 'ideal' destiny. Although there is some research on dogs who partner homeless people (for example Williams and Hogg 2016), and on free-ranging and feral dogs (for example Boitani *et al.* 2017; Bonanni and Cafazzo 2014; Coppinger and Coppinger 2016), 'cultures where dogs function mainly as food or pelt' are seriously underrepresented (Kubinyi *et al.* 2011: 260; although see Serpell (2017: 305–307) for a review of the literature on dogs as food, and also Dugnoille (2018)).

2 The other researcher is Ádám Miklósi, who has yet to write a popular book. I will address this new field of research, and Miklósi's scientific contribution to it, in Chapter 5.

3 www.dognition.com/the-genius-of-dogs (accessed August 2023).

4 Despite Wynne's claim to have abandoned at least two of his behaviourist convictions, *Dog Is Love* bears many of the hallmarks of behaviourism, not least its author's focus on research topics that can be pinned down empirically. Behaviourists have historically bracketed out emotions because they consider them to be unobservable. If Wynne feels able to 'take on' emotions, I suspect it is because they have been rendered 'visible' and measurable, in his view, through technologies of genetics, neuroimaging, and neurochemistry.

5 Devised by Gordon Gallup in the late 1960s, the MSR test is a test for self-recognition (which is often conflated with self-awareness). See Despret (2016: 97–104) for an insightful and humorous critique of the MSR test.

6 Note that domestication (intentional or not) is not for Hare and Woods selection *for* 'cleverness' (Hare and Woods 2020a: Chapter 4). Rather, selection against aggression produces 'cleverness' – understood as dogs' ability to understand human intentions – as an unintentional by-product (Hare and Woods 2020a: 88).

7 Berns has always been clear about his positive methods of training dogs to lie still in an fMRI scanner – the first dog he trained was his own dog, Callie – and the dogs' comfort/discomfort is obviously a high priority for him (see below). Nonetheless, one cannot but wonder how the context (a dog in an fMRI machine) shapes their preference in that moment for social praise or, perhaps, social reassurance, over food.

8 See below, where I offer a possible reason as to why Berns would consider dogs' relations to humans to have ethical significance in the context of his experiments, but not more widely.

9 This definition also has implications for the perceived difference between 'pets' and other domesticated animals. For Porcher, this difference inheres not in the animals themselves – all of whom are

domesticated – but rather in human distinctions (Porcher and Nicod 2020: 251). And as she also notes, 'the market for pet animals is worldwide, and resembles in many ways that of farm animals. There are dog breeders, but there are also those who farm dogs industrially, as a product' (Porcher 2017: 20).

10 Porcher is not alone in believing that the lives of animals can be expanded through work. Both Donna Haraway (2003, 2008) and Vicki Hearne (1991) argue that work with humans offers profound rewards for animals and that 'plumbing the category of labor more than the category of rights' is the route to 'nurtur[ing] responsibility with and for other animals' (Haraway 2008: 73) and/or is the route to animal 'happiness' (Hearne 1991).

11 This paper was first published as a journal article in French (Porcher and Lécrivain 2017) and later as a chapter in an edited collection in English (Porcher and Lécrivain 2019). I will use both versions interchangeably.

12 This may explain why 'companionship' is rarely considered to be work. Not because it is the most natural thing that a dog could ever do, but because companionship is not usually seen by *humans* to be a form of work.

13 My analysis here is addressed to the specificity of the reasons as to why dog 'resistance' is difficult to see and, more importantly, to accept. I am not suggesting that the challenges of recognising and identifying animal resistance – however resistance is articulated (see Chapter 5, this book) – are unique to dogs.

14 I will return to this issue, of 'our own ability to think beyond ourselves' (Fudge 2002: 27), in Chapter 5.

15 It is salutary to remember that, as recently as the 1980s in the UK, a dog could take himself out for a walk on his own (Bradshaw 2012: xvi).

5

Dog disputes: Scientific research with dogs

> Because human beings and dogs are aspects of each other, empirical analysis of the relationship may be confounded.
>
> (Paxton 2011: 5)
>
> Is contact with humans a necessary part of what it means to be a dog? No.
>
> (Pierce and Bekoff 2021: 163)

In Chapters 2 and 4, I illustrated how '*the* bond', according to scientists, shapes the capabilities of all dogs generically. In this chapter, I illustrate how the particularity of *a* bond, especially a bond between a scientific researcher and a canine research subject, makes it difficult for scientists to identify the capabilities of a generic dog. Dog–human contact, scientists argue, engenders complex affective and emotional responses in both dogs and humans, and this, coupled with dogs' sophisticated communication skills, and their sensitivity to human gestures, makes it hard to contrive situations in which the relations between human researchers and canine research subjects can be disentangled. But also, more profoundly, it makes it hard to establish what scientific advantage would be gained by such disentanglement. It is against this complex backdrop – against the highly charged question of scientific generalisation in the context of dogs' species story – that this chapter puts three related issues into conversation with one another: dogs' perceived relationality, as it is defined as a methodological problem in science; intersubjectivity, as it is defined as the foundation of animal capability, agency and resistance in animal studies; and the contested place of singular individuality, in both.

Vinciane Depret's model of 'polite research' is the stitching that holds these three issues together in this chapter. In the first section, having explored how 'the bond' complicates canine science, I ask what methodological support polite research, which secures its authority not in spite of, but on account of, researcher–animal intersubjectivity, might offer canine scientists. Although, as I demonstrate, this method potentially yields rich rewards, it is unlikely that most scientists would pursue it, for it requires abandoning the idea of 'the dog'. It is precisely this idea, of 'the dog', that Jessica Pierce and Marc Bekoff dispute in *A Dog's World* (Pierce and Bekoff 2021), and in their popular guide to dog ownership *Unleashing Your Dog* (Bekoff and Pierce 2019). There is no 'Universal dog' (Pierce and Bekoff 2021: 160), the authors write, and certainly no dog who is universally defined by an orientation toward humans. In the second section of this chapter, I explore what methodological issues follow from Pierce and Bekoff's objection to dogs' species story, and how polite research is once again both relevant and not relevant to it. For while polite research usefully describes the ethics that characterises Pierce and Bekoff's approach not just to the scientific study of dogs but to *all* dog–human relations, the uncritical concept of 'the individual' that the authors adopt in opposition to the idea of a generic 'dog' is antithetical to it.

The contrasts here, between a vexatious relationality and a welcome one, and between relationality and individuality, illuminate the different ways in which scientific problems are being articulated and addressed. None of these counterpoints to scientific generalisation, however, in my view, quite suffices when it comes to the undoing of dogs' species story, nor can they wholly account for how dogs specifically might be enabled to object to the questions that are posed to them by scientists.[1] After extending my discussion of animal capabilities to animal agency and resistance, I illustrate why this is so with reference to Martin Seligman's 'learned helplessness' experiments. The 'learned helplessness' experiments involved the monstrous practice of giving 'inescapable' electric shocks to dogs, to dogs in a box from which they could not escape, and then shocking them again to test their responses against experimentally naïve dogs (that is, against dogs who had not previously been 'inescapably shocked'). The aim was to show that, once these canine research subjects had been exposed to uncontrollable aversive events (to aversive events over which their behaviour made no difference), they did not seek to 'help' themselves by escaping or by trying to escape, even if they had previously learned how to do so. Seligman's experiments certainly demonstrate how a research apparatus produces subjectivities, as Despret anticipates. But these experiments were in no way polite. On the contrary, as I will illustrate, Seligman *forced* the dogs to become what his research apparatus proposed to them (helpless subjects, and substitutable species members) and quashed the possibility of any kind of active resistance on the part of an individual dog. Yet in this way precisely, in its erasure both of meaningful intersubjectivity and of the individual agent, the extreme brutality of the experiments was revealing: it exposed a different kind of 'resistance', a resistance that was represented by the irreducible singularities of the dogs themselves, by the sheer existence of singularity, which exceeded the spatio-temporal context of the apparatus and, momentarily, disrupted it. I will argue in conclusion that there is a lesson to be learned here, with regard to the challenging of dogs' species story, that might be extended beyond the research context.

One reason why I call attention to the singular individual is because, as I explored in Chapters 3 and 4, and will explore again, more forcefully, in Chapter 6, species categories tend to, perhaps even aim to, render that individual irrelevant – theoretically, methodologically, ethically and politically. Since indifference is often a death sentence, dispensing too hastily with this figure feels to me to be a luxury that most animals can ill afford humans to hold. I develop this argument, alongside a full interrogation and critique of the concept of species, in Chapters 6 and 7. I also, in Chapter 7, elaborate more fully on what I mean by an enduring individual.

Dogs, scientists and intersubjectivity

The late 1990s and early 2000s are usually identified, by canine scientists, as the beginning of the 'dog paper boom', of an explosion of interest in dogs' behaviour 'for its own sake' (Horowitz 2014b: vi; Miklósi 2017: 1–15).[2] This has led dogs, the canine ethologist Alexandra Horowitz writes, to become 'some of the most well-researched and interesting subjects of contemporary psychology and ethology' (Horowitz 2014b: v; see also Feuerbach and Wynne

2011).³ The focus on 'dogs *qua* dogs' explains why many contemporary canine scientists consider their work to be distinguished from *all* earlier research on dogs, regardless of whether it is naturalistic or experimental. Horowitz, for example, writes critically of Darwin, who, she argues, for all 'his great personal interest in dogs, studied domesticated animals as a means to understand how artificial selection worked' (Horowitz 2014b: vi). Or consider ethologist Ádám Miklósi's condemnation of Seligman's 'learned helplessness' experiments. The fact that dogs were chosen as research subjects because they 'are more similar to humans than are other species', Miklósi writes, makes the 'lack of concern about dogs' suffering' all the more 'staggering' (Miklósi 2017: 3).

Miklósi is one of two scientists – the other is Brian Hare – who, while working in different disciplines and countries, are commonly said to have ignited the dog paper boom. In Hungary and the USA respectively, Miklósi and Hare independently conducted similar experiments illustrating that dogs have communication skills that are not shared by primates (i.e. they are a potentially special kind of cognitive ability) or wolves (i.e. they are not inherited by descent), and which are not solely a consequence of their ontogenetic experiences of humans (Miklósi *et al.* 1998; Hare *et al.* 2002; Hare and Tomasello 2005; for Hare on Miklósi, see Hare and Woods (2020a: 14 and 231)). Hare *et al.* concluded from these experiments that, on account of the process of domestication in dogs, 'the social-cognitive abilities of dogs … have converged with those of humans' (Hare *et al.* 2002: 1636). Both Hare and Miklósi have elaborated on this argument over the past twenty-five years. Since I have already addressed Hare's position in Chapter 4, I will use an illustrative example from Miklósi's vast body of work to signal the direction in which canine science is currently travelling.

Miklósi *et al.* (2021) have recently argued that 'companion' should be understood not as a description of species such as cats and dogs, but rather as a biological function (meaning, minimally, a behavioural trait) that contributes to the well-being of both the human and the animal in a 'human companion animal partnership' (HCAP). 'Not surprisingly', the authors write, 'the dog (*Canis familiaris*) could be regarded as the core (reference) species for the development of such partnership[s]' (Miklósi *et al.* 2021: 2). The key point for Miklósi (as for Hare) is that the 'social competence' of dogs amounts to more than a reduced flight distance, as argued by Coppinger and Coppinger, among others (Miklósi *et al.* 2021: 4; see Chapter 2 of this book on Coppinger and Coppinger's theory of dog speciation). Social competence is a complex phenomena, characterised for instance by the ability to minimise conflict by following social rules; to form close relationships; to concede to a relaxed hierarchical structure (i.e. not to wish to be the pack 'leader'); to be attentive and interested in others; to understand social context; to use different communication tools to manage interaction; to be able to engage in social learning; and to engage in cooperative interactions (Miklósi *et al.* 2021: 5; for an earlier, less theoretically developed, but fuller account, see Topál *et al.* (2009)). If this sounds a lot like humans, it is because it *is* a lot like humans. Miklósi argues that 'the evolution of dogs mirrors some aspects of hominization' (Topál *et al.* 2009: 84). That is, the 'dog behaviour complex' and the 'human behaviour complex' are analogous; they evolved in parallel, and they are 'functionally convergent' (Topál *et al.* 2009: 77).

In view of this species story – wherein 'companion' is no longer a description of a relationship, but an evolutionary behavioural trait – it is not surprising to learn that contemporary experiments on dogs typically interrogate, for instance: the implications of different forms and degrees of socialisation on dogs' ability to live with and work for humans; dogs' ability to understand different kinds of human gestures; dogs' ability to make their own gestures understood to humans through various communicative channels (such as 'gaze alternation'); dogs' capacity to learn human words; the relation between dogs' contested theory of mind and domestication; dogs' capacity for empathy with humans; dog–human emotional 'contagion'; dog behavioural problems, as they affect life in the human home (such as fear, frustration, intra- and interspecies aggression, anxiety, boredom); etc. There are other experiments too, of course, especially on dogs' intraspecific behaviours (such as dog play), but the orientation of the study of 'dogs *qua* dogs' is substantially directed to dogs *qua* humans.

The trouble this engenders, for canine scientists, is this: on account of the dog–human 'special relationship', individual human researchers and individual dog research subjects are likely to form 'unique' bonds (Miklósi 2017: 6), and those bonds will necessarily have qualifying implications for the research. Since dogs' species story virtually defines dogs by way of their bonds with humans, it is not only the forming of bonds, or the failing to recognise the formation of bonds, that is problematic, but also the contrived absence of bonds/bonding. Enikő Kubinyi *et al.* gently criticise John Scott and John Fuller's (1965) classic *Genetics and the Social Behavior of the Dog*, 'the bible of dog researchers', on the grounds that, '[a]lthough all the dogs were socialized to laboratory staff, no individual social relationships developed … [T]hese subjects could not be considered to have experienced "normal" environmental input' (Kubinyi *et al.* 2011: 258). The tension here is between the goal of scientific research, which is to produce generalisable knowledge about 'the dog', and dogs' species story, which points to the unavoidable significance (especially the methodological significance) of particular individual dogs, in particular individual or small-scale sets of relationships with humans (such as scientific researchers), in particular contexts.

This 'problem' is exacerbated by the concentration of the major part of scientific research on what are usually called 'family dogs'. In fact, canine research subjects are often the scientists' *own* 'family' dogs. The neuroscientist Gregory Berns's dog Callie, for example, was the first dog to be trained to lie quietly in an fMRI (Berns *et al.* 2012), while Chaser, the Collie who learned more than 1,000 words, was trained by his guardian, the ethologist John W. Pilley (Pilley 2013). 'Family dogs' are probably among the most individualised of all animals in human societies. Indeed, it is in part on account of this individualisation that the historian Erica Fudge is prompted to ask whether a 'pet' is an animal at all (Fudge 2002: 27). Her answer: 'because [they live] with us in our homes … it is possible to see pets as making up a different class of creature' (Fudge 2002: 28; see also Chapter 6 in this book on the distinctiveness of pets). 'A pet', she continues, 'is a pet first, an animal second' (Fudge 2002: 32).

This question, 'is a pet an animal?' (Fudge 2002: 27), or versions of it, has haunted the scientific study of dogs. Serpell argues that 'the domestic dog … is an interstitial creature – neither person nor beast – forever oscillating uncomfortably between the roles of high-status animal and low-status human' (Serpell 2017: 312; see Chapter 6 of this book for an analysis of the racialised aspects of this status). One expression of the ambivalence that this oscillation creates is that, unlike most other research animals, dogs were sometimes named in scientific publications. As if simultaneously to disavow this individualisation however, these names often appeared in inverted commas. W. Horsley Gantt, for instance, who conducted torturous experiments on two dogs for fourteen years, refers to them in his publications as 'Nick' and 'V3' (Gantt 1962). The dog- and horse trainer and philosopher Vicki Hearne proposes that this use of inverted commas, which seems to indicate that the researcher is referring to creatures to whom they 'won't and can't talk', 'is extraordinarily weird, evidence of the superstitions that control the institutionalisation of thought' (Hearne 2007a: 169). Weird it is, but it may also be a symptom of the 'suspicion', Miklósi writes, with which 'scientists have viewed dogs', and which has led dogs, '[f]or many years', to be denied 'the status of "real" animals' (Miklósi 2017: x). So 'un-animal' are dogs, that scientists, Pierce and Bekoff argue, tend to view them 'as outside the sphere of natural taxa': 'dogs are often excluded from biological classification schemes, and they rarely appear in zoology textbooks' (Pierce and Bekoff 2021: 17). The authors object: '[d]ogs are not outside of nature' (161).

Because Miklósi, like Bekoff, is an ethologist, and because ethology is usually defined by scientists as the study of animals in their 'natural' or naturalistic environments, Miklósi proposes that 'in order to allow the dog into the club of "real" animals, we have to find a natural environment for it' (Miklósi 2017: 1). But what is a dog's 'natural environment'? Kubinyi *et al.* answer: 'the human social setting' (Kubinyi *et al.* 2011: 259). As such, research on dogs can be conducted just about anywhere (Kubinyi *et al.* 2011: 259). Yet because 'family' dogs are the most common subjects of scientific research, in practice most research is conducted in and/or near the 'family home'. And the 'family home', as Kubinyi *et al.* write, is a 'complicated, and often uncertain environment' in which the dog is 'highly dependent on their owner' (Kubinyi *et al.* 2011: 260). Studying dogs in their 'natural environment', therefore, means conceding to 'many uncontrolled environmental variables', such as the country, region or city in which a dog lives; the gender of the dog guardian; the perception of dogs in a particular culture or context (and especially differing perceptions of particular breeds); specific human individuals' perceptions of their specific individual dogs; culturally specific dog-keeping practices; as well as the fact that 'dogs themselves may vary around the world' (Kubinyi et al. 2011: 259–260). Who is to say what is a dog under such 'variable' conditions?!

Moreover, the focus on *the* family dog raises the question as to who exactly is the 'expert' with regard to *this* specific family dog. As in the case of veterinary medicine, the 'complex triad' (Hobson-West and Jutel 2020: 397) of the animal, their guardian and the 'expert' may raise questions of authority. Who is best positioned to interpret a dog's behaviour? In the best possible circumstances, the guardian should know more about 'their' individual dog than anybody else (Susan Close, personal correspondence). But their knowledge will be of a particular kind (Lestel *et al.* 2006: 170) and, from the perspective of science, a kind that is often marked as anecdotal (see Chapter 3 of this book). Ergo, in what looks distinctly like a distancing tactic, Miklósi notes that although he and his team listened to 'hundreds of casual observations of dog–human interaction (many people would call these anecdotes)', *their* aim was to provide 'an observational and experimental background to these ideas' (Miklósi 2017: ix).

I have used Miklósi's (2017) *Dog Behavior, Evolution, and Cognition* to give a rough structure the above discussion because Miklósi offers a clarifying portrait of the burdens on the canine scientist. Within only a few pages, Miklósi is obliged to establish: that a dog is a real animal; that in scientific studies dogs are more often subject to individualisation than are other animals (through naming, for instance) but that, despite this, the individuality of dogs has been historically neglected in canine research; that dogs have a natural environment in which humans play a pivotal role; that for various reasons this natural environment tends to mitigate against scientific generalisation; and that the study of dogs – the study that nearly everyone who lives or works with a dog cannot help but do – is science and not anecdotalism. In short, dogs' proximity to humans is destined to affect the research, for better or for worse. Finally, while ethologists usually study the efforts of animals to survive – survival being one of Tinbergen's four questions (Tinbergen 2005 [1963]) – as Miklósi points out, with no apparent humour (or reflexivity with regard to the scientific focus on western family dogs), '[d]ogs are not the best candidates for studying survival in nature, mainly because most present-day dogs live with humans and have access to vets, and people do their best to save their companions from the challenges of nature' (Miklósi 2017: 1). Indeed.

The problems facing these scientists are not superficial. They could not be resolved, for instance, by only ever observing dogs in situations that do not involve humans because, by the very definition of dogs, such situations would be atypical of the species. Nor can scientists ignore the impacts of humans on dogs who are participating, by choice or not, in research. To go back to Seligman's learned helplessness experiments: in Miklósi's analysis, the dogs' 'ambiguous social situation' – wherein they had a 'positive social relationship with the researcher both before and after the experiment was conducted' (Miklósi 2017: 4) (i.e. before and after they were electrocuted) – would have made it difficult, if not impossible, to distinguish between the 'neurosis', as Miklósi describes it, that this ambiguity engendered and the 'effect of [the dogs'] lack of control over the situation' (Miklósi 2017: 4). In other words, Seligman not only did not, but *could not* explain 'learned helplessness' in dogs, because he neglected to address the part played by dog–human relationships in his research.[4]

Another alternative, of course, would be to adopt a different relation to the 'problem' of dogs' so-called hard-wired responsiveness to humans. Rather than regret the difficulty of maintaining distinct boundaries between observer and observed, for instance, a researcher might choose to press further into this perceived dog–human responsiveness, and to rely on the reliability of dogs not just as interpreting subjects (Lestel 2011: 87), but as especially reliable interpreters of humans' intentions (Bradshaw and Rooney 2017: 134). An increasingly large body of work, developed in the social sciences and humanities, could offer philosophical and methodological support for such an approach. Much of this work is indebted to Vinciane Despret, who has articulated a clear model for research that actively turns on human–animal intersubjectivity (e.g. Despret 2016, 2015a, 2008; see also Lestel 2011). Here, I want just briefly to outline the implications of Despret's (2008) 'polite research' as it bears on the issue of generalisation, and especially generalisations based on species.

Brett Buchanan explains 'politeness' thus:

> Animals ... are not 'texts' awaiting hermeneutic interpretation any more than they are 'objects' that can be explained through scientific experiments; both are suggestive of a detached objectivity ill-placed with respect to subjective agents. Rather, asking the right questions demonstrates a form of 'politeness' towards other beings, not only giving animals the benefit of the doubt of being able to respond but doing so in a way that allows them to respond on their own terms and to answer questions that are of interest to them.
>
> (Buchanan 2015: 22)

'Questions that are of interest to them' is the starting point of polite research. Although the reasons for engaging an animal's curiosity, and identifying what matters to them, might seem obvious – octopi are more interested in 'squirting the experimenters' than pulling at levers (Godfrey-Smith 2016: 58) – in fact, in Despret's methodology, it serves the rather more opaque purpose of luring an animal 'to take a position' on the researcher's conjectures as to why they behave as they do. As Despret explains in her analysis of Berndt Heinrich's research on ravens:

> All the work of the researcher consists ... in leading the ravens to take a position in relation to [Heinrich's] fictions and hypotheses: resisting those that do not explain them; clarifying, in those that seem to be able to, that which counted for them. The scientist must, in other words, create a dispositive that confers on the ravens 'the power not to submit to his interpretations'. It is in this way that the politeness of 'getting to know' presents itself.
>
> (Despret 2015a: 62)

A 'dispositive' – or research 'apparatus'[5] – then, is successful, for Despret, to the extent that it enables an animal to refute and/ or clarify the researcher's assumptions. One exemplary illustration of a successful apparatus, Despret argues, can be found in Irene Pepperberg's research with the African Grey parrot, Alex. Pepperberg gave Alex the power to actively shape her research not by teaching him how to speak English, but by teaching him how to *use* language to control his environment and the behaviours of the researchers. The result? Alex 'accomplish[ed] tasks that were hitherto considered as exceeding the capacities of non-humans' (Despret 2008: 125). Included among those tasks were 'speak[ing], describ[ing], count[ing]' and 'classify[ing] objects in abstract categories' (Despret 2008: 125–126).

By way of example of an *un*successful apparatus, Despret draws on Vicki Hearne's engaging analysis of 'the silence of parrots' in the face of philosophers' refusal to allow parrots to control the conversation (Despret 2008: 124). A similar example can be found elsewhere in Hearne's work, in her assessment of the relationship between dogs and behaviourists:

> We can now say something about how the story the behaviorist brings into the laboratory affects not only his or her interpretation of what goes on but also what actually does go on. To the extent that the behaviorist manages to deny any belief in the dog's potential for believing, intending, meaning, etc., there will be no flow of intention, meaning, believing, hoping going on. The dog may try to respond to the behaviorist, but the behaviorist won't respond to the dog's response.
>
> (Hearne 2007a: 58)

What Hearne is saying here is that the behaviourist's failure to respond to the dog's response not only shapes their interpretation of the dog, but also what the dog is capable of: '[t]he behaviorist's dog will not only *seem* stupid, she *will be* stupid' (Hearne 2007a: 59; my emphasis). Despret's concept of polite research is designed to avoid exactly this kind of research relation, which diminishes the animal participants and leaves them no room to show what they are capable of. Politeness, Buchanan writes, is more than an 'approach *to* animals', it is also an invitation to a 'different response *from* animals' (Buchanan 2015: 22, emphasis in the original).

Would this, then, offer an alternative methodological model for research with (rather than on) dogs? Unfortunately, I anticipate that the answer would probably be no. Not because canine scientists are averse to encouraging an expansion of dogs' agency – on the contrary, they would surely welcome it – but because Despret's 'methodological courtesy' (Buchanan 2015: 22) derives its authority not 'merely' from the interactions between the research participants, but from the interactions between these *particular* research participants, organised according to this *particular* research apparatus. Alex, Despret writes, 'doesn't talk in the name of a "we" of parrots successfully imposed by scientists, but in the name of a "we" ' constituted by the assemblage of a parrot and human beings equipped with an apparatus aimed at making the parrot talk well' (Despret 2008: 127–128). Even when two further parrots, Kyaro and Alo, joined Pepperberg's team, and even when they too illustrated that they shared the capabilities of Alex, still Despret considers their testimony to refer to the apparatuses through which their capabilities were realised, rather than to any capabilities that might be 'guaranteed by the identity of the species and the stability of its repertoire of behaviour' (Despret 2008: 126). Polite research does not render generalisation impossible, but it does mean that it will be 'constructed bit by bit', and that the generalisable knowledge it produces will tell not about species, or even about scientists, but about the apparatus (Despret 2008: 128).

Which is not to say that many canine researchers today do not seek to qualify their results. Horowitz, for instance, advises her reader that 'when I talk about *the dog*, I am talking implicitly about *those dogs studied to date*' (Horowitz 2012: 9, emphasis in the original). Although 'well-performed experiments', she continues, 'may eventually allow us to reasonably generalize to *all dogs*, period … even then, the variations among individual dogs will be great' (9, emphasis in the original). Nevertheless, despite Horowitz's sensitivity here, it is clear that 'individual dogs' do not matter as singular dogs; rather, as the concept 'variation' implies, they matter as a departure from a generalisable group ('*all dogs*, period'). Horowitz, who was long ago Marc Bekoff's doctoral student, is unquestionably among the most reflexive canine researchers working today. Yet even she claims to be reporting on 'the known capacity of *the dog*' (9, emphasis in the original), i.e. on 'the dog' as a species.

One reason why I feel sure that my proposal of polite research with dogs would be rejected by most canine scientists is that their reflections on the methodological problems posed by dogs make sense only if one *already knows* what a dog is. For the question for most canine researchers is not *whether* dogs are especially responsive to humans; it is what to do, methodologically, *given that* dogs are especially responsive to humans. This starting assumption not only reconfirms dogs' species story and legitimates the practices that support it, it also makes it difficult to invite a 'different response', as Buchanan puts it, from a dog. Difficult, but not impossible – as the following section demonstrates.

Posthuman dogs

In this book, I essentially ask: what are the implications, for dogs, of dogs' species story, a story that constitutes dogs as always having been and being in relations with humans? In *A Dog's World: Imagining the Lives of Dogs in a World without Humans*, Jessica Pierce and March Bekoff (2021) ask: *is* there a dog without humans? The way they answer this question is far from direct. Theirs is an experiment in 'speculative biology', which means speculating about '[w]hat would happen (or would have happened) *if* ...' (Pierce and Bekoff 2021: 8, emphasis in the original). Pierce and Bekoff's *if* is a science fiction scenario in which humans no longer inhabit the earth. As in the first section of this chapter, my preliminary intentions are to explore how scientists perceive and manage the methodological tensions that are raised by the study of dogs. For Pierce and Bekoff, such tensions follow not from an inherent dog–human relationality that potentially compromises the research relationship and makes it difficult to draw generalisable conclusions about 'the dog'. Quite conversely, they proceed from a 'science fiction' scenario that seems to be intentionally designed to *avoid* generalisations about dogs. The question, for them, as I noted in the introduction to this book, is how to articulate this project within the domain of canine 'science fact'.

Since the core of their scenario – a world without humans – has also been explored by other authors, Pierce and Bekoff begin the book by introducing their readers to what these authors have said (usually in passing) about the possible futures of dogs. Such reflections are a showcase for species stories in the present:

> '[W]ild predators would finish off the descendants of pet dogs' (though 'a wily population of feral house cats' will persist by feeding on starlings).
> (Alan Weisman in Pierce and Bekoff 2021: 3)

> [C]ats are self-reliant and skilled enough to survive without people ... Is it possible, [Markham Heid] asks, that after millennia of domestication 'the entire species [of dogs] may have lost its ability to live independently?'.
> (Pierce and Bekoff 2021: 4)

A Dog's World responds to these kinds of conjectures by proposing that scientists cannot know what dogs might be or become in an imaginary future, because they do not know what dogs are in the present. The assumption that dogs are not 'wily', or that they are not 'independent', cannot, at this point (or perhaps at any point), be either established or refuted. Although Pierce and Bekoff ultimately object to nearly all generalisations about dogs, they object especially strongly to portrayals that take dogs' dependence on humans for granted.

More specifically, Pierce and Bekoff object to the idea that the 'purpose' of a dog is to be a human 'help-mate' and 'companion' (Pierce and Bekoff 2021: 15), to representations of the evolution of dogs that assume that 'dogs have evolved to communicate *with us*' (88, emphasis in the original) and to the claim that dogs 'are emotionally attuned to humans and bonded to them' (117). By way of example, Pierce and Bekoff offer 'puppy dog eyes, gaze-following behaviour, oxytocin feedback loops, and even dog ESP' (88). '[T]he extent to which these emotional skills in dogs are dependent upon or uniquely directed to humans', they write, 'is often overstated' (117). In summary: '[d]ogs clearly form social relationships with humans … But it is far too human-centric to say that … the ur-dog would say to the ur-human (in the voice of Tom Cruise), "You complete me"' (91).

Pierce and Bekoff's objection to the narcissism that characterises so many accounts of 'what is a dog' puts them in an awkward position with regard to the dominant dog species story. They negotiate this by neither wholly disputing nor fully endorsing it. 'The origin of modern dogs', the authors write, is 'hotly contested' (Pierce and Bekoff 2021: 22). Scientific questions regarding the relation of dogs to wolves, for example, are 'likely to get muddier before they get clearer' (23). The field is riddled with controversies. Here Pierce and Bekoff refer to the recent discovery, in November 2019, of the body of puppy in eastern Siberia. Dated to approximately 18,000 years ago, the question remains as to whether the pup was 'a wolf or a dog or perhaps an animal that was ancestral to both' (23; see also Chapter 2 of this book on the difficulties of classifying potential ancestral wolf or dog remains).

This is obviously not a dispute with evolutionary theory itself, given that speculative biology, as Pierce and Bekoff define it, 'makes[s] predictions about the trajectory of evolution' (Pierce and Bekoff 2021: 8). One dramatic change in evolutionary direction that would follow from a world without humans – to take a single example – is that the dog population that constitutes the main object of most scientific research (companion and working dogs in the Global North) would be subject to natural rather than artificial selection.[6] In keeping with the attentiveness to time that generally characterises the work of evolutionists (see Chapters 2, 4 and 6 of this book), Pierce and Bekoff note that this change will affect different populations of dogs differently over time. Only 'later-generation' dogs – dogs who after thirty years or so will replace 'transition dogs' (alive when humans disappear) and 'first-generation' dogs (born to mothers who had contact with humans) – will be 'truly posthuman' (Pierce and Bekoff 2021: 13). Posthuman, for Pierce and Bekoff, does not in any way refer, as it does in the social sciences and humanities, to (broadly speaking) the desubjectifying entanglements that reveal the autonomous, independent, Cartesian individual to be a fiction (and which, by the same token, reveal the very concept of *post*human to be a fiction, for 'we have never been human'). Posthuman dogs are what it says on the tin: they are the dogs who live on when 'all humans are gone' (Pierce and Bekoff 2021: 12).

The most common strategy deployed by Pierce and Bekoff in their protest against generalising categories – be they a taxonomic category, such as canid, or a biological concept, such as phenotype (Pierce and Bekoff 2021: 46) – is to outline the characteristics that are indexed to the category or concept, and then to dissolve its intelligibility by pointing to the variability that exists within it. Yes, canids, for instance, are defined by particular physical features and behavioural traits. But these features are extremely diverse, especially with regard to size, which can vary between 2 and 150 lb (Pierce and Bekoff 2021: 21). Put this together with the differences that can be identified within every other physical feature and behavioural trait, and the implications for making generalisations about the future of any single posthuman dog multiply exponentially. Add experience into the mix, and the future of even the famously 'intelligent' Border Collie (see Chapter 1 of this book) cannot be guaranteed. For breed, which is a generalising category, is trumped by individual experience:

> [N]o two border collies are alike, and each will respond to a posthuman future in unique ways ... [T]wo border collies who were raised under the same circumstances and exposed to the same environment will respond differently to future events ... Breeds don't have personalities; individual dogs have personalities.
>
> (Pierce and Bekoff 2021: 36)

The conceit of speculative biology comes into its own here, for by exploring the consequences, in an imaginary future, that follow from even a single difference, the authors are enabled to shine a light on the significance of the multiplicities of differences among dogs in the present. In Pierce and Bekoff's analysis, 'difference' means the difference between individuals,[7] and as the examples stack up and up, the reader is confirmed in thinking that the real methodological function of the thought experiment is to put an end to nearly all kinds of generalisations about dogs.

The agenda of *A Dog's World* is explicit:

> Imagining a future for dogs without their human counterparts is an interesting exercise in biology, but the real value of the thought experiment ... is that it can help us think more clearly about who dogs are in the present and this, in turn, can clarify the moral contours of human–canine relationships.
>
> (Pierce and Bekoff 2021: 13–14)

No reader can be in doubt about those moral contours by the time they reach the end of Chapter 8. In this penultimate chapter, Pierce and Bekoff balance a speculative list of dogs' 'losses' against dogs' 'gains' in a posthuman world. Not only is the list of losses short by comparison, the *kind* of items on this list (nutritious food, water, shelter, friendship, 'toys') are, as the authors note, 'replaceable' (Pierce and Bekoff 2021: 153). To describe what dogs would gain in a posthuman world – and this is presumably the purpose of the exercise – is to describe what dogs lose in *this*, human, world. The physical losses to dogs of living in this world, now, include: human constraints (collars, leashes, fences, cages), intensive captivity (puppy mills, laboratories, dog meat farming), experimentation, abuse, sexual exploitation, dog fighting, forced breeding, the killing of healthy dogs, artificial selection for maladaptive traits, obesity, desexing (with all its attendant health implications), surgical mutilations (docking, debarking, ear cropping), shelters and shelter-related mortality, and breed-specific genetic disorders (Pierce and Bekoff 2021: 146). They also lose: potentially better nutrition, a greater range of sensory experiences, a natural level of hormones and development, and levels of physical activity that suit and are decided upon by dogs themselves (146). As well as the physical losses incurred by their lives with humans, Pierce and Bekoff also review the 'social'

Dog disputes 171

and 'psychological' losses. Suffice it to say that these latter lists make my Chapter 1 look like a wan description of dog despair.

Pierce and Bekoff's 'gains and losses' chapter gives the reader some insight into how dogs' species story is operationalised in practice, through vast and complex networks of human control, and especially human control over dogs' reproduction. As I understand it, their point is not really that a change in evolutionary trajectory would be transformative of dogs (that much is obvious); it is, more radically, that if dogs were 'free', in *this* world, and especially if they were free to choose when and with whom to mate (Pierce and Bekoff 2021: 136–139), then the 'fiction' of 'what is a dog' would become visible. With what consequences? 'We could still live with dogs as companions, although over time they might become less tame, less docile, and less interested in being our pets' (138). In other words, if humans did not exercise such tight control over dogs, the true fragility of the (story of the) 'dog–human bond' would be exposed for what it is: a retrospective explanation, naturalisation and justification of contemporary dog–human relations.

Before reading *A Dog's World*, I read Bekoff and Pierce's *Unleashing Your Dog: A Field Guide to Giving Your Dog the Best Life Possible* (Bekoff and Pierce 2019). In this ostensibly 'lightweight' book, I thought that I had, somewhat surprisingly, found a critique of dogs' species story. So surprising was this to me, that I feared that I had perhaps read too much against the grain of Bekoff and Pierce's argument, or had read too much into it, or had been a little too wishful. With the publication of *A Dog's World*, however, the unusual tone of *Unleashing* makes better sense to me, and gives me confidence in my interpretation of it. *Unleashing* is, quite simply, not written with dogs' species story in mind. This immediately liberates the authors from the classic 'dog book' structure, which usually starts with the domestication-as-speciation story, and indeed from any structure that would support the substitution of one 'essence' of dog with another (cf. Coppinger and Coppinger 2016, as discussed in Chapter 2 of this book; Wynne 2020a, as discussed in Chapter 4 of this book). Instead, they organise each of their chapters around one of dogs' senses, with a final chapter on play, which the authors describe as 'a kaleidoscope of senses' (Bekoff and Pierce 2019: 139). In keeping with *A Dog's World*, Bekoff and Pierce are quick to foreground the obvious artificiality of the chapter divisions (Bekoff and Pierce 2019: 35), and urge their readers to remember that 'even' when it comes to the senses, one individual dog will experience particular forms of sensory deprivation more or less 'keenly' than another (Bekoff and Pierce 2019: 10).

All this has implications for the dog owners to whom the book is addressed. Although the authors make some small effort to soothe the multifaceted anxieties of people who live with dogs, on the whole their portrait of dog guardians is relentlessly unflattering. This is largely due to their uncompromising starting point, which is that companion dogs should be understood as 'canine captives':[8] '[T]here's no getting around this' (Bekoff and Pierce 2019: 9). And, in case any reader is in doubt as to what captivity means, Bekoff and Pierce helpfully provide a definition: 'from the Latin *captivus*, "caught, taken prisoner", and from *capere*, "to take, hold, seize"' (5).

Although Bekoff and Pierce do not deny 'that celebrated "bond"' (Bekoff and Pierce 2019: 8) between dogs and humans, for them the form the bond takes, the form of the relation, is captivity. In a vague address to an unidentified group of scientists who 'argue that the long association with humans has changed what is "natural" for dogs', Bekoff and Pierce insist instead that '[d]ogs will never fit easily and without negotiation into human homes and lifestyles' (9). The reasons are many and include, alongside the more familiar deprivations (under-exercise, long periods of isolation, being treated like a 'furry human'), a detailed account of how the very sensory architecture of a human home – its lighting, sounds, smells, spatial organisation – can be an assault on a dog's senses and on their person. For Bekoff and Pierce, the 'bond' between dogs and humans is a 'Faustian bargain', a bargain based on a desire not for 'knowledge' but for 'love and companionship' (Bekoff and Pierce 2019: 8). That desire is located not on the side of dogs, however, as in Clive Wynne's (2020a) *Dog Is Love*, for example (see Chapter 4 of this book), but firmly on the side of humans. It is humans who seek to 'capitalize' (Bekoff and Pierce 2019: 8) on the dog–human relationship, and it is this asymmetry that transforms 'the bond' into a bondage for dogs. The interface between humans and dogs, for dogs, is not a zone of 'bonding' but rather a 'zone of uncertainty', where uncertainty is the tension between 'captivity and freedom' (Bekoff and Pierce 2019: 9).

Bekoff and Pierce frame *Unleashing* in terms of ethics (Bekoff and Pierce 2019: 8). To me, however, it reads more like a political manifesto that is essentially concerned with the struggle for freedom for dogs. Not for total freedom, not for a freedom 'outside' what exists now (for that, one must turn to *A Dog's World*), but for greater 'degrees of freedom' (Bekoff and Pierce 2019: 9) within the current (political) structure. Just as Porcher and Schmitt (see Chapter 4 of this book) argue that, even though domestication never differs, the conditions might – 'a dog, like a pig, may be treated well or badly' (Porcher and Schmitt 2012: 40) – so Bekoff and Pierce similarly argue that captivity 'refers to a type of existence, not its quality' (Bekoff and Pierce 2019: 5). Although this existence cannot be 'otherwise', it can be improved to the extent that the so-called dog–human bond that defines and shapes that existence is loosened. The title of the book *Unleashing Your Dog*, ultimately, means unleashing your dog from you. Bekoff and Pierce's book is characterised by a deadly seriousness, which is belied by its populist tone.

For Bekoff and Pierce it is not the relational intersubjectivity of dogs and humans that poses a problem for science; rather, it is that each dog differs from another, and so too do their own behaviours, over time, or in particular contexts (Bekoff and Pierce 2019: 19, 23). Science, in short, does not know as much about dogs as some science writers imply (Bekoff and Pierce 2019: 16) and, in view of the authors' consistent (perhaps even militant) emphasis on the individuality of every dog in both *Unleashing* and *A Dog's World*, it is difficult not to conclude that it never will. What does it mean, then, to do research on or with 'dogs'? The argument in *Unleashing*, and especially in *A Dog's World*, suggests that the questions 'what is a dog?' and 'what can a dog do?' still have relevance, but that they must be posed to each and every 'truly … distinct individual' (Bekoff and Pierce 2019: 150). It is *because* individual dogs are 'truly distinct' that the answers to these questions cannot be anticipated in advance. Moreover, whether the questions are posited by scientists, owners, trainers, or by whomever it is who enters into relations with a dog, they necessarily incur the obligation of allowing (if not enabling) the dog to answer in their own specific and unique way – again, *because* they are unique. This is, in effect, Despret's notion of polite research, which emphasises particularity in its every dimension, refracted through the individual and extended to all dog–human relations.

Animal capabilities, agency and resistance

Except, of course, it is *not* Despret's polite research because there is no place in Despret's work for an unreflexive conception of 'the individual'. I will address some of the very good reasons for this rejection of the individual, in animal studies and in the social sciences more broadly, in Chapter 7. Here, I confine my comments to what is problematic about it in the context of debates about animal agency and resistance. One most obvious problem concerns the rapid cascade of interlocking assumptions that usually follows from the notion that, in order to 'have' agency, one must be an individual (that is, that agency is a property of individuals). This idea, which is both philosophical (Pearson 2014) and common-sensical (Meijer and Bovenkerk 2021: 52), often goes hand in hand with the conviction that agency is synonymous with intentionality (Meijer and Bovenkerk 2021: 52). And, further, that in order to act with intention, the individual must be cognitively capable of reasoning. 'The ability to reason', the historian Chris Pearson writes, 'is central to the human-centered concept of agency because it allows people to break free, to an extent, of their instincts, emotions, traditions, and political and social structures' (Pearson 2014: 133). Perspective too, then, co-exists with this conception of agency. For no one can 'break free' of their circumstances unless (presumably) they have a point of view on them.

While some authors consider this model of agency to be relevant to animals – in his much-cited *Fear of the Animal Planet*, Jason Hribal, Pearson argues, transforms animals into 'four-legged agitators, to file alongside human radicals and revolutionaries' (Pearson 2014: 251) – there are other, less anthropomorphic, ways to conceive of an animal's relations to their conditions, and of their objections to it. Susan Nance, for instance, in her analysis of elephants in the entertainment industry in the USA, argues that is not necessary to speak of elephants 'rejecting the circus or capitalism', nor is it necessary to identify 'what a given elephant's intentions or internal experience was at every moment', in order to be able to prove, based on 'a body of evidence', that elephants 'rejected their conditions of existence' (Nance 2013: 10). Nevertheless, even without assuming that elephants have a 'political' take on their conditions, or that their every action is informed by intentionality, the notion that an elephant 'has' agency tends to confine questions of agency to questions of the individual. One is prompted to ask, for example, in what situations an individual elephant is able to exercise 'their' agency or not, etc.

This is partly why, for Despret, the problematic coupling together of agency and perspective runs deeper than the 'anthropomorphic conception of subjectivity' (Despret 2013: 30) that undergirds it, and which is the product of a long history of 'intellectual and cultural shifts that created the perspectival mode' (Daston in Despret 2013: 30).[9] More significantly, for her, this coupling makes it difficult to describe 'unfamiliar beings, such as bees or even flowers' as agents because they appear not to have a perspective (29). In order to develop a theory of agency that is 'much more extensively shared in the living world' (29), Despret identifies agency not as a property of a subject with a point of view but as the product of a 'rapport of forces' in which '[e]ach living being renders other creatures capable (of affecting and of being affected), and they are entangled in a myriad of rapports of forces, all which are *"agencements"*' (37).

Let me step back for a moment. As discussed above, in Despret's model of polite research, an animal's authorisation is achieved not solely by creating a research apparatus that engages their interests, but also by giving the animal the 'power' to resist the researcher's hypotheses.[10] It should be noted that this robust animal, this animal who is capable of resisting the researcher's explanations of their behaviours, is not a fortified individual who has the 'freedom to …' or the 'freedom of …', as Pierce and Bekoff put it (Pierce and Bekoff 2021: 146). On the contrary, a productive research apparatus achieves results precisely to the extent that it engenders 'an unprecedented, creative, improvised, queer "becoming together"' (Despret 2013: 33). Berndt Heinrich's invitation to the ravens to activity, his invitation to them to take a position on his hypotheses, is in effect an invitation to intersubjectivity, by which Despret means: 'becoming what the other suggests to you, accepting a proposal of subjectivity, acting in the manner in which the other addresses you, actualizing and verifying this proposal, in the sense of rendering it true' (Despret 2008: 135).

To pose the question of animal agency is, thus, to make a proposal of subjectivity, a proposal that can transform an animal from something that looks like a machine (say) into someone who looks like a subject, a subject with a point of view. This, according to Despret, was Jocelyn Porcher and Tiphaine Schmitt's (2012) achievement when they illustrated that cows 'do more than simply function' at work (Porcher and Schmitt 2012: 55, emphasis omitted; see Chapter 4 of this book). In a stroke of methodological genius, Porcher and Schmitt showed that cows actively cooperate at work, that they actively invest their affects in their work, by demonstrating how, on occasion, they refused to work, refused to cooperate and made it hard for the farmers to do their jobs. For Despret, however, even if an animal – a cow in this instance – looks as though they 'have' capabilities or 'have' agency, this appearance is always subtended by a 'rapport of forces that makes some beings capable of making other beings capable, in a plurivocal manner' (Despret 2013: 38).

If agency is, in effect, 'activated' by affective relationality, then it is as relevant to flowers as it is to cows. Despret writes:

> This is how flowers gain agency, through becoming enabled to make their companion pollinators [bees] be moved by them, and this is how the latter could themselves be agents, through becoming enabled to make the flowers able to attract them, and in turn to be moved by them. This is why agency always appears in a flow of forces. Agencies spring in a flow of forces, in *agencements* that makes more agencies.
>
> (Despret 2013: 40)

The appearance of agency is the product of an *agencement*: 'there is no agency without *agencement*. In other words, a being's agency testifies to the existence of an *agencement*' (Despret 2013: 38). Like the specificity of a research apparatus, which enables or delimits a being's intersubjective capabilities, the specificity of an *agencement* enables or delimits a being's agency. In both cases, these qualities are the product of the assemblage, and not the property of the human, animal, insect or plant.

I began this section with a model of agency that attributes agency to individuals, and conflates it with intentionality and reasoning. This sets the bar for agency very 'high', and sets it in favour of humans. Indeed, to the extent that it relies on a normative, even idealised, notion of the human agent, it not only fails to recognise 'that agency can be exercised by different beings in different ways' (Meijer and Bovenkerk 2021: 53), but also 'exaggerates the gap between humans and other animals' (Meijer and Bovenkerk 2021: 52). Relational conceptions of subjectivity and agency, such as Despret's, are hugely valuable in terms of moving away from this exclusive and exclusionary model. And yet, in some ways, I find the implications that follow from her attribution of agency to bees and flowers, who seemingly do not have a perspective, less startling than the implications that potentially follow from her use of the concept of an *agencement* to explain the appearance of an agential subject, with a point of view, within a research apparatus. Startling, not because this position insists that subjectivity is created rather than given, or that all agency is interagency, but rather because it implies, first, that the most significant feature of this figure *is* 'their' point of view (which is why it needs explaining) and, second, that the capabilities of an animal can in theory be reduced to the relations that are underpinned by a particular *agencement*. In other words, that the capabilities of a 'subject' within an experiment, say, and indeed the very subject itself, can be wholly explained *by* the experiment. This closes off the possibility of the significance of an 'outside', and also the possibility that there might be something about the figure of the subject which is also 'capable', and capable of 'resistance', that is not tied to a point of view.

In Martin Seligman's 'learned helplessness' experiments, it was the eruption of an outside inside the experiments – an outside that assumed the form of dogs' unique individual biographies – that opened up the research to forces beyond it, and ensured that some of the dogs did not respond as Seligman anticipated.

Intersubjectivity *and* enduring singularity

As I have already indicated, Seligman's learned helplessness experiments are, for many contemporary canine researchers, exemplary of scientific and moral failure. Astonishing as it seems, however, the early controversies surrounding Seligman's research stemmed less from solicitude about the dogs' welfare and more from Seligman's 'clash with traditional stimulus–response theories of learning', and also the use he made of 'mentalist' concepts to explain his results (Peterson 2004: 517).[11] As I noted in Chapter 3, behaviourism sequesters any analysis of the private, interior worlds of living creatures in favour of empirically observable behaviours. Methodological behaviourists do this because they consider those worlds to be inaccessible. For radical behaviourists, such as John Watson and, later, B. F. Skinner, that private, interior, world does not exist at all (Schneider and Morris 1987: 33; Boakes 2008: 153). Either way, behaviourism renders mentation an 'irrelevance' (Rollin 1998: 207). In its place, learning is *the* mark of the mental' (Rollin 1998: 208–209, emphasis in the original).

With regard to learning: behaviourist theories typically argue that learning is produced either when two events occur in contiguity (when this happens, learning leads to the 'acquisition' of behaviours), or when two events, once associated with each other, become non-contiguous (when this happens, learning leads to the 'extinguishment' of behaviours). In a departure from this model, Seligman added a third form of learning, 'independence between events' (Seligman and Maier 1967: 8), i.e. non-contingency. Seligman argued that when a dog has learned that distressing events are contingent upon nothing, and that there is nothing she can do to change or control them, then – and this was the controversial part – she will do nothing in response, even when an alternative, one with which she is familiar, is presented to her. Exposure to uncontrollable events, Seligman concluded, produces a series of 'motivational, cognitive and emotional deficits' (Maier and Seligman 1976: 3).

Seligman arrived at his conclusions by dividing his dogs into two groups. One group, prior to being put into a shuttle box (a box that contains a means of escape), were given electric shocks from which they could not escape, either because they were yoked into a hammock or because they had been temporarily paralysed by curare (a neuromuscular blocking agent) (Overmier and Seligman 1967). This group of dogs – which numbered 150 (Seligman 1972: 408) – was distinguished from another group who had not been inescapably shocked. When put into the shuttle box, both groups had ten seconds, from the start of a conditioned stimulus (dimmed lights), to jump a barrier that would enable them to escape the shock chamber. If they did not jump, the shock – 'administered through the grid floor' (Overmier and Seligman 1967: 28) – would start and continue for sixty seconds (Overmier and Seligman 1967: 29).

Bruce Overmier and Seligman 'discovered' that dogs who had not previously been inescapably shocked more frequently jumped the barrier. Those who had been inescapably shocked before entering the shuttle box learned more slowly that jumping the barrier was a means of escape, often failed to retain this learning and, even when they did learn and retain it, frequently '[gave] up and passively [accepted] the shock' (Seligman 1972: 407). These, then, are the 'motivational, cognitive, and emotional deficits' produced by this research apparatus: motivational, in the sense that the dogs were not motivated even to attempt to escape, having been subjected to uncontrollable aversive events; cognitive, in the sense that these uncontrollable aversive events interfered with the dogs' ability to establish contingent connections between behaviours and outcomes; and emotional, in the sense that the dogs were more greatly distressed by uncontrollable than by controllable events (Maier and Seligman 1976: 3).

In his brilliant analysis of fish agency and resistance, Dinesh Wadiwel argues that one can identify agential resistance in the designs of instruments that are used to control, capture and kill animals. What these designs illustrate, Wadiwel writes, is that 'the resisting body generates the need for the instrument of violence, and technological refinement in the instrument of violence corresponds with the continuing creativity and innovation of those who resist' (Wadiwel 2016: 210). The shuttle box/shock chamber, the hammock, the curare: these horrifying instruments of violence offer evidence of the efforts required to make shock inescapable to a subject who wants nothing but to escape.[12] Their very pitilessness indicates that the dogs' 'resisting bodies' obliged the researchers to actively *produce* passivity in order to discover passivity, to actively *produce* submission in order to discover submission. In addition to this physical coercion, the dogs were also emotionally coerced by their relations with the researchers. In his book on animal pain, the philosopher Bernard Rollin argues that the pain that the dogs experienced in Seligman's studies would have been 'deepened and rendered more extreme by its total incomprehensibility' (Rollin 1998: 145), an incomprehensibility made all the more abysmal by the friendliness of the people who electrocuted them.

This is why, as I discussed earlier in this chapter, Miklósi argues that Seligman could not isolate 'lack of control over aversive events' as a cause of learned helplessness: because the dogs' 'motivational, cognitive and emotional deficits' would also have been shaped by the ambiguous relations with humans that were instantiated by the research apparatus. A research apparatus always produces something, even if what it produces is negative (such as the silence of the parrots when faced with philosophers). Seligman's apparatus produced passivity and 'neurosis', as Miklósi characterises it. For the ambiguous, intersubjective relations between the researchers and the dogs were, in their own degenerate way, a proposal of subjectivity to the dogs, even though the nature of that proposal, and the manner in which they were to act in response, must surely have been impenetrable to them, as Rollin says. The dogs' 'neurosis' is an intelligible response in this context, a response that renders true an abusive and violating proposal of subjectivity.

The violence of Seligman's research is significant: because *even still*, he could not immediately produce helpless passivity in every dog who had been inescapably shocked. Not, in this instance, because his apparatus produced resisting subjects (what room for resistance, with the shock chamber, the hammock, the curare?), but because, conversely, something in some of the dogs' pre-laboratory biographies ensured that they were, at least initially, insulated from its purpose. The fact that individual animal biographies are rarely recorded does not mean that animals do not have them (Fudge 2004; Baratay 2022): 'have them', not in the sense that animals are potential autobiographical subjects – which is what the writing of biography usually implies – but in the sense that animals are individuals who are shaped by their histories of experience. Although Seligman could not identify what exactly in these dogs' experiences 'protected' them from his proposal of helpless subjectivity (because their pre-laboratory histories were unknown to the researchers), they made a difference to it nevertheless.

Seligman's apparatus did not *produce* these dogs as particular, singular individuals; their singularity was derived from experiences (undoubtedly also relational) that preceded the time, space and context of the experiments. It did draw attention, however, to their *being* singular, and it made that mode of being matter. It prompted Seligman to ask more questions and to 'commit to more activities' (Despret 2015a: 64). Those questions and activities, however, unlike in a polite research apparatus, were not designed by Seligman to encourage activities in the dogs 'in return' (Despret 2015a: 64). On the contrary, Seligman repeated his original question, and demanded that his hypothesis be confirmed as true: '[c]ould it be possible that those dogs … have had a prelaboratory history of controllable trauma while dogs who are helpless without any previous shock have experienced uncontrollable trauma before arriving at the lab?' (Seligman 1972: 410). And confirmation indeed he received, by the method of comparing dogs with pre-laboratory histories of experience to 'cage-reared dogs' who 'have very limited experience controlling anything' (410).

The problem with not encouraging activity in return – the problem with confirmation – is that there is nothing to be learned from it. The comparison between dogs with unique personal histories and cage-reared dogs ensured that Seligman was obliged neither to investigate what precisely about those pre-laboratory histories was significant, nor to question any aspect of the apparatus, for the cage-reared dogs were essentially bred to bear witness to its purpose (which was to 'demonstrate' that exposure to uncontrollable events leads to helplessness). For what chance would a cage-reared dog, with 'limited experience of controlling anything', have of exerting control over an apparatus that is specifically designed to disestablish it? This is a comparison, in other words, defined by ignorance on the one hand and enforcement on the other. In this way, Seligman bullied his hypothesis into truth. For those readers who are interested: '[w]hile it took four sessions of inescapable shock to produce helplessness one week later in dogs of unknown history, two sessions of inescapable shock in the hammock were sufficient to cause helplessness in the cage-reared dogs' (Seligman 1972: 410).

The point here is that the significance of the pre-laboratory histories of some of the dogs in Seligman's study could not be erased, despite the unrestrained violence of the research apparatus, which sought to impose its proposal of neurotic subjectivity on all of the dogs. Of Porcher's analysis of cow cooperation and resistance, Despret writes: 'when everything happens as it should, we don't see the work' (Despret 2013: 42). One might say of Seligman's experiments that *had* everything happened as it should, we wouldn't have seen the singular individual. Animals, Dominique Lestel writes, 'are individuals which do not always behave as they "should"' (Lestel 2011: 84). I would push this point further and argue that it is *because* animals are individuals that they do not always behave as they should. In response, Seligman sought to breed experience- and individuality-free dogs – 'generic' dogs, one might say – whose invariability approximates the invariability that is supposed to characterise a representative of a species.

But a cage-reared dog is not 'experience-free'. A cage-reared dog has unique experiences of being cage-reared, which will shape a uniquely singular individual, irreducible, and thus resistant, to species. 'Submission' may be a part of the story of that experience, but it is not the whole of it.

Conclusion

This chapter began by addressing the methodological challenges that dogs' species story poses to those scientists who are invested in it. Pierce and Bekoff's somewhat anfractuous science fiction scenario – in effect, an alternative methodology by alternative means – illustrates how difficult it is to confront that story, much less to overturn it. Dogs' species story is not, I have argued, undermined by the 'problems' raised by canine research. On the contrary, those problems serve only to verify the 'truth' of it. There is an underlying irony here, which is that the particular relationships established in research, between particular researchers and particular dogs, confirms to scientists the defining characteristic (relationality) of dogs 'as a species'. When we look at animals, Erica Fudge writes, we see 'something dangerously recognizable. We see, in fact, a version of ourselves' (Fudge 2002: 40). Is there any animal about whom this is more true, in science, than the domesticated dog?

Polite research is both about ourselves and about getting away from ourselves. It is about ourselves in the sense that it does not assume that the researcher and the research subject can be disaggregated either from each other or from the research apparatus. To ask a question is, necessarily, to enter into relations. But it is also about getting away from ourselves, for the aim is to enable animals to object to (and thereby to refine) the questions that are posed to them. The problem for dogs, however, as I have argued throughout this book, is that intersubjectivity and interagency, in the context of dogs' species story, are not necessarily polite; that is, they do not necessarily enable dogs to show what they are capable of (the irony to which I refer, above). I am returned again, then, to the tensions around which this chapter has circled: species and the question of generalisation more broadly, relationality, capabilities, individual agency, resistance. It has not been the aim of this chapter to try to resolve these tensions. On the contrary, this chapter has been driven by their irreconcilability, and by the implications of that irreconcilability with regard to the potential dismantling of dogs' species story in science.

Seligman's research was paralysing, both physically and emotionally. Yet still the dogs in these experiments could not be reduced entirely to the proposals that Seligman put to them, of helpless subjectivity, and of species. What 'resistance' they put up, however, derived not from some quality or attribute smuggled in under the category of the individual (freedom to act, some inherent capability, a point of view that was permitted to matter). More simply, it issued from the assemblages of experiences (whether they were experienced as such or not) that constituted the dogs' singularities. In the context of these violent experiments, only these irreducible singularities could disrupt Seligman's practice and oblige him, at least momentarily, to question his assumptions. And perhaps, *because* this minimal conception of individuality is somewhat less relational and somewhat more defined by the boundaries of a life lived uniquely (this happened to this dog, this did not happen to this dog; this dog did this, this dog did that), it might also offer a portal to thinking 'beyond ourselves' (Fudge 2002: 22). Revolting as Seligman's experiments were, they also, inadvertently, posed a question that I would argue is rarely extended to dogs. Crudely: who are you, beyond what I know of you, what I see of you, what I project onto you, and what I want from you?

In this chapter, I have emphasised the methodological and ethical significance of a singular life. In the following chapter, I address the political significance of a singular death.

Notes

1 By 'dogs specifically', I mean dogs as they are specifically understood through dogs' species story, which constitutes them as relational by definition.
2 *Why* some of these scientists seek to research dogs' behaviour 'for its own sake' – i.e. for what purpose – is an open question. See for example my discussion of Dognition.com in Chapter 4.
3 Horowitz mentions psychology and ethology here, but dog behaviours and biology are of considerable interest across a wider range of

scientific disciplines than this, including, since the genomic sequencing of a purebred Boxer, Tasha, in 2004, comparative genetics (e.g. Lindblad-Toh *et al.* 2005; Ostrander 2012).

4 Seligman was not the first to fail to recognise the impact on the dogs of their relationships with the researchers who electrocuted them. Gantt, in his research on the 'effect of person' (1962), neglected to account for the familiarity of the dogs with the experimenters who were stroking them as they were being shocked. Both Gantt and Seligman recorded the significance of dog–human relationships to dogs in *general*, but neither investigated how their own *particular* dogs' responses were affected by 'specificity to a particular person' (Feuerbacher and Wynne 2011: 52).

5 See Jeffrey Bussolini's helpful comment on this problematic translation (Bussolini in Despret 2015a: 71n).

6 This would also bear on free-roaming dogs, however, given that 'sterilisation is a core activity of free-roaming dog population management' globally (Collinson *et al.* 2021: 1).

7 'Individual' is not to be conflated with 'sameness' over a lifetime, however, because for Pierce and Bekoff a dog's changing experiences will change the dog (Pierce and Bekoff 2021: 32).

8 I deduce that Bekoff and Pierce make a distinction between 'captive' dogs, who are companion and working dogs, and 'intensely captive' dogs, who are dogs held in puppy mills, laboratories etc.

9 See Lorraine Daston's excellent summary of this history (Daston in Despret 2013: 30)

10 Herein lies a key distinction between polite research and anecdotes (see Chapter 3): polite researchers are obliged to have their interpretations (or versions) of events authorised by their animal research participants. An anecdote demands no such authorisation, which is why anthropomorphism so often runs free.

11 Despite objections from behaviourists that this helplessness could be explained by 'motor response deficits' (that is, by the dogs not being physically able to help themselves), in the end the cognitive interpretation won out, as 'psychologists … [saw] the parallels between learned helplessness as produced in the laboratory and maladaptive passivity as it exists in the real world [in humans]' (Peterson 2004: 517).

12 There are many more examples of 'learned helplessness' apparatuses that were 'tailored' to the resistant capabilities of other animal bodies, including cats, rats, mice and fish.

6

On the deathlessness of 'the dog': Species, 'race' and individuals

[A]nalogy may be a deceitful guide.

(Darwin 2008: 356)

I arrive finally at the concept of species, which is also necessarily to arrive at the concept of 'race'. 'Race' is folded into my discussion of species for two reasons: first, because as many theorists have illustrated, and as the first half of this chapter will confirm, it is difficult if not impossible to disentangle species and species thinking from 'race' and racism; second, because it is the argument of this book that species thinking erases the significance of particularity: in practice, the particularity of the individual animal. One question that arises, therefore, is how the individual animal might be 'recovered' – if not in science, then in politics. This chapter proposes that there is no route 'back' to individuality via species. The racialisation of dogs, however, offers one potential point of entry to individuation and/or individualisation. I illustrate this in the second half of the chapter, by analysing mainstream North American public discourses about pit bulls, as they played out in the context of the Michael Vick dog fighting controversy.

Racialisation individuates and/or individualises dogs not because racism pertains primarily to individuals or because it is individualistic. Rather, it is because racism often operates through the constitution of racialised populations, which are usually understood to be composed of identifiable (targetable) individuals. It should go without saying that this route to individuation and/or individualisation is objectionable both for humans and for dogs. For dogs, however, it represents a significant change in the *kind* of category to which they are allocated (to populations, as well as to species) from which real implications flow, for their lives as well as for their deaths. To repeat the point I made in the introduction and that I will develop more fully in Chapter 7: my aim here is not to advocate 'for' temporary, contingent, and often politicised populations 'as opposed' to species which, although theoretically themselves populations (or fluctuating patterns of difference and similarity), are often reified, as I will demonstrate, as a 'thing'. Instead, it is to use the concept of populations as a means to illuminate the implications of that species reification for animals.

The entanglement of species thinking (and especially speciesism) and racism is enduring. *How* exactly these prejudices are entangled in each other, however, is determined in part by the different ways that the categories of species and of 'race' are conceived of in science. This is a key preoccupation of this chapter, which traces changing conceptions of species and of 'race' over several centuries, with the aim of better understanding the traffic between them. Failure to appreciate the significance of the temporal similarities between species and 'race' in the nineteenth century, for example, can lead to misplaced political optimism, as I demonstrate in my analysis of two contemporary readings of Darwin's 'parasol anecdote'. Conversely, recognising the significance of the bifurcation of the concepts of species and of 'race' post-population thinking – and especially the significance of their differing time scales – brings nuance to the analysis of the contemporary intersections between speciesism and racism. This chapter teases out, for instance, how the implications of the co-racialisation of pit bulls and of humans differs for dogs and for humans, given that dogs are first gathered under the sign of species.

For the sake of clarity, this chapter is schematic. The contribution I hope to make to the debates about the relations among 'race', species, racism and species thinking is conceptual rather than empirical. In the first part of the chapter, I ask what are the consequences – in a somewhat abstract, even generic, way – for those individuals who are defined first and foremost by a species category. In the second part, I ask how their racialisation first as black and then as white transforms those consequences for pit bulls, as pit bulls are conceived of in US public discourses. Public discourses are usually simplistic, and often reductive. The life and death of an individual pit bull will be far more complex than such discourses allow, as Katja Guenther's affecting ethnography of shelter animals, which includes a chapter on 'the peculiar problem of pit bulls' (Guenther 2020: Chapter 6), illustrates. An empirical analysis of the relations among racialising public discourses, species categories and the reality of the lives of individual pit bulls is, unfortunately, beyond the scope of this book. Suffice it to note that this chapter is indebted to Dinesh Wadiwel's analysis of 'exception', and of the work it does in making violence against animals, 'on a massive scale', possible: '[t]he gap between the human and non-human', Wadiwel writes, 'is constituted purely by exception – in the belief that humans are deserving of something more than that of the animal, or alternatively, that the animal may be subject to that [to] which human life should never be subjected' (Wadiwel 2002: para. 17). The exception with which I will be concerned in this chapter – the 'something more' of which humans are deserving – is the conceptual possibility of a death, which I contrast with the conceptual deathlessness of animals, when they are defined as species. What the 'simplicity' – even the crudeness – of public, and especially public media, discourses makes transparent, is that the acquisition of the identity of an individual confers on pit bulls the 'privilege' of a death that always counts,[1] and sometimes matters. This is important, because by lifting these dogs out of the deathlessness of species, their lives and deaths can at least potentially stand as testimony to the ways in which they are bound up in the connected violences of racism and species thinking.

What is a species?

John Wilkins argues that the 'received view' of species, which is mostly written by biologists (Wilkins 2017: xxix), 'has taken biologists and philosophers by storm' (xxi). The received view goes something like this: prior to Darwin, an understanding of species, which was derived from Plato's essential forms and from Aristotle's conception of individuals as sharing the essence of their species (which in turn share the essence of the genus), dominated natural philosophy and natural history.[2] Although the gap between Plato and Carolus Linnaeus (1707–1770) was long (2,000 years long), Linnaeus's 'universal system for the naming and classification of all organisms', which turned species and genera into fixed and stable ranks, continued and consolidated the essentialism tradition (Wilkins 2017: 81). According to this tradition, 'all members of a type were defined by their possession of a set of necessary and sufficient properties or traits, which were fixed, and between which there was no transformation. This is variously called *essentialism, typological* or *morphological thinking*, and *fixism*' (Wilkins 2017: xxi, emphasis in the original). In this manifestation of essentialism, variation within species was unimportant, and 'represented mere imperfections in creatures' (Futuyma 1986: 107).

In the modern view of species by contrast (so the received view continues), variation is 'pivotal' (Futuyma 1986: 108). The hero here is Charles Darwin, who developed a conception of taxonomic groups (taxa) in which

> taxa are populations of organisms with variable traits, which are polytypic (have many different types) and which can transform over time from one to another taxon, as the species that comprise them, or the populations that comprise a species, evolve. There are no necessary and sufficient traits. This is called *population thinking*.
> (Wilkins 2017: xxi, emphasis in the original)

'No necessary and sufficient traits' does not necessarily point to species nominalism (to the idea that species is 'just' a name without an objective referent). Rather, evolutionary thinking, perhaps inevitably, 'made it harder to be exact about species' (Wilkins 2017: 308). If species are populations undergoing constant transmutation (see below), it is harder, for example, to identify whether/when the rank of species had been achieved. Thus it was that Darwin's view of species changed considerably over time (Wilkins 2017: 153–182).

The 'received view' of species outlined above – which pits essentialist, typological thinking against, variously, 'common descent, statistical properties of [genetic] populations, and biological relationships' (Wilkins 2017: xxx) – is given greater complexity and depth when its relation to racism is acknowledged and interrogated. To this end, I trace now a brief history of the relations between species and 'race', as these relations unfolded in the eighteenth century, and then in nineteenth-century racist science.

When the evolutionary biologist Douglas Futuyma describes variation, prior to Darwin, as 'mere imperfections', he means they are 'mere' in a philosophical sense, not in a political sense. Consider, for example, the doctrine of monogenism, which characterised the beliefs of most British and European scientists up to about 1800 (Stepan 1982: 1). Monogenism is often associated with a relatively 'universalistic, egalitarian and humanistic' attitude to human differences because its roots in Christian theology, and especially the philosophy of Augustine of Hippo, decreed that no matter how 'peculiar' humans are, all are 'descended from Adam' (Stepan 1982: 1). Yet modern monogenists ascribed differences among humans to 'degeneration from Eden's perfection' (Gould 1996: 71): to degeneration, that is, from an original type, the closest representative of which were 'none other than Europeans' (Smith 2015: 118). 'Imperfections', in this imperialist and colonialist context, are hardly 'mere'.

Prior to the eighteenth century, and indeed during it, Roxann Wheeler argues, there was little consensus as to *which* humans differed from each other, and no single 'register of human difference' (Wheeler 2000: 44). Climate, Christianity, clothing and commerce were all potential contenders (Wheeler 2000). A number of developments during the course of this century, however, revivified the hierarchical notion of a 'great chain of being', which had its roots in Aristotle's *scala naturae*. As Wilkins explains: 'the second plank of the Great Chain is the *law of continuity* (Leibniz calls it the *lex continui*) – that all qualities must be continuous, not discrete … [Aristotle] require[d] that there be no sudden "jumps", from which the medieval claim *natura non facit saltus* (nature does not make leaps) came' (Wilkins 2017: 53, emphasis in the original). The discovery in geology and palaeontology, for instance, that 'extinction was a reality' served to extend 'the chain of organic beings' back in time, while in comparative anatomy, Nancy Stepan argues, Cuvier and Lamarck (despite their differences) were both inspired to find 'an organisational rationale for a scale of intelligence' (Stepan 1982: 13).

Linnaeus's work is indicative of the return of the 'great chain' and its contribution to the consolidation of hierarchies of fixed identities. In the first nine editions of *Systema naturae* (1735–1756), which introduced Linnaeus's classification scheme, Linnaeus identified what he believed were four 'varieties' of humans (varieties, rather than fixed, stable subspecies), whose distinctions he explained with reference to geography and climate. These classifications went some way to derail the great chain, because the 'alignment of races with four continents … put them all on the same level' (Charmantier 2020: para. 26).

By the tenth edition (1758), however, Linnaeus had expanded his group of four human varieties to six, and also added to the defining properties of geography and climate, personality and moral characteristics, including modes of governance. The evaluative criteria that characterised this expanded reclassification, and particularly the negative description of the variety 'Africanus' (which, despite Linnaeus's reshuffling, always appeared at the bottom), was 'viewed by contemporaries in a hierarchical manner, and carried on being used in such a way through the following decades' (Charmantier 2020: para. 26).

Until the end of the eighteenth century, the terms 'varieties' and 'races' were used interchangeably to designate different groups of humans, animals and plants. 'Varieties' was the more common term (Wheeler 2000: 31). This is not to imply, however, that 'race' was neutral, as Amir Zelinger explains:

> When *race*, a word that does not exist in Greek or Latin, was mentioned for the first time – in French – in the fifteenth century, it was applied to the pedigrees of dogs that accompanied aristocrats on their hunting expeditions. Already then, discourses of race represented more than an 'objective' classification of different types of dogs. They were part of a social ideology that connected dog 'races' to symbols of nobility and aristocratic supremacy and facilitated the production of class hierarchies.
>
> (Zelinger 2019: 363, emphasis in the original)

During the nineteenth century, the terms 'race' and 'species' were used mostly synonymously (Peterson 2019: 445) – 'races' could be applied as much to cabbages as it could to humans (444) – while 'variety' and 'variation' became the ground on which arguments about the boundaries between species were won or lost. These disputes informed (and were informed by) the racial and class hierarchies that were at this time supporting and justifying colonialism, imperialism and slavery. Indeed, it was in the 'two hostile camps' of monogenism and polygenism, Adrian Desmond and James Moore write, that nearly all the 'emotive racial signifiers' that shaped debates about 'race' and slavery between the British colonial emancipation of slaves in the 1830s and the American civil war in the 1860s could be found (Desmond and Moore 2009: 243).

As noted above, in 1800, most British and European scientists could be identified as monogenists. The doctrine of pluralism/polygenism, of separate creations or origins, by contrast, was considered 'heretical and "atheistic"', and was adopted solely by 'the most isolated and heterodox thinkers' (Thomas 1984: 135). Yet only fifty years later, by the mid-nineteenth century, polygenism was an 'anthropological orthodoxy' (Thomas 1984: 135). As well as absorbing Joseph Arthur de Gobineau in France and Robert Knox in Scotland, polygenism was instrumental in motivating 'a collection of eclectic amateurs' to transform themselves into a specifically North American science, the American school of anthropology (Gould 1996: 74). Key members of this school included 'the blatant racists' (Bernasconi 2007: 17) George Robbins Gliddon and Josiah Clark Nott,[3] the craniometrist Samuel George Morton, and Professor Louis Agassiz. Wilkins describes Agassiz, who was Cuvier's 'devotee and intellectual successor', as 'the last fixist' (Wilkins 2017: 130) – i.e. the last to believe in a conception of species as fixed.

The polygenists, Stephen J. Gould writes, 'abandoned scripture as allegorical and held that human races were separate biological species' (Gould 1996: 71).[4] This served both 'Southern slavery and Northern craniologists' (Desmond and Moore 2009: 166) well, for it gave justification to slave owners to enslave and reason to craniologists to measure. It gave, in short, new 'scientific' solidity to long-standing racial prejudices. Desmond and Moore attribute the reification of monogenism and polygenism largely to the English-born Gliddon, an Egyptologist and one-time United States Vice-Consul at Cairo, who had a 'zeal to falsify scripture' (Erikson 1986: 111). Gliddon coined the epithets monogenism and polygenism in 1857 in his and Nott's co-edited volume *Indigenous Races of the Earth* (Desmond and Moore 2009: 288).[5] In doing so, Gliddon 'captured the momentum of the age' and, together with Nott, ensured that monogenism became 'tainted' with the stain of religious dogma. This taint was significant because, in both England and North America, the 'harder racist attitudes [that] were spreading through the classes' were linked to an aggressive secularism that took aim at the Church's authority and militated against missionary support for, for example, Maori land rights and struggles against slavery (Desmond and Moore 2009: 222). Polygenism, meantime, was cast as 'a dispassionate and fearless' modern science that found empirical evidence of separate black and white ancestry in rocks and tombs (Desmond and Moore 2009: 289).

Darwin's thesis was relevant to these disputes not solely because it posited a shared ancestry for all humans and animals, but because, unlike *both* the monogenists and polygenists, who believed that the limits of species could never be transcended – '[w]ith me', said Knox in 1850, 'race or hereditary descent is everything; it stamps the man' (Knox in Stepan 1982: 4) – Darwin argued that substantial variations could exist *within* a species, and that, under the right conditions, these variations could convert to differences *between* species. With regard to the former, just as dog breeding helped Darwin to articulate the concept of natural selection (see Chapter 2 of this book), so the wide range of dogs' sizes and shapes, coupled with the diversity of their behaviours, gave evidence of intraspecies variability. Herein lies the significance of Darwin's stories about his dogs – about his surly dog's unemotional greeting on return from his five-year-and-two-day voyage on the Beagle, which appeared in *The Descent of Man* (Darwin 1981: 45), or the 'hot house face' of Bob, which is the source of an anecdote in *The Expression of Emotions* (Darwin 2009: 113). 'Courage and timidity', Darwin wrote, 'are extremely variable qualities in the individuals of the same species, as is plainly seen in our dogs' (Darwin 1981: 39–40) (see below, on Darwin's 'essentialism of individuals').

With regard to the latter, variability, Eileen Crist writes, was 'the mainspring of [Darwin's] devastating attack on the idea of the fixity of the species' (Crist 2000: 41). Where the polygenists attributed the differences they identified in humans and animals to separate origins – as in Nott's chapter on the separate origins of dogs in *Types of Mankind* and in a later article called 'A Natural History of Dogs' (Brace 1974: 521) – and where the monogenists attributed them to 'deviations from some fixed type', Darwin's argument turned on the claim that variability is 'the material basis of evolution' (Crist 2000: 41). It was Darwin's hope, clearly expressed in *The Descent of Man*, that 'when the principles of evolution are generally accepted, as they surely will be before long, the dispute between the monogenists and the polygenists will die a silent and unobserved death' (Darwin 1981: 235).[6]

Becoming biological

In his analysis of the concept of race in early modern philosophy, Justin Smith hypothesises that, where 'a belief in the transcendent essence of the human soul' (Smith 2015: 8) once served as a bulwark against racial thinking (because no difference between humans could be said to mark an *essential* difference), the naturalisation of human beings made it possible for different groups of humans to be classified – as all animals, plants and minerals were classified – in terms of their different 'natures' (Smith 2015: 18). Perhaps more significant than 'Darwin's theory itself' (Foucault 2003: 256), then, was the fundamental shift of emphasis, during the nineteenth century, 'from a sense of man as primarily a social being, governed by social laws and standing apart from nature, to a sense of man as primarily a biological being, embedded in nature and governed by biological laws' (Stepan 1982: 4). Although the insertion of humans into nature started long before Darwin began talking to dog breeders, his evolutionary theory of biological descent unquestionably represents one of its consummate moments. So ruthless was Darwin's naturalism that, his dispute with the polygenists aside, it seemed not to matter too greatly to him whether humans were defined in terms of races *or* of species. In a note on Gliddon and Nott's *Types of Mankind* – the 'American manifesto for polygenesis' (Bernasconi 2007: 15) – Darwin wrote that, either way, humans are 'descended from common stock' and so, in the end, it (race or species) will ' "come back" to the same thing' (Darwin in Desmond and Moore 2009: 265).

How could Darwin possibly think that 'race' and species 'come back' to the same thing? One answer – which I will return to complicate below – is that, for him, neither 'race' nor species refers to unchanging essences. Darwin's essentialism was rather, as Elizabeth Grosz notes, an 'essentialism of individuals' (Grosz 2004: 42). This is the foundation of populational biology, in which 'continuously varying individuals ... undergo evolutionary changes' (Stepan 1982: 86). Insofar as species are 'a post hoc aggregation of individuals', they cannot be said to be constituted 'by essential features, abilities, or forms' (Grosz 2004: 42). Indeed, one could go further, as Grosz does. 'What evolves', she argues, 'are not individuals or even species, which are forms of relative fixity or stability, but oscillations of difference (which underlie and make possible individuals and species) that can consolidate themselves, more or less temporarily, into cohesive groupings only to disperse and disappear or else reappear in other terms at different times' (Grosz 2004: 24).

Although Grosz is not addressing the question of 'race' here specifically, this is arguably exactly why population thinking – especially in combination with genetics – ultimately led to the dissolution of 'race' as a biological category: because the 'relative fixity' that is *Homo sapiens* includes within it very *little* oscillation of differences that could be identified as racial. The first draft of the Human Genome Project, which was released in 2000, 'revealed' that there is more genetic variation among individual humans than there is among human populations, which show roughly 99 percent similarity. '[A]s species goes', writes Dorothy Roberts, professor in law, sociology and civil rights, '*Homo sapiens* stand out as remarkably homogeneous. There is less genetic variation in the entire human race than in a typical wild population of chimpanzees' (Roberts 2012: 51).

At least to some degree, histories of concepts of species and histories of concepts of race appear to share a common trope. First they describe the invention of essentialist typologies in Europe over the course of several centuries, then they describe how the expunction (at least in theory) of this essentialism was prompted by a shift in scientific thinking toward populations composed of ceaselessly mutable individuals. Staffan Müller-Wille writes of 'race':

> The concept of race is one of the most problematic legacies of the Enlightenment. Most existing historiography on this concept frames its subject by two discontinuities. At the beginning of the story, we have the invention of race by European naturalists and anthropologists, marked by the publication of the book *Systema naturae* in 1735, in which the Swedish naturalist Carl Linnaeus proposed a classification of humankind into four distinct races. At its end stands the demise of race as a viable biological concept after World War II in favour of population-genetic conceptions of human diversity, again prominently marked by the UNESCO Statement on Race issues in 1950.
> (Müller-Wille 2014: 598)

As its history indicates, and especially its historical reluctance to 'give up' the category of race, population thinking in biology was hardly the sole contributor to the dissolution of biological 'race'.[7] The horrors of eugenic claims and of the Second World War, coupled with the civil rights movement, had important roles to play in the appreciation of the new genetic science, as did 'the confidence of the social anthropologists and sociologists, from diverse schools, that the psychic and social life of human beings was not reducible to the biology of race' (Stepan 1982: 172). Franz Boas, for example, and 'his prestigious cast of students' (which included Margaret Mead, Otto

Klineberg, Ruth Benedict, Ashley Montagu and Melville Herskovits) reconstituted anthropology as 'a respected discipline focused on studying culture instead of race' (Roberts 2012: 43). And their legacy has been enduring. Racism and processes of racialisation, as they are understood in the social sciences today, may well include real, material, embodied, structural, organised effects – including biological effects (Jackson 2020: Coda) – but they do not produce biological races. In place of biology, *racism* explains the ascription of individuals or groups of individuals to (usually negative) categories that may be wrongly perceived as biological.

The fact that any claim about 'race' today is rightly understood to be political rather than biological does not render incidental the relations between evolutionary biology and the power of critiques of 'race', racism and processes of racialisation. On the contrary, as Roberts's concise summary (above) of the implications of the findings of the Human Genome Project indicates, the scientific erasure of 'race' as a biological category *depends*, at least to some degree, on the maintenance of the category *Homo sapiens*, for it is precisely the species boundary that enables proportions of human similarity (greatly similar) and difference (not very different at all) to be identified. Where science was once, as in Darwin's century, the backdrop for the division of humans into species and/or 'races', now it is the backdrop for human unity. Post-Darwin, and especially post-population genetics, biology constitutes *the* evidence for the claim that 'race' can have no origin or source *other* than politics. This politicisation is important because it enables processes of racialisation and racism to be analysed and critiqued and, further, to be understood as subject to identifiable change and transformation. Forms of racism can harden, but also they can be modified and perhaps even dismantled. Racism itself may be abiding but, importantly, particular *modes* of racialisation and racism are confined to the relatively short time span of specific histories, cultures and societies. Relatively short, that is, compared to the deep time of evolution. Simply put: 'race' and species are now broadly understood to operate on and across different time scales.

This temporal rupture between 'race' and species suggests that the similarities between the trope that characterises histories of 'race' and histories of species (from typologies to populations) disguises a deeper fracture between them. As Grosz writes, the question converts from 'How can individuals vary so widely? to How can species maintain their identity and cohesion over time?' (Grosz 2004: 42). 'Cohesion over time' is exactly the issue. Even though, post-Darwin, species cannot be said to be '*fixed* natural kinds' (Smith 2015: 51, emphasis in the original), the pace of zoological evolutionary change, from a human perspective, makes it feel for the most part *as if* they are. Species are largely perceived – by both scientists and non-scientists (Smith 2015: 51) – to endure, if not for all time, then at least for a very long time. In this regard, as Smith writes, it is almost '[universal] to suppose in our ordinary lives that a species is a really existing kind of thing' (51).

To return to Darwin's claim that 'race' and species ' "come back" to the same thing', this temporal fracture is important, for it explains how Darwin could de-essentialise 'race' and species with one hand, only to re-essentialise them with the other. For sure, 'race' may have been no more or less fixed than species in Darwin's evolutionary theory, but in Darwin's era they were often perceived to share the same, long – *very* long – *durée*. As with species today, 'race' thus appeared, in effect, to be 'a really existing kind of thing'. In the following section, in order to illustrate this point, I will briefly reflect on two contemporary readings of Darwin's well-known parasol anecdote, in which Darwin uses the fierce growling and barking of his dog (at a parasol) to try to explain the evolutionary relation between religious and non-religious people. I choose these readings, by Matthew Day and David Chidester (both of whom are scholars of religion) because, in my view, they fail to recognise how differences between historical and contemporary perceptions of the temporalities of 'race'/racialisation and of species shape the political significance of the relations between them. This failure leads both authors to draw what, to my mind, are misguidedly optimistic conclusions. Today, 'race' and species do *not*, as Darwin imagined, ' "come back" to the same thing' at all.

The parasol anecdote

Despite Darwin's own scientific and moral objections to both monogenism and polygenism, and even though, according to the 'received view' of species, his theory of evolution marks the end of typological thinking, Darwin himself was bound, in different ways, by the prejudices of race and class that defined his era. With regard to typology, Darwin did not consider racial traits to be useful for survival, and therefore did not consider them subject to natural selection. In other words, he 'plac[ed] man's racial traits outside evolution' (Stepan 1982: 175). How else, then, to explain the so-called racial differences among humans? Since there existed no 'theory of genetics with which to explain the source of variation in organisms' (Stepan 1982: 87), Stepan argues that there was 'some biological validity' (86) in both Darwin's and Alfred Russell Wallace's view that 'racial categories' arose in human prehistory. Nevertheless, the notion that races were 'extremely old and fixed' (85) looked very much like a confirmation of 'races' as static types.

Darwin's legacy of scientific racism cannot be attributed solely to this typological remainder in his thinking. The issue of continuity – of evolution as a process of gradual and continuous change – kept open, more fundamentally, the possibility that all living creatures, including humans, could be situated on an evolutionary scale. As I began to discuss in Chapter 2, the linear notion of time that undergirds the idea of continuity was not, Grosz argues, Darwin's own. On the contrary, she writes, Darwin 'construed [life] as a confrontation with the accidental as well as the expected, a consequence of the random as well as the predictable. It is the response, the very openness, of material organization to the dynamism of time' (Grosz 2004: 7). Unlike that of 'virtually all of his followers', therefore, Darwin's 'model of time and development ... refuses any pregiven aim, goal, or destination for natural selection' (Grosz 2004: 90):

> [Darwin] refuses anything like the telos or directionality of the dialectic, or a commitment to progressivism in which we must always regard what presently exists as superior to or more developed than its predecessors. We cannot assume that the goal of natural selection is the survival of the individual or the species, nor can we assume that the goal of evolution is the proliferation of progeny.
>
> (Grosz 2004: 90)

Despite the persuasiveness of Grosz's understanding of Darwin, it remains difficult to grasp exactly how '[d]escent, the continuity of life through time', allows for a conception of life that generates 'divergences rather than convergences, variations rather than resemblances' (Grosz 2004: 7). The very concept of descent lends itself more readily to the mistaken idea of 'the transmission of invariable or clearly defined characteristics over regular, measurable periods of time' (7). Darwin himself did not help here, for in order to illustrate that 'there is no fundamental difference between man and the higher mammals in their mental faculties' (Darwin in Grosz 2004: 58) – 'and by "fundamental", [Darwin] means unbridgeable, unobtainable by small gradations, gradual increments, or elaborations' (58) – he used the expression *natura non facit saltum* (nature makes no leaps) at least eight times in *On the Origin of Species*.

Why did he do this? Arguably, because he was grappling with the counterintuitive, perhaps almost unbelievable, relation between present discontinuity (the vast number of different 'varieties' of dogs, for example, *today*) and past continuity (could they *really* all share a common ancestor?).[8] In place of the polygenist contention of separate origins, Darwin argued that what may *look like* leaps – the radical discontinuity between humans and frogs, say, that led Nott to state that '[y]ou [Darwin] may be kin to frogs but I ain't' (Nott in Erikson 1986: 114) – are *not* in fact leaps at all, if one goes far enough back in time.[9] 'This canon [nature does not make leaps]', Darwin wrote, 'if we look only to the present inhabitants of the world, is not strictly correct, but if we include all those of past times, it must by my theory be strictly true' (Darwin 2008: 154). Despite his fidelity to branching processes (see Chapter 2 of this book), and the radical evolutionary implications to which they point, 'the notion of evolution as a linear progression, with existing species and races providing living evidence of continuity, [was] never far away' (Boakes 2008: 21). Or, as Stepan puts it: given 'the type of argument he was making', later scientists 'would find it only too easy to interpret Darwin as meaning that the races of man now formed an evolutionary scale' (Stepan 1982: 55). Herein lies the problem with Darwin's famous parasol anecdote, in which Darwin draws an analogy between, as Matthew Day puts it, 'Godless savages and superstitious dogs' (Day 2008: 49).

The parasol anecdote appears in a section of *The Descent of Man* entitled 'Belief in God – religion' (Darwin 1981: 65). If it is difficult, today, to appreciate how significant was Darwin's attempt to explain the evolution of religion, it is worth recalling that religion had for centuries served in Europe as a proto-racial ideology (Wheeler 2000: 15) and that, in the nineteenth century, it had an important role to play in science, particularly in Britain. The rigid distinction between religious and non-religious people was 'theoretically unacceptable' to Darwin, writes Day, 'because it established an absolute gap between two points in evolutionary history that could not, in principle, be bridged by gradual descent with modification' (Day 2008: 50). The parasol anecdote is one of Darwin's answers to that problem. I quote it here in full:

> The tendency in savages to imagine that natural objects and agencies are animated by spiritual or living essences, is perhaps illustrated by a little fact which I once noticed: my dog, a full-grown and very sensible animal, was lying on the lawn during a hot and still day; but at a little distance a slight breeze occasionally moved an open parasol, which would have been wholly disregarded by the dog, had any one stood near it. As it was, every time that the parasol slightly moved, the dog growled fiercely and barked. He must, I think, have reasoned to himself in a rapid and unconscious manner, that movement without any apparent cause indicated the presence of some strange living agent, and no stranger had a right to be on his territory.
>
> (Darwin 1981: 67)

Day argues that Darwin viewed religion as a 'by-product of three separate psychological faculties acting in concert' (Day 2008: 60): causality, reason and curiosity. The parasol anecdote was important, he writes, because, by showing that dogs have curiosity, coupled with the ability to understand (or to imagine they understand) causality, Darwin was able 'to narrow the cultural and biological space that separates religious and non-religious humans. Both the pre-scientific savage and the non-human animal are navigating the world with the same instinctive but untutored notion of causality' (Day 2008: 64).

Elsewhere, Darwin proposed that the roots of religious devotion – which he conceded is a 'complex emotion' (Darwin 1981: 67) – could be identified in a dog's feelings toward his 'master': 'we see some distant approach to this state of mind, in the deep love of a dog for his master, associated with complete submission, some fear, and perhaps other feelings' (Darwin 1981: 68). Day writes:

> The tactical significance of the savage/dog comparison, then, is clear: the 'savages' of the colonized world presented a kind of intermediate form of natural religiosity, a stage betwixt and between the crude, incipient worship of a dog for his master and the cultivated, self-reflective devotion of a Victorian Christian to her God.
>
> (Day 2008: 65)

In short, by way of 'intermediacy', Darwin sought – Day argues – to contest not simply human exceptionalism (what today might be called speciesism), but more particularly the exceptionalism of white, God-fearing Europeans (racism).

It is interesting to reflect on what role the concept of animal–human continuity plays in both Day's and Chidester's similar evaluations of this anecdote. On the whole, both attribute Darwin's imperialism to benign paternalism and cultural prejudice *because* they understand the concept of continuity to be evidence of Darwin's objection to polygenism and his commitment to anti-slavery. Chidester writes:

> Arguably, this identification of indigenous people with dogs can be read as a political subtext in imperial theorizing about religion – colonizers are to humans as colonized are to animals. But Darwin insisted on the continuity between animals and humans. As a result, religion was recast from a marker of difference between savage and civilized to a medium of continuity between animals and human beings.
> (Chidester 2009: 67)

Or, as Day puts it: 'Darwin solved the problem of intra-species variation by appealing to inter-species continuity' (Day 2008: 59).

Yet it takes only the gentlest of nudges to slip from an understanding of continuity as *bridging* a 'gap' to an understanding of continuity as *filling* a gap. Although Darwin's analogy *could* potentially illustrate why 'humans like us' might nevertheless not be religious, it would more likely 'confirm', to a Victorian public steeped in the ideologies of colonialism, that non-religious people, unlike religious people, are like animals (if not, at least in some respects, synonymous with them). From this perspective, being not religious is in fact being not *yet* religious, not yet *capable* of being religious.[10] Continuity (in this case, interspecies continuity) and division (in this case, the moral/political divisions between animals and humans, and between different groups of humans) are not, in other words, mutually exclusive, as both Day and Chidester seem to suppose.

My point is that the analogy is troubling not solely on account of the racist, imperialist context in which it is situated, but also because, in the nineteenth century, a particular conception of evolutionary time could apply as much to 'race' as it did to species. Understanding this historically and culturally specific conception of the shared temporalities of species and of 'race' in the nineteenth century is important because, without it, one might miss how Darwin's 'bridge' between humans and animals, the unity of descent, could be interpreted as a racialised gradation of humans and animals. Understood thus, the parasol anecdote looks less like an argument for interspecies continuity, and more like an illustration of how dogs, 'savages' and God-fearing Europeans fit on to a continuous, linear and 'progressive' evolutionary scale.

By the end of Darwin's century, 'mankind (*le genre humain*)' had shrunk into 'the human species (*l'espèce humaine*)' (Foucault 2009: 75) (as all other creatures had shrunk into species) and, no less significantly, race had mostly contracted to human phenotypical difference (Peterson 2019: 445). The 'capacious' definition of race, which had applied as much to cabbages as to humans, was supplanted toward the end of the nineteenth century, and certainly by the beginning of the twentieth century, by 'a human-centred definition' (Peterson 2019: 444). Race itself, as Christopher Peterson succinctly puts it, was racialised (Peterson 2019: 444). In 1932, the concept of racism entered the *Oxford English Dictionary* in the context of the rise of European fascism (Peterson 2019: 449). Today, the conjoined becoming-species of humans (and, more specifically, the becoming *one* species of human) and the becoming-human of 'race' make it inconceivable that religion – or indeed any other non-biological quality or characteristic – could define separate human species or human 'races'. The very mode of my analysis of the parasol anecdote is indicative of this: it implicitly reflects my understanding of racism as a force that assumes many different forms, draws on many supporting actors (such as dogs), and can be interrogated in its historical and cultural specificity. Biology is relevant here, not for what it says about 'race' *per se*, but because the real, material substance of biology (life, reproduction, sexuality, nutrition, disease, death) is deployed to do biopolitical work. A key technique of that biopolitical work is racism, which Foucault describes as 'a biological-type caesura within a population that appears to be a biological domain' (Foucault 2003: 255). In other words, racism fractures what is now understood to be a 'biological' field. This does not mean that 'race' is biological. On the contrary, it illustrates that it is not. What it means, is that racist forms of politics exploit biology.

The contrast with species could not be more stark.

Who needs species?

Importantly, the 'framing' of the history of the concept of race as a move from typological- to population-thinking, Müller-Wille writes,

> serves a similar function as the quotation marks – 'speech act condoms', as Jacques Derrida once called them – that habitually encase the term [race]. As a potential pollutant, race is excluded from proper and rational discourse and treated as a subject that can only be understood as a residue of long outdated forms of typological and hierarchical thinking, if it can be understood at all.
>
> (Müller-Wille 2014: 598)

There are no such 'speech act condoms' around the category species. Where biology itself – or rather, the privileged status accorded to biology now that human beings are 'naturalised' – enables the history of the concept of 'race' to be 'told as the history of a *false idea*' (Müller-Wille 2014: 599, emphasis in the original), the truth or falsity of the idea of species – *is it* an idea, or not? – remains unclear. '[S]pecies?', John Wilkins writes: '[n]o biological theory *requires* them' (Wilkins 2017: 342, emphasis in the original). Yet species remains a driving category in biology, even though none of the six basic species concepts identified by Wilkins – '*biospecies* (reproductively isolated sexual species), *ecospecies* (ecological niche occupiers), *evolutionary species* (evolving lineages), *genetic species* (common gene pool), *morphospecies* (species defined by their form, or phenotypes), and *taxonomic species* (whatever a taxonomist calls a species)' (Wilkins 2017: 305, emphasis in the original; see also 348–350) – cover all the different 'modes of being a species' on the evolutionary 'tree' (350).

In a survey of over 150 universities in the USA and Europe, Bruno Pušić, Pavel Gregorić and Damjan Franjević asked biologists 'what they made of the species problem' (Pušić et al. 2017). Their results were startling. Almost none of these biologists believed that species is the unit of evolution, that there is or should be a single definition of species or that species are real, and virtually nobody believed that species are individuals, as Michael Ghiselin (1987) has controversially argued (Pušić et al. 2017: 195–197). Nevertheless, nearly all the biologists considered species to be *a basic concept in biology* (Pušić et al. 2017: 185). This ambivalence and ambiguity are reflected in the social sciences and humanities, which explains perhaps why a social scientist might argue that species is an actual biological infrastructure that is torqued, but neither produced nor determined, by political and economic factors (Kirksey 2015) – or that the limits, fuzziness, breaches, hierarchical subversions and reworkings of the borders and barriers around species are valuable objects of analysis, while the category itself is nevertheless accepted as 'ontological distinction between different forms of biological life (species)' (Livingston and Puar 2011: 7). Meanwhile, in the public domain, the concept of species is saturated, if not totally overloaded, with ethical and political value. In environmental and ecological debates, it lends power and meaning to ideas of extinction, endangerment and protection. It is the barometer of biodiversity loss and the warning signal of the collapse of ecosystems (cf. Heise 2010). It drives the Promethean discourse of *Homo sapiens* as a destructive geological super-agent (Crist 2013; Harari 2011). In animal activism and scholarship, the concept of species necessarily subtends the charge of speciesism (Singer 2015 [1976]).

Does it matter that, while critiques of racism are often simultaneously critiques of the category 'race' (as the 'speech act condoms' indicate), critiques of speciesism only rarely address the category species? After all, as Smith notes, 'distinctions that are not about something real are not for that reason not real distinctions' (Smith 2015: 52). Clearly, the formal evacuation of 'race' from biology (by way, in part, of population genetics) has made very little difference to the reality of racism (Duster 2015), just as the concept of unity of descent, which constitutes humans and animals as part of the same evolutionary 'family', makes no difference at all to speciesism. But surely it *does* matter, because a classification of 'race' is called out as racist precisely because it classifies falsely. This is why genetic science, even though it disputes biological race, continues, rightly, to be critically identified as a racist science. The National Institutes of Health's (NIH) Revitalisation Act, for instance, mandates that any clinical practitioner or biomedical researcher who receives federal funding 'should report on the diversity of their research subjects according to racial and ethnic categories designated by the OMB [White House Office of Management and Budget]' (Fujimura and Rajagopalan 2011: 17). '[T]he entire enterprise', Roberts writes, 'from beginning to end – identifying populations to enter into data sets, determining which and how many genetic clusters matter, and applying the findings to our everyday lives – inescapably depends on preconceived notions of race' (Roberts 2012: 58).

Among the many possible critiques that one might raise against the NIH's use of the OMB categories is that they turn 'distinctions that are not about something real' into 'real distinctions'. Specifically, they turn 'preconceived notions of race', as Roberts put it, into racialised realities. Research subjects are not possessed of intrinsic characteristics that would justify their allocation to racial groups; rather, their allocation to such groups (even if by way of self-identification) is one aspect of a process of their racialisation. The OMB categories *determine* that the research and its research subjects will be racialised, regardless of the particularity of any individual research subject, or the particularity of patterns of health and/or genetic similarities and differences (which may or may not map on to groups of individuals). Particularity is important here as a referent beyond the category: it can serve as evidence of the fiction of the category 'race' (because nobody actually embodies a biological race), as well as evidence of the fact of its effects (the embodied effects of racism, which may be manifested in individuals and/or across communities).

Again, the contrast between 'race' and species is striking. As I have already noted, it is difficult to call out species as 'not about something real' because, to all intents and purposes, species appear, to quote Smith again, to be 'a really existing kind of thing' (Smith 2015: 51). With what implications, for particularity? Where the *falsity* of 'race' makes it important, in the struggle against racism, to be interested in forms of particularity (as I have just noted), the ostensible *truth* of species makes it difficult to find any reason to be interested in, or concerned about, such forms, including the form of particularity that is the singular individual animal. In the passage from induction to species classification, individual animals, who exist in relation to other individual animals with whom they may constitute *a* group, are transformed into members of *the* group. Once *the* species group is established, it is the species that counts, and not the individual. This is why, even though individual animals are allocated to species groups, such groups are not usually conceived to be composed *of* them (see Chapter 7 for more on this point). A species can be considered extinct, for example, even if some small number of individuals who are assigned to that species category are still alive (Van Dooren 2016). Or consider those individual 'examples' of endangered species who are constituted by law as not killable. These individuals are special not because they are individuals, but because they are members of a special species, a protected species. Mourning the extinction of 'a species', therefore, would appear to be mourning the extinction of the *idea* of individuals, which may be why species extinction is often dramatised through the fictional portrayal of the death of an endling (the final member of a species) (see for example Heise 2010: 61–63).

Individual particularity, difference or variability is certainly important with regard to population level processes of *speciation*, but once the stage of 'fixity' (through reproductive isolation, say) has been achieved, the relevance of particular individuals to their species category is nullified. Once a species rank has been identified – regardless of whatever model of species is being deployed, and whatever different mode of qualification for membership of the category species is being advanced – what that rank 'means' for and about an individual is already decided for that and every other individual who is a member. This is especially clear in scientific studies and experiments in which, Alexandra Horowitz writes,

> [i]f one man fails to solve a Rubik's cube in an hour, we do not extrapolate from that that all men will so fail. When it comes to describing our potential physical and cognitive capacities, we are individuals first, and members of the human race second. By contrast, with animals the order is reversed ... [A]nimals [are] representatives of their species first, and ... individuals second.
> (Horowitz 2012: 8)[11]

The fact that biologists do not wholly endorse or even believe in the concept of species; that it is very hard, and has always been hard, to identify a species in practice (Ereshefsky 2017); and that no biological theory requires them anyway; is not, therefore, what matters. What matters is that the concept of species remains central to all kinds of debates about animals – whether it is deployed scientifically or casually – while the category itself, at the very same time, obliterates the relevance of the individuals who are apparently the subjects of discussion and concern.

In her book *Elephants on the Edge*, the trans-species ecologist and psychologist Gay Bradshaw asks: 'Who is an elephant?' (Bradshaw 2009: 2). Although Bradshaw describes this question as 'unfamiliar' (2), to me, it is jarring. It is jarring, because it is underlined by a violence, by the abrogation of the 'who' by way of the category 'elephant'. The question does not need to be asked, because the answer is given within it: an elephant is an elephant. The question one asks of species is *what*. What is an elephant? What is a dog? The answer will pertain to *all* elephants, to *all* dogs, regardless of 'who' they are. It is surely significant that Bradshaw, who is concerned with 'whos', prefers the terms 'deportation' to 'translocation', and 'genocide' to 'culls' and 'harvesting'. The terms deportation and genocide, she writes, cast the consequences of the 'appropriat[ion] of wildlife lands and the reshap[ing] of animal societies' in a radically different light, by making visible that they are usually imposed on animals – i.e. on individual animals – 'without animal consent' (Bradshaw 2010: 15). But of course they are imposed without consent, for one cannot ask consent from a species. When individual animals are understood as representatives or ambassadors for a species, it means that they exemplify the species, not that they speak for it. Can speciesism explain the widespread deportation and genocide of animals? The charge of speciesism is not directed at the classification species. Rather, it is directed at the prejudicial attitudes of humans toward those whose species classification differs from their own. In this respect, the charge of speciesism reaffirms the validity of species, if not its 'truth'.

Species appear to be real, and this 'reality' is everywhere instantiated and affirmed, often without notice. To be clear, I am less concerned with the 'truth', or not, of species, and more with how species, and especially species stories, *work*. What is the work of species? I have argued throughout this book, and in this chapter, that one of the key achievements of species thinking is that it erases the significance of particularity, and especially the particular individual animal as a figure of relevance in science and elsewhere.[12] This is what prompts me to ask how else, by what method or mechanism, an animal can come to acquire the identity of an individual, at least in those places, be they geographical, philosophical, scientific, political ... where individuality matters. Necessarily, this is a question to be investigated empirically, for the answer will always be specific to the 'species' of animal (i.e. to what their species story allows or not), and to their historical and cultural location. As I illustrated in Chapter 5, one way that a dog acquires individuality in science and more broadly is by being in a relationship with a human (with a human researcher, say, or with a human guardian). Another way, as I will illustrate now, is by being identified as 'a threat to the corporate *bios*' (McWhorter 2010: 77), that is, as a 'dangerous' dog. These two modes of individuation are in many ways quite different: what is politically and socially important about a population of dogs in relationships with humans is that the individual dogs matter in some way to those humans. While individual 'dangerous' dogs also matter to individual people, the political and social significance of that population lies elsewhere: in its dangerousness. Nevertheless, these two populations, very differently constituted, have something significant in common, as I will return to discuss in conclusion.

Black pit bulls

Even though it is the case that 'race unlike species has turned out to be biologically insignificant' (Smith 2015: 52), so saturated do these two concepts remain in the twentieth and twenty-first centuries that, Claire Jean Kim writes, there can be 'no race-free space' from which to talk about animals (Kim 2015: 185, emphasis omitted). In her book *Dangerous Crossings: Race, Species, and Nature in a Multicultural Age*, Kim argues that 'race, which borrows from species, gives back to it; race is part of the lexicon by which species is made just as species is part of the lexicon by which race is made' (Kim 2015: 272). Importantly, scholars – and especially those who draw inspiration from the framework of intersectionality – are careful to distinguish this *traffic* between 'race' and species from *analogies* between 'race' and species. For example: the term 'canine racism' is derived from contemporary US debates about breed-specific legislation (BSL) and especially the banning or strict regulation of the bull breeds (Weaver 2013: 693). Opponents of BSL argue that, since young black men began dog fighting in the 1980s, and especially fighting pit bulls, pit bulls in particular have been unfairly demonised by the North American press as dangerous dogs. Drawing on the vocabulary of race-related struggles, BSL opponents not only characterise the prejudice against these dogs as 'canine racism', but also deploy terms such as 'breed discrimination legislation' and 'canine profiling' (Kim 2015: 273). In other words, they evoke 'the analogy to racial discrimination to awaken sympathy for the pit bull' (Kim 2015: 273). In response, many researchers have criticised analogous thinking both because it 'unavoidably reproduce[s] the association [of animals] with Blackness' (Kim 2015: 273), and also because it does not comprehensively illustrate how the exploitation of black men and pit bulls are connected.

In 2007, National Football League (NFL) player Michael Vick was arrested and indicted for dog fighting, and given a twenty-three-month prison sentence. The case was especially explosive, as Kim shows, because its 'central players' were the 'most animal of humans (the Black man)' and the 'most human of animals (the dog)' (Kim 2015: 255). Moreover, the criss-crossing between 'race' and animality was especially pronounced in this controversy because Vick had 'superstar' (Kim 2015: 253) status as an NFL athlete, and '[a]nimal tropes', Kim writes, 'pervade discussions of Black male athletes to the point where they have become normalized, working synergistically with tropes about Black male violence, brutality, and dangerousness' (Kim 2015: 268).

Kim describes the polarisation of the public debates around Vick in terms of an 'optic of cruelty' and an 'optic of racism' (Kim 2015: 254). With regard to the former, 'animal advocates' focused almost exclusively on Vick's cruel treatment of his dogs, failing to recognise the racialised aspects of the case, or of their own discourse. With regard to the latter, 'Vick's defenders' drew attention to racism, and especially to the racism of the North American criminal justice system, while simultaneously assuming that concern for Vick's dogs was 'perverse and morally out of joint' (Kim 2015: 277). In her 'ethics of avowal', by contrast, Kim seeks to interrogate the intersection between 'the institutionalized violence against Blacks *and* the institutionalized violence against dogs in contemporary society' (Kim 2015: 255, my emphasis). She writes:

> Like Blacks, pit bulls have been constructed as a group of beings whose behavior is biologically determined as violent, ruthless, and dangerous. Like Blacks, pit bulls are often victims of a 'shoot first and ask questions later' policy by police. Like Blacks, they are objects of public loathing and fear whose very presence provokes a strongly disciplinary (if not murderous) response ... Pit bulls are dying for being Black'.
>
> (Kim 2015: 272–273)

Before addressing the implications of the racialisation of pit bulls for their status as individuals, I want to pause for a moment to clarify exactly what versions of the concepts of 'race' and of species make it possible for Kim to claim intelligibly that '[p]it bulls are dying for being Black'.

The statement '[p]it bulls are dying for being Black' makes a particular, twenty-first century, kind of sense. It is comprehensible to the extent that one understands that pit bulls are dying because, like black men in North America, they have been 'constructed', as Kim puts it in the above extract, 'as a group of beings whose behavior is biologically determined as violent, ruthless, and dangerous'. While the attribution of these characteristics (violence, ruthlessness, dangerousness) to biology has real, material implications, 'in truth' it is incidental; it is 'a way', as Foucault puts it, 'of transcribing a political discourse into biological terms' (Foucault 2003: 257).[13] One might compare and contrast the discrimination against pit bulls in the twentieth and twenty-first centuries with the discrimination that English colonists directed against Indian 'races' of dogs in the seventeenth century (see Chapter 1). On the one hand, this racism – to use the word anachronistically – can be understood to be similarly extrinsic,[14] insofar as it maps onto Indian dogs the 'savagery' that the English attributed to Indian people. But English racism was intrinsic too, because the colonists identified, in English dogs, the civilisation that they believed to be characteristic of the English race. Indeed, this intrinsic racism – understood as 'the bare fact of being the same race' (Kwame Anthony Appiah in Peterson 2019: 448) – extended to nearly all their animals: '[c]onvinced that their beasts could not forfeit their identity as English chattel, colonists could safely regard domestic animals as extensions of themselves. Even the scrawniest cow wandering aimlessly through the woods advanced the cause of civilizing the wilderness' (Anderson 2004: 140). In other words, English colonists, English dogs and other English animals shared a 'race' that was uninterrupted by species difference. One reason why this continuity may have been intelligible is that, as I have already discussed, 'race' was no less real than species, and shared roughly the same time scale. Generations of English dogs and cows were imbued with the characteristics of English 'civilisation'.

Today, the racism toward black men and pit bulls *must* be identified as extrinsic, because 'race' has no biological or other intrinsic foundation. This is what enables the commonalities between the racialisation and racist treatment of men and pit bulls to be identified and analysed, and it is also what ensures that these commonalities are understood to be contingent and temporary. The different temporalities and durations of 'race' and species are relevant here: the time of processes of racialisation brings men and dogs 'together' in a very specific (racist) way. The time of species holds them apart. Since 'race' does not run continuously between species (as it did in the seventeenth century), to slip over this difference would be to turn analysis into an analogy – into an analogy such as 'canine racism' – which would strengthen the association between men who are racialised black and dogs/animals, just as the analogy between 'Godless savages' and 'superstitious dogs' strengthened the association between non-believers and dogs in the nineteenth century.

I pay attention to how 'race' and species are operating as categories here, not in order to dispute the traffic between racism and species thinking that informs the racist co-racialisation of men and dogs, but rather to propose, in light of the fact that men are *not* dogs, that the implications that follow for men and for dogs – in this mainstream, media-saturated context – are not identical. 'Violent, ruthless, and dangerous', when ascribed to men who are racialised black, recalls essentialist thinking, where essentialism is indexed, as Kim notes, to biology. Perhaps it even recalls typological thinking, insofar as the duration of the narrative 'violent, ruthless, and dangerous' extends back *at least* to the early 1800s. Kim argues that the 'parable of Black recalcitrance', wherein 'Vick made the right choice at first but then *slipped back* … echoes across the centuries with Southern plantation owners' antebellum arguments that freed slaves would revert to (bestial) type as soon as the civilizing, disciplining influence of slavery was lifted' (Kim 2015: 255, emphasis in the original). Racist 'history', here, supports the perceived eternalism of biology.

Pit bulls, however, are not transformed by racism into a type. Pit bulls are *already* a type: they are a type of dog (not a breed), and they are, in effect, a type of animal (a species). I would tentatively propose, therefore, that what is of specific significance to pit bulls, as dogs, of their racialisation as black, is that it marks them out as a population, a population comprising identifiable individual dogs, 'dangerous' dogs, who are subject to a ' "shoot first, ask questions later" policy' (Kim 2015: 272). Although this identification as the object and target of power (of State power, and of institutionalised State violence) – this individuation – is shared by both men who are racialised black and by pit bulls, for pit bulls it is transformative of the kind of group to which they 'belong'. Now, in the public eye, a pit bull is somehow more than 'just' a dog, more than 'just' a representative of *Canis familiaris* (where one representative can as well be replaced with another). Now, a pit bull is a dog who has been singled out and made newly visible – distinguished from most other dogs.

Since my argument here risks homogenising all other dogs, i.e., all dogs who are not pit bulls, this is perhaps an opportune moment to remind the reader, as I noted in the introduction, that my analysis in this chapter is somewhat schematic (not least for the sake of brevity). In theory and probably in practice, numerous dog populations are being constituted, each of which, in its empirical specificity, challenges the relationship of the dogs who constitute them to the species category *Canis familiaris*. But this is precisely my point: there is almost no route back to particularity via species; nearly always, some other mode of individuation is required. The constitution of pit bulls as a population of 'violent, ruthless, and dangerous' individuals is in no way positive. To repeat again: '[l]ike Blacks, [pit bulls] are objects of public loathing and fear whose very presence provokes a strongly disciplinary (if not murderous) response' (Kim 2015: 272).

I have argued that species categories are not usually understood to be composed of individuals. One consequence of this evacuation of the individual is that species categories are also somewhat disconnected from death. Insofar as examples – especially examples of a domesticated species – can be on-goingly replicated, one might even claim rhetorically that animals, when they are defined by their species, are in fact deathless (see also Chapter 7). One conspicuous aspect of the Michael Vick controversy, therefore, and of BSL more generally, is that they constitute pit bulls as a population of individuals whose deaths are of considerable public concern. The very point of BSL is that it legitimates surveillance and control of pit bulls and their handlers. Vast numbers of statistics pertaining to individual pit bull lives, and especially their deaths, are collected not only by those who support BSL, but also by those who oppose it. Pit bull deaths are a topic of concern, in other words, whether that concern stems from a belief that pit bulls *should* die, or from the belief that they should *not*. Kim herself offers plenty of statistics with regard to pit bull deaths (Kim 2015: 274), as have other scholars over the decades. In one of the earliest accounts, Vicki Hearne, writing in 1991, noted that in 1987 the Endangered Breed Association recorded that '35,000 people took their bull breed dogs to pounds and humane societies to be killed ... because they had read in a newspaper that their dogs were dangerous' (Hearne 2007b: 278). Clearly, not much has changed. Pit bulls in shelters, Katja Guenther writes, are routinely 'killed in large numbers' not because they are associated with dog fighting specifically, but because they are seen to be 'higher risk and more dangerous than other types of dogs' (Guenther 2020: 157).

This concern with pit bull deaths should come as no surprise – as no surprise at all – for, to state the obvious, individuation/individualisation is one of the principal apparatuses through which a life is recognised not 'merely' as a life, but as a life that ends with a death. Nonetheless, in the public domain, these deaths remain largely anonymous (cf. Guenther 2020: Chapter 5). A pit bull died. Or: 35,000 pit bulls died. Or: 3 million pit bulls died (in shelters, in a year, in the USA) (Kim 2015: 274). To be concerned with these deaths is not necessarily to be concerned with the loss of singularity that they represent, with the loss that, by definition, cannot be recovered. It would take the ostensibly neutral 'rehabilitation' and 'salvation' of Vick's dogs, which Harlan Weaver argues means in fact the re-racialisation of these dogs as white, to transform pit bull deaths from something that counts, to something that matters: to transform them, that is, into the deaths of irreducible, irreplaceable individuals.

White pit bulls

That these dogs were rehabilitated at all is unusual. More commonly, as Weaver explains, 'federal, state, and local governments [in the USA] euthanize all dogs present at a dogfighting bust, including those that work as government informants (as participants in fighting rinks staged to set up busts)' (Weaver 2021: 111). A shift in policy made the dogs' rescue possible, and this, Weaver argues, 'changed the connections between the category of pit bull and race' (111). In particular, a narrative of citizenship, closely tied to the normative kinship practices of marriage (including gay marriage) and family (Lauren Berlant in Weaver 2021: 111–112), was central to the dogs' rehabilitation, as were certain citizenship practices: 'one of the rescuers' main goals for all the dogs', Weaver reports, 'was that they pass the American Kennel Club's Canine Good Citizen test' (112). 'No longer partnered with "thugs"', he writes, Vick's dogs 'became pit bulls committed to the greater social good, pit bulls with stakes in home lives, pit bulls with loving families needed to advocate for them in order to distance them from their "bad rap"' (113).[15] All of which, Weaver argues, amounts not to the 'absence of race' but, rather, to 'the active construction of whiteness' (112; see also Guenther (2020): 182–185 on the part played by feminisation in the construction of pit bulls as white).

Vick's dogs' re-racialisation as white was synonymous with their 'recod[ing] as "unique individuals"' (Weaver 2021: 113). This was largely achieved through some of the most classic techniques of individualisation: naming, portraiture, photography, storying etc.; and, in addition, details of the dogs' perceived personalities were widely disseminated (see for example Giambalvo 2019). It was also achieved, however, by way of public scrutiny of their deaths. Considerable attention was paid, for instance, to the four (out of fifty-one) dogs who died soon after being rescued: two in shelters, and two who were euthanised, one for being 'too violent' and one for medical reasons (*Sports Illustrated* 2008: para. 47). The Best Friends Animal Society, which took in twenty-two of the remaining forty-seven dogs, and which rehomed all but two of them (Lucas and Meryl), posted mini 'obituaries' when any of the dogs died: obituaries that included, importantly, the reasons for their deaths. Bonita, for example, whom Vick used as a bait dog, 'passed away from anesthesia complications during a dental surgery' in 2009 (Dickson 2009: para. 1); Georgia lost a 'battle with kidney failure' in 2013 (Harmon 2013: para. 1); Mya died after 'a brief battle with cancer' in 2019 (Castle 2019: para. 3); and Frodo, 'the last surviving "Vicktory dog"', died of old age in 2021 (Castle 2021).

To my mind, this preoccupation with the dogs' deaths constitutes them as a new kind of population. No longer are they a population of 'violent, ruthless, and dangerous' individuals; now, they are a population of individuals who are at risk of a wrongful death. Not merely individuated, these pit bulls are, further, individualised, and as individuals they not only *can* die, their deaths at both individual and group level are open to moral evaluation (could this death have been avoided? Is it a just or an unjust death?). Herein lies the significance of the listing of the causes of death – it does not *really* matter how these dogs died, only that their deaths were distinguished from the injustices of dog fighting: 'distinguished', as opposed to 'distinct', from. It is notable, for instance, that several of the dogs' obituaries recorded babesia as a cause of ill health and/or death. *Babesia gibsoni* is tick-borne blood disease that, because it can be transmitted through bites, is commonly found in fighting dogs (Niestat *et al.* 2022). Dying of causes related to babesia, however, surrounded – as nearly all the obituaries emphasise – by tender loving care (including veterinary care), is perceived to be morally quite different from being killed in a dog fighting pit, being tortured to death, being shot for losing a dog fight, being shot by police or being euthanised by a humane society for being 'beyond rehabilitation'. All of these are unjust deaths. Having introduced their readers to Sweet Jasmine: to what she looks like – '35 pounds of twitchy curiosity with a coat the color of fried chicken, a pink nose and brown eyes' (*Sports Illustrated* 2008: para. 2) – and to how traumatised her life has been, *Sports Illustrated* switches immediately to:

> PETA [People for the Ethical Treatment of Animals] wanted Jasmine dead. Not just Jasmine, and not just PETA. The Humane Society of the US, agreeing with PETA, took the position that Michael Vick's pit bulls, like all dogs saved from fight rings, were beyond rehabilitation and that trying to save them was a misappropriation of time and money.
>
> (*Sports Illustrated* 2008: para. 5)

The moral outrage here is that Sweet Jasmine would have suffered an unnatural death, having endured a life of unnatural suffering that itself could have killed her. This outrage is only possible, however, if the individuated pit bull, now steeped in individuality, is perceived to be a morally relevant unit of analysis: a figure not just of particular significance, but of significance because they are particular.

Conclusion

I noted earlier Kim's claim that dogs are the 'most human of animals' (Kim 2015: 255): human 'not in terms of appearance or cognitive ability or percentage of shared DNA, but in terms of intimacy, familiarity, and identification' (Kim 2015: 271). There is nothing especially controversial about this.[16] I have already illustrated in the previous chapter, for example, how the question 'is a pet an animal?' (Fudge 2002: 27) torments the scientific study of dogs. In her book, *Animal*, Erica Fudge offers a historical analysis of how this distinction between a pet and an animal came about during the early modern period, and how it includes not only individualisation (especially by naming), but also co-habitation and taboos on pet consumption (Fudge 2002: 27–46; see also Thomas 1984: 112–115). To this list of three, I would add a fourth distinguishing feature, which is that 'pets' are not animals because their individual deaths (usually) matter, at least to those who know them. What ties Vick's dogs specifically with 'pet' dogs more generally is that they are both illustrative of how limited are the routes by which an animal can acquire the identity of an individual and, relatedly, escape the deathlessness of species. In this case, the racialisation of Michael Vick's dogs as black lifted them out of the undifferentiated species blur that is 'the dog' (constituting them as a population of identifiable 'dangerous' individuals), while their re-racialisation as white obviated their melting back into it.[17]

I am not suggesting that all humans enjoy the privilege of a death that counts. They do not (ICRC 2022; Lo and Horton 2015). Mine is not an argument aimed at securing for animals what humans have supposedly secured for themselves. My point simply is that the issue of individual particularity is intensely relevant to animals because they are usually classified by a sign (species) whose very 'success' depends upon its erasure. Truly, as Kim says, 'race' and species give and take from one another. But my own view is that they do so discriminately. Species thinking, because species are considered to be 'real', offers up the substance of biology to biopower. But the power to individuate, a key technique of biopolitical racism, is one that species thinking neither cares for nor covets. Species thinking does not (wish to) produce individuals, in the way that racism sometimes can. Should racism seek to convert an individual, or group of individuals, into a racialised type, however, where better to go than to species, which is a type of type like no other, for it offers no possibility of return to particularity. This matters for animals, but also for humans, for as Wadiwel writes: '[i]f the *destiny of humanity lies in the animal*, then the true political challenge of the contemporary era revolves around the removal of the gap in its entirety' (Wadiwel 2002: para. 17, emphasis in the original).

Political challenge and transformation, in the context of the conjoined lexicons of 'race' and of species, often turn on identifying the *falseness* of 'the type' and the *wrongness* of an individual's relation or allocation to it. But when animals are identified as species, the falseness of the category and the wrongness of the allocation hang suspended. This is in part what has motivated my writing of this book, and the grief that lies behind it. The idea that it is possibly-not-wrong to allocate an animal to a not-exactly-false category ensures that when species thinking kills, nobody dies.

Notes

1 Always counts, that is, in those countries – currently numbering around forty – that have passed some form of partial or full breed-specific legislation against pit bull types. (For details, see https://worldpopulationreview.com/country-rankings/countries-that-ban-pit-bulls (accessed August 2023)).
2 Both Plato and Aristotle believed in essential forms. Aristotle, however, was 'eager to distance himself from Plato's theory of Forms, which exist quite apart from the material world. He does so in part by insisting that his own forms are somehow enmeshed in matter' (Ainsworth 2020).
3 I will return to Gliddon below. Nott was a physician and 'medical anthropologist', who spent most of his life in Mobile, Alabama. Loring Brace describes him as a 'prototypical Southern racist' (Brace 1974: 516). Among his many publications, Nott was responsible for the English translation of Gobineau's *Essai sur l'inégalité des races* (Erikson 1986: 112).
4 See Smith (2015) for a more detailed analysis of how the theory of separate origins has historically been linked to disputes over scriptural authority.
5 *Indigenous Races of the Earth* was the follow-up to Gliddon and Nott's *Types of Mankind*, which was published in 1854 and written in memory of Samuel Morton, who died in 1851.

6 Darwin was drawn into these debates as a scientist, and also because he came from a family that for two generations had been well established as anti-slavery campaigners (Desmond and Moore 2009, esp. Chapter 1). The hope expressed in *The Descent of Man* stemmed in part from Darwin's revulsion at the way monogenism often, and polygenism always, sanctified slavery by insisting that 'savagism' and 'civilisation' were given and unchanging states.

7 Biologists in the early part of the twentieth century, Richard Lewontin writes, 'were loath to abandon the idea of race entirely' (Lewontin 2006: para. 11). Theodosius Dobzhansky's notion of 'geographical race', for instance – of race as a genetically distinct geographical population – was an effort, Lewontin argues, 'to hold on to the concept [of race] while mak[ing] it objective and generalizable' (Lewontin 2006: para. 11; see Gannett (2013) on the three conceptions of race held by Dobzhansky during his lifetime).

8 So varied are dogs that even Darwin was tripped up by them: 'I fully admit', he wrote, that domestic dogs 'have probably descended from several wild species' (Darwin 2008: 18).

9 This is why the comparatively speedy time span of modification by artificial selection was a helpful metaphor for Darwin (see Chapter 2), and also why so much turned on the answers to questions about geological time in the nineteenth century (Boakes 2008: 49–52; Van Grouw 2018: 62–65). The issue, simply put, was this: is the earth *old enough* to support theories of evolution?

10 Gradation, with the possibility of improvement, can make colonialism easier to justify than does the idea that some groups of humans are irredeemably inferior (Smith 2015: 33). This 'liberal racism' involves 'making the best of the European experience the model for everyone, and the eventual perfection of mankind consisting in everyone becoming creative Europeans' (Richard Popkin in Smith 2015: 33).

11 *If* they are individuals at all (see Chapter 7).

12 Which is not to deny that particular animals may be relevant, in different and often unpredictable ways, to particular scientists, or that a generic conception of 'the individual' is not important in science (see Chapter 7). This is especially well illustrated by the biological species concept, in which the individual is usually, but not always, considered to be the unit of inheritance.

13 The BVA, the British Small Animal Veterinary Association (BSAVA), the RSPCA and other UK bodies such as the Dogs Trust, as well as similar organisations in the United States, Australia and elsewhere, are all opposed to breed-specific legislation, citing literature that indicates that there is no scientific evidence to support the claim that pit bull types are inherently dangerous (see for example Collier 2006).

14 As Peterson, drawing on Kwame Anthony Appiah, defines it: '[e]xtrinsic racism identifies morally relevant criteria (alleged intellectual weakness, dishonesty, criminality and so on) as warranting discrimination' (Peterson 2019: 448).
15 As Weaver notes, these narratives are not only raced, but classed. They assume, for example, the existence of homes – homes on which mortgages can be raised and in which dogs are actually permitted to be accommodated – and on homes as opposed to woods or streets or shelters (Weaver 2021: 114; on dogs and class in the USA, including especially pit bulls, see also Dayan (2016)).
16 Except that Kim is probably referring to companion and working dogs, who make up only a small proportion of the total global dog population (see Chapters 2 and 5 of this book).
17 One might object that the deaths of this group of approximately fifty dogs were *able* to be singularised on account of their relatively small number. In Chapter 7, I will argue that while the 'numbering up' of animals is a key factor in their de-individualisation, it is the concept species itself that is more significant.

7

Dog politics

> Man's best friends are storybook dogs.
> (Coppinger and Coppinger 2016: 21)

Except: they are not storybook dogs. They are dogs whose lives are mostly organised by a storybook story that tells of a special relationship between dogs and humans; a storybook story that serves, whether by design or not, to legitimise human governance of dogs. Because dogs, so the story goes, 'belong' with us. Perhaps, like no other animal, they belong *to* us. The very name, *Canis familiaris*.

In 2009, in the first issue of the first volume of the now well-established journal *Humanimalia*, the sociologist and ethologist Lynda Birke wrote an article entitled 'Naming names – or, what's in it for the animals?'. In it, she argues that '[n]aming, describing other animals is, in the story, a way of not communicating, of not understanding who they are' (Birke 2009: 1). 'The story' to which Birke is referring is Ursula Le Guin's 'She unnames them'. But the point she is making could apply as well to the story that I have been addressing in this book, which is a story about dogs as a species. I have called this dogs' species story. I do not think that dogs' species story is a way of not communicating or not understanding *per se*. I think it is about communicating and understanding in a very *particular* way, a way that is of considerable benefit to humans. Much has been tested on dogs; much has been learned about dogs; and much, arguably, is known about dogs. But mostly, this is dogs in relations with humans.

A lot of Birke's article is about whether animals benefit from animal studies research. 'Does this research I read about take seriously the animals' point of view', she asks, 'or only the viewpoint of the humans thinking about animals?' (Birke 2009: 1). The question is relevant fourteen years later not only because, some would argue, animal studies is no better placed to address an animal's point of view than it was when Birke raised it as an issue (see for example Blattner's (2021) rather sharp critique of animal studies), but also because part of the answer as to why one might not take 'seriously' an animal's point of view is that to do so would be to reinstate problematic, possibly anthropomorphic, conceptions of individual subjectivity, which a long history of philosophical, social science and humanities thinking has attempted to overturn (see for example Chapter 5 of this book; cf. Baratay 2022). I mention this quandary because it is pertinent to this book specifically, and because it is more generally indicative of why it might be difficult to conduct research that benefits animals. Animals are often 'invited in' to debates in which so much energy has already been expended defending or challenging long-standing theoretical preoccupations that it is ultimately simpler to sacrifice the animal to the debate than to change it. Species, in science, is one of these preoccupations. 'The individual', in the social sciences, is another. This leaves dogs in a particularly difficult place with regard to conducting research that benefits them, as I have argued throughout this book, because one key alternative to the individual in animal studies – relationality, entanglement, intersubjectivity – is precisely the defining characteristic of dogs' species story in science.

Even though it is impossible (and arguably undesirable) to cast these theoretical and philosophical preoccupations aside, it is surely worth being sensitive to how they shape and constrain what critiques and interventions are likely to be imaginable, and also, therefore, how important it is to try to reset at least some of the parameters. In the following, rather abstract, discussion, I will illustrate all the points I have been making here by tracing a very brief history of 'the individual' as it is understood, by social scientists and humanities scholars, to be connected to and embedded in modern science – and therefore why it is problematic – and one scientific counterpoint to this figure, the holobiont, which has been warmly welcomed in response. I also ask, however, where these debates leave the *actual* individual, as Alfred North Whitehead might put it: where it leaves, that is, the individual animal, with a specific 'point of view', to whom animal studies researchers, Birke argues, are accountable (Birke 2009: 3). I use Whitehead's work here for two reasons. It enables me, first, to illustrate that there are ways to understand 'the individual', and even 'a point of view', that are not antithetical to relationality; and, second, that relationality itself can delimit an individual's potential. Having cleared this theoretical space, the rest of the chapter addresses some of the more practical and pragmatic implications of my analysis of dogs' species story in this book, and the directions that might follow from it.

'We have never been individuals'

It is no accident that modern science, which proceeds on the basis of the bifurcation of nature into subjects and objects (Whitehead 1985), should bind itself to a most problematic conception of the subject. The founding gesture of modern science, Jessica Riskin argues, is Descartes's. Not because Descartes did away with two of Aristotle's souls (the vegetative soul, present in plants, animals and humans, and the sensitive soul, present in animals and humans), or even because he introduced the idea of 'living machines'. Rather, for Riskin, it is because he introduced a mechanistic view of life *and at once posited an exception to it*, by retaining for humans Aristotle's rational soul. By this gesture, Descartes established the indivisibility of modern subjectivity and modern science:

> Seeing the world as a pure machine, lifting his thinking soul out of the world, even out of its own bodily interface with the world, Descartes accomplished the distancing of self from world that defines modern subjectivity, the sense of fully autonomous, inner selfhood, and modern objectivity, the sense of regarding the world from a neutral position outside of it. It was in Descartes's philosophy that modern selfhood and modern science created one another.
> (Riskin 2016: 61–62)

Descartes's aim was not to 'reduce life to mechanism' but 'to elevate mechanism to life: to explain life, never to explain it away' (Riskin 2016: 45). Nevertheless, it is by way of this mechanistic conception of life that animals (and indeed 'nature') are constituted as objects, and distinguished from the human subject. Whitehead demonstrates the inadequacy, if not the absurdity, of this bifurcation in the broader context of his critique of what he calls the materialist theory of evolution – which in fact, according to him, is no evolutionary theory at all, because '[t]here is nothing to evolve' (Whitehead 1985: 136). Nothing, because the bifurcation of nature reduces the relations between subjects and objects to 'the bare relation between knower to known. The subject is the knower, the object is the known' (Whitehead 1967: 175). As a consequence, all meaning, experience and value are assumed to originate with the human subject, while nature appears as an altogether 'dull affair': 'soundless, scentless, colourless; merely the hurrying of material, endlessly, meaninglessly' (Whitehead 1985: 69). Or perhaps, in more contemporary parlance, the hurrying of material, endlessly, mindlessly (see Chapter 3 of this book).

Descartes's subject has bounced down the centuries, and down numerous units of scientific analysis. It is Haraway's modest witness, exemplified by Robert Boyle, 'the legitimate and authorised ventriloquist for the object world, adding nothing from his mere opinions, his biasing embodiment' (Haraway 1997: 24). It is the genetic individual, as described by the modern synthesis, who is characterised by 'autonomy and physiological unity', internal genetic homogeneity, and genetic uniqueness (Bernabé Santelices in Godfrey-Smith 2009: 85), and whose reproduction depends on the identification of individuals and their parents (Godfrey-Smith 2009: 69). It is the germ cell, which lies at the heart of a 'clean', self-contained theory of species self-replication, guaranteeing that offspring will be protected from genetic changes in the parent, as long as those changes 'do not affect the germ cells' chromosomes' (Tsing 2015: 140).

What all these figures (and there are many others) have in common is that, by way of their boundedness and autonomy, they are assumed or assume themselves to be 'protected from the vicissitudes of ecological encounter and history' (Tsing 2015: 140), and protected especially from the vicissitudes of relationality, of being in and of the world. It is into this specific context, a context in which worldly units take on, troublingly, some of the characteristics of the Cartesian subject (the subject constituted hand-in-hand with modern science), that the principle of symbiosis and the holobiont erupt. And they erupt not only into science. As Scott Gilbert, Jan Sapp and Alfred Tauber anticipate, part of the attraction of symbiosis lies in the challenge it poses to some of the axioms of majoritarian western philosophy (Gilbert et al. 2012: 326).[1] Evidence of symbiosis, they write, is fundamentally transforming 'the classical conception of an insular individuality into one in which interactive relationships among species blurs the boundaries of the organism and obscures the notion of essential identity' (325). Although microbial and botanical sciences have long challenged 'the autonomous individual' and an 'individualist conception of the organism', '[t]he discovery of symbiosis throughout the animal kingdom' finally offers some resistance, 'even' within the zoological sciences, to that bastion tenet of genomic individuality: 'one genome/one organism' (327). '[A]nimals are composites of many species living, developing, and evolving together' (325).

Concepts such as symbiosis, or the holobiont, can be an '[incitement] to theory' (Tsing 2015: 38) because they reveal that no individual, 'in reality', is bounded and/or autonomous. An example of a holobiont might be a human or an animal, plus the bacteria and other microbial and eukaryotic species that the organism 'hosts' and without which it would lose 'functionality'.[2] They are an incitement to theory and, arguably, a confirmation of it, for by returning not only history, the contingency of encounterings and relationality to evolutionary biology, disciplines such as evolutionary developmental biology ('evo-devo') and ecological evolutionary developmental biology ('eco-evo-devo') support and offer further impetus to those analyses of the social world that are organised around, for example, contact zones, relatings and entanglements. In effect, the figure of the holobiont not only challenges and disputes the existence of the autonomous individual but also, seemingly, offers scientific 'proof' of heterogeneous, contingent and temporary processes of making-with, becoming-with, worlding-with etc. (Haraway 2008, 2016). As Haraway puts it:

> Critters do not precede their relatings; they make each other through semiotic material involution, out of the beings of previous such entanglements. Lynn Margulis knew a great deal about 'the intimacy of strangers', a phrase she proposed to describe the most fundamental practices of critters becoming-with each other at every node of intraaction in earth history.
>
> (Haraway 2016: 60)

'Encounter-thinking', whether in the biological or social sciences, posits that the world is different from what we thought it was. Just as 'we have never been modern' (Latour 1993), so 'we have never been individuals' (Gilbert *et al.* 2012: 336). Instead, Gilbert *et al.* conclude, '[w]e are all lichen' (336) – i.e., associational.³ Nature selects relationships (Gilbert *et al.* in Tsing 2015: 142).

And yet. To return to Birke's version of the question *cui bono?* (Star 1990: 43), one might ask how, from the 'point of view' of an animal, this version of the world differs from the one that it replaces, or whether it is the same story, differently told: animals are not individuals. In *How Forests Think*, Eduardo Kohn asks whether attention to relations, encounters and entanglements is an invitation to think about ethics and politics differently, or whether it an ethics or a politics in and of itself. On the one hand, he writes, '[t]he multispecies encounter is, as Haraway has intimated, a particularly important domain for *cultivating* an ethical practice' (Kohn 2013: 134, my emphasis). On the other hand, 'in the hopeful politics we seek to cultivate, we privilege heterarchy over hierarchy, the rhizomatic over the arborescent, and we celebrate the fact that such horizontal processes – lateral gene transfer, symbiosis, commensalism, and the like – can be found in the nonhuman living world' (Kohn 2013: 19). Kohn makes this point because he finds evidence of hierarchy – verticality, one might say – in the living world (19). But one also finds in the living world horizontal processes (as Kohn puts it), such as becomings, that do not necessarily bear positive ethical or political value.

The notion that horizontal processes, entanglements, relationality etc. are inherently ethical implicitly subtends much of my previous work (see for example Motamedi Fraser 2019). The more I have focused on animals, however, and specifically dogs, the more this position seems problematic to me, as this book has illustrated. My argument throughout the book has been that this story of relationality – or associationality – is very often a problem for dogs; that, where dogs are concerned, relationality itself has become reified, not only as a concept, but as a series of expectations and practices that shape what a dog should and must be; and that, as such, relationality is now potentially a violent abstraction that limits what dogs, and especially those dogs who live and work closely with humans, are able to become. This is a difficult conclusion to draw, however, for one can hardly return again to the very figure that has been instrumental in justifying centuries of violence against both animals and humans. For not only is Descartes's subject cleaved from animals, to the extent that only he – that bounded, adult, autonomous, self-governing, white, male, bourgeois, heteronormative, able-bodied individual (to offer something of a caricature), replete with his box of 'god-tricks' (Haraway 1991: 188–196) – can truly achieve this separation, animality remains a key part of racist, sexist and ableist constructions of distinctions among humans. No amount of 'inclusion' can erase that 'originary' splinter, for it defines the normative human subject (Derrida 2008: 45). Herein lies the problem with liberal humanism, as Cary Wolfe summarises it, which has a 'penchant for the sort of "pluralism" that extends the sphere of consideration (intellectual or ethical) to previously marginalized groups without in the least destabilizing or throwing into question the schema of the human who undertakes such pluralisation' (Wolfe 2009: 568).

My argument in this book, therefore, obliges me to find a way to conceive of individuality (or singularity) differently, preferably without compromising relationality. I find that way in Whitehead's concept of endurance, and of an enduring concrete percipient. I will sketch out Whitehead's thesis very briefly here, for what it offers in itself, but also – to go back to Birke's question as to who benefits from animal studies research – because it offers a kind of guide by which to establish how something (research, in this instance) might become relevant to animals and also how it might be recognised as having been achieved.

Whitehead is best known for his argument, essentially captured in the title of his magnum opus, *Process and Reality*, 'that the actual world is a process, and that the process is the becoming of actual entities' (Whitehead 1978: 22). But this is only the half of it, for becomings perish, while actual entities, or societies, as Whitehead also sometimes calls them, endure. Whitehead gives the example of '[a] man, defined as an enduring percipient, [as] such a society' (Mays 2013 [1959]: 263). The word 'society' is significant here. In Whitehead's schema an 'enduring percipient' must be understood to be a society (or nexus) of societies, '[y]oking together all the way down' (Haraway 2008: 31). And all the way 'up', too, for 'there is no society in isolation' (Whitehead 1978: 90). '[T]he single organism', Whitehead writes, 'is almost helpless' (Whitehead 1985: 140).

Nevertheless, the fact that 'everything is connected!', as Martin Savranksy (2016: 90) drily puts it, does not mean that an enduring percipient (a dog, say) experiences the entirety of the world. Rather, it is the connectedness of the world that experiences the singularity of the percipient, as Vinciane Despret explains in her moving account of extinction:

> What the world has lost, and what truly matters, is a part of what invents and maintains it as a world. The world dies from each absence; the world bursts from absence … When a being is no more, the world narrows all of a sudden, and a part of reality collapses. Each time an existence disappears, it is a piece of the universe of sensations that fades away.
> (Despret 2017: 219–220)

To understand a dog as an enduring percipient is to understand them to be both 'connected' and singular. That singularity derives not from a projection of a unique essence of individuality (as in the liberal humanist subject), but from the particularity of the processes of unification (particular processes, out of all potential processes, out of potentiality itself) that give rise to a dog. A dog is, in effect, 'the decision amid "potentiality". It represents the stubborn fact that cannot be evaded' (Whitehead 1978: 43). Although this specificity of existence is not 'proof of subjectivity', it does nevertheless define 'a point of view, a locus' (Latour 2005: 230). It is a temporary occupation of a position or, 'much more accurately … [it is] what keeps you busy' (Whitehead in Latour 2005: 229). This is how Whitehead makes it possible to speak of a point of view, without simultaneously implying that an anthropomorphic conception of the subject underlies it.[4]

The salient issue here, however, is that while Whitehead's enduring percipient, a dog, is connected to 'the world', not *everything* – not the everything that is connected – is relevant from that particular dog's point of view. Yes, when we analyse the society that is the individual dog, we find, as Gilbert *et al.* argue, a society of symbionts, for unification 'yokes' them, as Haraway puts it, indivisibly and irreversibly together.[5] But whether the specific modes of becoming of a society of symbionts, as they complete an animal's metabolic pathways, are relevant to that dog's experience of herself *as* an enduring percipient is an open question. And if it is relevant, then there is also the question of *how* it is relevant, or, by what selected mode of unification it becomes relevant. Does a dog experience being a holobiont in the mode of a philosophical challenge to individuality? I doubt it. Could they potentially experience it in the mode of illness (as they would, if a microbe were to evade the immune system and become a cancer or pathogen)? Probably. Similarly, will a dog appreciate, as I have just argued, that their singularity 'is made up of myriad multiplicities of unification' (Donaldson 2013: 191)? Frankly, no. Will she appreciate that the significance of her singular unification is erased by the concept of species? In terms of its consequences, this is more than likely. In fact, it is why I give the epigraph of this book to Lynda Birke, who argues that while animals 'may indeed be supremely indifferent to the names we give them ... they are not indifferent to the naming of oppression' (Birke 2009: 7).

In *Staying with the Trouble*, Donna Haraway writes that '[t]he fusion of genomes in symbioses, followed by natural selection – with a very modest role for mutation as a motor of system level change – leads to increasingly complex levels of good-enough quasi-individuality to get through the day, or the aeon' (Haraway 2016: 60). This is characteristically funny: nothing more than a comma separates this unexpected temporal leap from the day to the aeon. But it also points to a kind of disregard for quasi-individuality. It suggests that there is no difference between being a quasi-individual for a day or being a quasi-individual for an aeon, between being a particular, singular individual and being an individual member of a species. Part of the problem for animals, however, is that 'what it is to be an individual', or a quasi-individual, for a day is strongly affected by human perceptions of animals as aeonic individuals. It is in part *because* particular individuals are seen to be aeonic individuals – at some level all the same – that they often *cannot* get through the day. I opened this book with an account of Beth, who was euthanised for her disinterest in humans. *This* Beth could not be an aeonic dog. *This* Beth could not get through the day.

Despite the significant influence of Whitehead's work on contemporary social theory, the concept of endurance is often overlooked. One reason for this neglect might be that endurance has been used – by human scientists specifically, Isabelle Stengers argues – to validate what exists now, over what could be (Stengers 1999: 204). And it is true: the on-going iteration of 'now' is baked into Whitehead's concept of endurance insofar as endurance is, in large part, the successful demand that new becomings comply to an 'order' that has already been established – to an order, in other words, that exists here, now, today.[6]

One might understand dogs' species story thus: as a largely enforced mode of becoming in the present, a pattern or an order of becoming, to which most dogs are obliged to conform and from which they depart at their peril. This particular mode of becoming – lured by a story that privileges the becoming of dogs with and through humans, a mode of becoming that is widely relayed in science, as well as in the popular domain, and which, in practice, bears daily upon and shapes the lives of individual dogs from their births through to their deaths – is less about novelty and difference, less about the boundless potentiality that is the vector for creative actualisation, and more about conformity to likeness. Endurance is both the product (achievement) of the becoming of the species 'dog', and the price paid by individual dogs.

Where violence lies

Disputes with the figure of the individual can, in my view, be problematic, given that the classification 'animal', and the classification of animals into species, depend in large part on the erasure of animals as individuals, which in turn contributes significantly to and legitimates the on-going war against them (Wadiwel 2015). 'The very definition of the creation act' (Stengers 2010: 6), as Haraway said in a joint seminar with Isabelle Stengers in 2006, constitutes creatures 'not as individuals but according to a "kind" that prepares them for use and classification by Adam and Eve ... and justifies the dominion given to humans over everything else on earth' (Stengers 2010: 6–7). Or, as Henry Buller puts it: the 'challenge to [animal] individualisation ... has been singularly useful to humankind ... It is, after all, through this rendering plural of non-human "beasts" that *Homo sapiens* takes its dominant place in the driving seat of the anthropological machine and has done so ever since' (Buller 2013: 157).

Because classification, among other practices, renders animals 'plural', many theorists have rightly addressed how numbers or multitudes 'help us to stop thinking' (Despret and Porcher in Buller

2013: 158) and/or have sought to find ways to make the 'multitude without power' (Buller 2013: 156) ethically meaningful (for example Davies 2012). While I agree that the 'numbering up' of animals certainly contributes to their de-individualisation, some distinction between how different 'numbering-up categories' operate and what they achieve might be useful. For example: Buller cites James Serpell, who argues that '[t]reating animals as groups of organisms (populations, species, ecosystems and so on) creates ethical problems when it encourages people to ignore or devalue the well-being of individual animals comprising those groups' (Serpell in Buller 2013: 161). And Buller himself writes that 'there is no herd nor shoal – no "heap of stones" – without the individual animals that compose it' (Buller 2013: 158). The words 'comprise' and 'compose' are an important part of what Serpell and Buller are saying here, because they serve to connect these 'groups' – populations, species, herds etc. – to individuals by implying that such groups would be meaningless without the individuals who constitute them.

While this is usually the case as far as the concept of a population is concerned, for a population must at least pay lip service to being populated (I am not sure about herds or shoals or heaps), it has been the argument of *Dog Politics* that it is not often the case with regard to species concepts. Species concepts, as I have illustrated (see Chapters 3 and 6 especially), give no *reason* to recognise the particular individual animal because they gather together animals not on the basis of who they are, but of what they represent.[7] Just one representative, therefore, is enough. Or even, where extinct species are concerned, none is enough. Herein lies the atrocity of species thinking, and its injury: with no reason to recognise an individual life, and no reason, therefore, to recognise an individual death, where lies evidence of a life destroyed by violence? In her important analysis of how identity serves to create a cause for a death, and drawing on the work of sociologists Luc Boltanski and Laurent Thévenot, Despret writes that:

> a cause results from the collective work of production of an identity that aims to mobilize, in order to denounce and stop an injustice … What ties [deaths with causes] together is that they would not have happened if something had been done, if those who have been victims were taken into account, if their causes had been acted on behalf of.
>
> (Despret 2016: 82)

For Boltanski and Thévenot, statistics on the causes of human deaths 'desingularise' humans, because 'it is only through their deaths that victims are presently defined' (Despret 2016: 82). Despret gently objects. When it comes to the billions of deaths of food-farmed animals, 'desingularization does not operate in a consistent manner: animals that are killed are translated into pounds of meat, deceased humans into persons' (82). But perhaps food-farmed animals are not *even* desingularised by their deaths, for that would assume that they were perceived to be singular in life. Without the identity of an individual, is there a difference between the living and the dead? Can there *be* a cause of death?

In her book *Afro-Dog: Blackness and the Animal Question*, Bénédicte Boisseron argues that neither animals nor oppressed groups of people are perceived as individuals. Instead, '[a]nimals, women, blacks, and Jews become merely ideas and concepts, caught in a rhetoric of similes, analogies and metaphors' (Boisseron 2018: 22). If there is a difference, it is perhaps that the rhetoric of similes, analogies and metaphors in which animals are routinely caught is only very rarely called out, in the public domain, as a form or symptom of oppression. The idea of 'an exaltation of larks' or 'an ostentation of peacocks' or 'an unkindness of ravens' is more likely to be considered lyrical than it is to be perceived as lethal.

Species as story

In her splendidly titled article 'Bad with names', Brianne Donaldson points to the senselessness of the word 'animal', which 'spans fairy flies to blue whales' (Donaldson 2013: 182), and suggests that, '[a]s a common-place word in biology, agriculture, popular culture, law, and the humanities, it has lost accurate meaning' (186). This loss of *accurate* meaning does not equate with the loss of *all* meaning, however. On the contrary, the word 'animal' is electric with meaning, for it denotes, Jacques Derrida argues, 'all the living things that man does not recognize as his fellows, his neighbors, or his brothers' (Derrida in Donaldson 2013: 182). In my view, species categories operate rather in the reverse. They disguise their political work precisely to the extent that, mostly, they appear to mean nothing much at all beyond their 'accurate' meanings – by which I assume

Donaldson means specific meanings – that are 'accurately' indexed to particular groups of animals. House sparrows, *Passer domesticus*. Dogs, *Canis familiaris*. Woolly mammoths, *Mammuthus primigenius*. It is this perceived accuracy, I think, that obscures the contribution that species thinking makes to the on-going exploitation and subjugation of living animals. Simply put, unlike the category 'animal', species categories appear to be relatively coherent, relatively empirical, and therefore less, or even not at all, political. Should a case be made, then, against species, as it is against 'animal'? I believe it should, although *how* to make that case, especially in a way that is of benefit to animals, deserves some reflection, for the problem of species is not purely conceptual. As I have argued throughout this book, species are stories that materially shape the lives of individual animals.

For example: Gilles Deleuze challenges the biological species concept by proposing that 'bodies change the most without any filial or hereditary modification at all ... The symbiosis between wasp and orchid is not at all due to descent or genes but to the circumstances and context of bodies colliding and cooperating' (Donaldson 2013: 184). Or affecting and being affected. In his book on Spinoza, Deleuze argues that an animal should be defined not 'by its form, its organs, and its functions', but by 'the affects of which it is capable' (Deleuze 1988: 124). This contribution is welcome because it cuts refreshingly through and across species lines. It enables Deleuze to propose, for instance, that there are greater differences between a race horse and a plough horse than there are between a plough horse and an ox (Deleuze 1988: 124). But it is also problematic, because the revised categorisation of plough horses and oxen by way of affects is no more likely to recover the singularity of an individual animal than is species, for it does not appear to be much bothered with *this* plough horse or with *that* ox. I have argued throughout this book that the negation of the significance of the singular individual is one of the most devastating consequences of species thinking. For me, therefore, any critique of, or alternative to, species must necessarily have something to say to the individual.

But not *solely* to the individual! The reason Donaldson finds value in being 'bad with names' is because, for her, names are bad: because names and naming are too often a way, to return to Birke's analysis of Le Guin's story, of not communicating and not understanding. Being bad with names, therefore, is a way of orienting oneself toward singularity. 'Our forgetfulness', Donaldson writes, 'may allow us to come to situations open to the demands of that moment, without recourse to prescriptive ethics or the fixed identities on which such ethics are based' (Donaldson 2013: 198). Although this too I very much welcome, I also think that more may be required – from 'the animals' point of view', as Birke puts it – than pitting species against singularity (and celebrating singularity), not least because the singularities of animals will be shaped by the names we call them. It does not seem possible to me, therefore, to forget. And even if it were possible, this is arguably not the moment for forgetting, as species concepts gain ever more traction, especially in the context of debates about anthropogenic climate catastrophe. Rather than forget species, I would argue that this is precisely the moment to make species visible and legible not as an 'accurate' classification, neutral and unbending, but as a *story*, decked with the power to frame, judge, legitimise and delegitimise animals' behaviours and, by extension, how they are treated; to make visible and legible that what matters about a species story is not its truth or falsity, but the forces it has the power to harness, and the modes of living and dying it facilitates and authorises. Although this attention to species stories risks giving new life and substance to the very category (species) it seeks to dismantle, the risk, I think, is worth it. Because unlike species thinking, species stories always lead back to individuals. Indeed, this is what they are: an invitation to ask how *this* individual's life is empirically and substantially shaped – how, even, it was ended – by the stories we are (or are not) telling.

'[A] focus on individual animals', Beth Greenhough and Emma Roe write, 'can be accused of misrepresenting the realities of animal lives, given many animals are rarely treated as individuals but as flocks of chickens, herds of pigs or tanks of exotic pet fish' (Greenhough and Roe 2019: 376). But this is the point: a flock is not a herd or a tank. How, exactly, does the story of a flock determine the life of *this* individual chicken, and how does it determine it differently from *that* pig in a herd or *that* exotic pet fish in a tank? Species stories may well have overlapping elements, but they will also vary, in their structure and content, and in their implications. Although relationality is the key driver of domesticated dogs' species story today, my guess is that it is unlikely to be the force behind domesticated cats' species story, just as I think the predator status of dogs probably carries less significance in their story than does the prey status of horses in theirs (see for example Tomlinson (2024)). How do these differences bear on the individual animal? And how do they determine what modes of (re)individualisation are possible? The answers to these questions depend on empirical investigation.

For the love of a dog

> 'Tied up?', said the wolf: 'so you don't run Where you want?' – 'Not always; but so what?'
> (Jean de La Fontaine in Porcher and Lécrivain 2019: 113)

This is the epigraph of Jocelyn Porcher and Élisabeth Lécrivain's article, discussed in Chapter 4, which is entitled 'The wolf and the patou dog: Freedom and work'. In it, Porcher and Lécrivain object to the opposition between freedom and work. Elsewhere, Porcher and Sophie Nicod argue that there is a freedom in labour that can be contrasted to the 'costly freedom' of 'wildlife' (Porcher and Nicod 2020: 255) that animal liberationists propose for domesticated animals. Theirs is a disingenuous proposal, Porcher and Nicod add, for it 'hides the fact that our social, political and environmental constraints, as well as the economic system in which we live as a whole – capitalism – leaves no place for animals' (256).

Like the wolf, I too have a question: why should the relevant comparison be between a 'free' wolf and a 'working' dog? Why should it not be between how domesticated dogs live with humans now, and how they *could* live with and alongside us? By this question I hope to indicate explicitly that the argument in this book is not an abolitionist one. I do not share Gary Francione's view that humans are so exploitative, and the lives of domesticated animals so impoverished by that exploitation, that the only alternative is extinction (extinction of domesticated animals, mind, Francione says, not of humans). Among the very many reasons for not supporting Francione's position is the fact that extinction, as Nicolas Delon points out, 'does not repair the historical injustices of domestication' (Delon 2020: 174). 'Reconstructing our relations with [domesticated animals]', however, might (Delon 2020: 174).

How our relations with animals, domesticated and otherwise, might be reconstructed is an open and urgent question. Among other tactics and strategies, it is a matter for public debate. What I hope this book has illustrated, among other things, is that there is no reason at all – above all, no reason such as 'the bond' – that would justify the exemption of dogs from such a discussion. In the USA, Karla Armbruster argues, dogs may feel to some people like 'beloved canine "family members"', but 'from a societal perspective they are categorized as something closer to pigeons and rats: potential or actual nuisances, indulged only as the lifestyle choice or accessory of a human being' (Armbruster 2019: 118). This contrast between a beloved family member on the one hand, and a lifestyle choice and a nuisance on the other, is a common one. It is easy to criticise the latter two. The notion of a dog as a 'lifestyle choice' can be condemned on the grounds that it equates a dog with a consumer object, and also because it obliges the dog to live their life in the mode of an embodiment of a 'reason' that is not their own. (As does, of course, the notion of a dog as a devoted companion, or an animal model, or an exercise regime, or a play partner, or a form of therapy, or a drug detector.)

As for being categorised as a public nuisance; again, this can and should be deplored. It might be noted, for example, that while pigeons and rats are subject to all kinds of violences, including enforced sterilisation and extermination, they are not required to live their public lives under the pressure of extreme behavioural and emotional control in order not to be a 'nuisance'. So great are the constraints on dogs today that one almost feels obliged to ask whether mechanism has made a come-back: not in science, maybe, but on the public street and in public policy. For it appears that the only way that a dog could meet the demand to be 'under control' – not to fart here, not to sniff there, not to get too close, not to bark in fright, not to growl in anger, not to jump from surprise, not to run up in delight – is to be a machine.

But what I have tried to argue in this book is that profoundly problematic practices, such as the objectification and 'machinisation' of dogs, are not the only reasons why we should be motivated to reconstruct our relations with them, as Delon advises. The third conception of dogs that Armbruster identifies, of dogs as a 'beloved family member', is perhaps the most wide-spread and intuitive source of 'evidence' for dogs' species story and the so-called bond that underpins it. Yet it is precisely *this* notion of dogs, of dogs as human kin, that poses, I think, a most dangerous threat to dogs today (especially to dogs in the Global North). In his book *Environmental Enrichment for Captive Animals*, Robert Young (2003) includes – unusually, especially given the date of publication – a chapter on companion animals. He begins with this statement, which I quote in full, because it exemplifies for me how obfuscating the love of an animal can be:

> Unfortunately, we have virtually no information on the welfare of these [companion] species within the home environment. People normally only become concerned about the welfare of their pet when it is physically injuring itself, for example, fur and feather plucking in mammals and birds, respectively. The reason why we do not investigate the psychological well-being of companion animals is something that is not understood. It has been suggested to me by various scientists that the topic is too controversial and emotionally charged to touch because we are often talking about a 'loved family member'. Thus, to imply the welfare of a pet animal is not good would be perceived by the owner as a direct criticism. There seems to be an unspoken sentiment that because we 'love' our companion animals then their welfare must be good. Yet, in the UK and North America the number of consultants dealing with behavioural problems is growing at a rapid rate; there are books on the subject in most languages and television programmes that specifically deal with such problems.
>
> (Young 2003: 76)

I wager that, over the past twenty years since this was written, the numbers of dog consultants, dog books and dog television programmes have increased in proportion to the tightening of dogs' species story. Love, as Young says, is too often mistaken for welfare. But where dogs' species story is concerned, the point extends still further, for here love, being loved by a human, is too often mistaken for life, for the meaning of a life for a dog.

Many people who live with dogs are likely to find something to identify with in Nigel Clark's description of a social life with domesticated animals. That life, Clark writes,

> can be seen to rest ... primordially on a kind of mutual *dis*possession [rather] than on the possession of animals by human actors; a letting go of customary precautions and boundary maintenance on the part

of each participating species. Whatever benefits and utilities might eventually emerge, any ongoing interspecies association ... hinges on 'a gift of the possibility of a common world'.

(Clark 2007: 57, emphasis in the original)

While I genuinely appreciate the spirit of Clark's dream here, it is difficult to imagine how living with dogs could be reconceived of in terms of a mutual dispossession, a 'letting go of ... boundary maintenance'. Because to my mind, one of the greatest obstacles to building a 'common world' with dogs is exactly the naturalisation of the blurring of dog–human boundaries in dogs' species story – the *dis*respect for those boundaries. Dogs' species story justifies and legitimates that disrespect at every level, from imagining that a dog welcomes every human touch to the notion that it is the *raison d'être* of a dog to be loved by, or to work for, or to be friends with, or to play with, or to simply *be*, with humans.

Humans create dependencies in dogs, and then use dogs' species story to claim those dependencies as an intrinsic, evolutionary characteristic of dogs. This story, as I have tried to demonstrate in this book, is in fact a prescription for 'normal' dog behaviour, a prescription to which individual dogs frequently object. For me, therefore, the first step toward the reconstruction of human relations with domesticated dogs would be to recognise – in theory and especially in practice, in our hearts and in our houses (and on the street, and in the workplace, and in kennels and shelters, and in every place where dogs are found) – that these prescribed behaviours are what humans demand of dogs, and not the inherent property of each and every member of the species *Canis familiaris*. The first and foremost gesture of 'dispossession' is thus the dispossession of this story of 'the dog', which judges every individual dog by how well they play their part in it. It is not that we who love dogs should not love them. Only, that we might love dogs differently.

Notes

1 The biologist Scott Gilbert, who is closely associated with these developments, has been especially good at drawing out the implications of his work for philosophy. It is interesting to note that, as well as a Ph.D. in biology, Gilbert has an M.A. in the history of science.

2 All animals are part of such holobiontic associations, because '[t]here are no germ-free animals in nature' (Gilbert *et al.* 2015: 612).
3 Lichen, as Peter Godfrey-Smith notes, are a 'classic example' of symbiosis, being 'associations between fungi and various kinds of green algae' (Godfrey-Smith 2009: 73): 'the fungi reproduce, the algae reproduce, and the lichen does as well' (75).
4 This notion of an individual, as a specific mode of unification of and abstraction from becomings/relationality, is not entirely dissimilar to Vinciane Despret's concept of an agent as the product of a rapport of forces (see Chapter 5 in this book). The difference for me is the important role played by potentiality, which ensures that the unification of the subject/agent is not reducible to any particular spatio-temporal assemblage (Fraser 2006).
5 Whitehead writes: '[t]here are not "the concrescence" and "the novel thing": when we analyse the novel thing we find nothing but the concrescence' (Whitehead 1985: 211).
6 How is compliance to an order of becoming achieved? '[T]here is a memory', Whitehead writes, 'of the antecedent life-history of its [the event's] own dominant pattern, as having formed an element of value in its own antecedent environment' (Whitehead 1985: 131). That value not only inheres in an entity's 'specious present' (131), it also reaches out to its future. '[T]he uniformity along the historic route increases the degree of conformity which that route exacts from the future' (Whitehead 1985: 56; on the immanence of the future, see Whitehead (1967): Chapter 12). Which means: a history of conformity to conformity is itself an accrued and accruing value, making conformity cumulatively more difficult to overturn.
7 Except, as I have explored at various points throughout this book, insofar as an animal departs from species norms. But as Buller notes in his discussion of 'mass' farm animals, the becoming 'visible and identifiable' as an individual, by way of such departure, also often signals an animal's 'undoing': '[t]heir moment of singularity is also that of their culling' (Buller 2013: 156).

References

Abramson, Charles I. (2009) 'A study in inspiration: Charles Henry Turner (1867–1923) and the investigation of insect behavior', *Annual Review of Entomology* 54: 343–359.

Ainsworth, Thomas Ross (2020) 'Form vs matter', in *Stanford Encyclopedia of Philosophy*. Available at https://plato.stanford.edu/entries/form-matter/ (accessed October 2021).

Alexander, Melissa (2006) 'The myth of "purely positive"', *Karen Pryor Clicker Training*. Available at www.clickertraining.com/node/988 (accessed August 2022).

Allen, Colin and Bekoff, Marc (1999) *Species of Mind: The Philosophy and Biology of Cognitive Ethology*. Cambridge, MA: MIT Press.

Anderson, Virginia DeJohn (2004) *Creatures of Empire: How Domestic Animals Transformed Early America*. Oxford: Oxford University Press.

Armbruster, Karla (2019) 'Dogs, dirt, and public space', in J. Sorenson and A. Matsuoka (eds), *Dog's Best Friend? Rethinking Canid–Human Relationships*. Chicago and London: McGill-Queen's University Press, pp. 113–134.

Arnet, Evan (2019) 'Conwy Lloyd Morgan, methodology, and the origins of comparative psychology', *Journal of the History of Biology* 52: 433–461.

Baratay, Éric (2015) 'Building an *animal* history', trans. Stephanie Posthumus, in Louisa Mackenzie and Stephanie Posthumus (eds), *French Thinking about Animals*. East Lansing: Michigan State University Press, pp. 3–14.

Baratay, Éric (2022) *Animal Biographies: Towards a History of Individuals*. Trans. Lindsay Turner. Athens: University of Georgia Press.

Bates, Lucy A. and Byrne, Richard W. (2007) 'Creative or created: Using anecdotes to investigate animal cognition', *Methods* 42(1): 12–21.

Battaglia, Carmen L. (2009) 'Periods of early development and the effects of stimulation and social experiences in the canine', *Journal of Veterinary Behaviour* 4: 203–210.

BBC [British Broadcasting Corporation] (2021) 'Households "buy 3.2 million pets in lockdown"', 12 March. Available at www.bbc.co.uk/news/business-56362987 (accessed August 2022).
BBC [British Broadcasting Corporation] (2022) 'Pug health so poor it "can't be considered a typical dog" – study'. Available at www.bbc.co.uk/news/newsbeat-61494094 (accessed August 2022).
Beer, Colin (2020) 'Niko Tinbergen and questions of instinct', *Animal Behaviour* 164: 261–265.
Bekoff, Marc (2003) *Minding Animals: Awareness, Emotions, and Heart*. Oxford: Oxford University Press.
Bekoff, Marc (2007) *The Emotional Lives of Animals*. Novato, CA: New World Library.
Bekoff, Marc (2018) *Canine Confidential: Why Dogs Do What They Do*. Chicago: Chicago University Press.
Bekoff, Marc and Jamieson, Dale (1992) 'On the aims and methods of cognitive ethology', in *PSA: Proceedings of the Biennial Meeting of the Philosophy of Science Association*, Vol. II, *Symposia and Invited Papers*. Chicago: Chicago University Press, pp. 110–124.
Bekoff, Marc and Pierce, Jessica (2019) *Unleashing Your Dog: A Field Guide to Giving Your Canine Companion the Best Life Possible*. Novato, CA: New World Library.
Benvegnú, Damiano (2018) *Animals and Animality in Primo Levi's Work*. London: Palgrave Macmillan.
Berger, John (2009) *Why Look at Animals?* London: Penguin.
Bernasconi, Robert (2007) 'Black skin, white skulls: The nineteenth century debate over the racial identity of the ancient Egyptians', *Parallax* 13(2): 6–20.
Berns, Gregory S., Brooks, Andrew M., Spivak, Mark and Levy, Kerinne (2017) 'Functional MRI in awake unrestrained dogs predicts suitability for assistance work', *Scientific Reports* 7(1): 43704.
Berns, Gregory S., Brooks, Andrew M. and Spivak, Mark (2012) 'Functional MRI in awake unrestrained dogs', *PLoS ONE* 7(5), e38027: 1–7.
Besky, Sarah and Blanchette, Alex (2019) 'The fragility of work', in S. Besky and A. Blanchette (eds), *How Nature Works: Rethinking Labor on a Troubled Planet*. Sante Fe: School for Advanced Research Press, pp. 1–22.
Birke, Lynda (2009) 'Naming names – or, what's in it for the animals?', *Humanimalia* 1(1): 1–7.
Blattner, Charlotte (2020) 'Animal labour: Toward a prohibition of forced labour and a right to freely choose one's own work', in C. E. Blattner, K. Coulter and W. Kymlicka (eds), *Animal Labour: A New Frontier of Interspecies Justice?* Oxford: Oxford University Press, pp. 91–115.
Blattner, Charlotte (2021) 'Turning to animal agency in the Anthropocene', in B. Bovenkerk and J. Keulartz (eds), *Animals in Our Midst: The Challenges of Co-Existing with Animals in the Anthropocene*. International Library

of Environmental, Agricultural and Food Ethics 33. Cham: Springer, pp. 65–78.

Blattner, Charlotte, Couter, Kendra and Kymlicka, Will (2020) 'Animal labour and the question for interspecies justice', in C. E. Blattner, K. Coulter and W. Kymlicka (eds), *Animal Labour: A New Frontier of Interspecies Justice?* Oxford: Oxford University Press, pp. 1–25.

Boakes, Robert (2008) *From Darwin to Behaviourism: Psychology and the Minds of Animals.* Cambridge: Cambridge University Press.

Boardman, Holly and Farnworth, Mark (2022) 'Changes to adult dog social behaviour during and after COVID-19 lockdowns in England: A qualitative analysis of owner perception', *Animals* 12: 1682.

Boisseron, Bénédicte (2018) *Afro-Dog: Blackness and the Animal Question.* New York: Columbia University Press.

Boitani, Luigi, Francisci, Francesco, Ciucci, Paolo and Andreoli, Giorgio (2017) 'The ecology and behavior of feral dogs: A case study from central Italy', in J. Serpell (ed.), *The Domestic Dog: Its Evolution, Behavior and Interactions with People.* Cambridge: Cambridge University Press, pp. 342–368.

Bonanni, Roberto and Cafazzo, Simona (2014) 'The social organisation of a population of free-ranging dogs in a suburban area of Rome: A reassessment of the effects of domestication on dogs' behaviour', in J. Kaminski and S. Marshall-Pescini (eds), *The Social Dog: Behavior and Cognition.* San Diego: Elsevier, pp. 65–104.

Boxall, Jackie, Heath, Sarah, Bate, Simon and Brautigam, John (2004) 'Modern concepts of socialisation for dogs: Implications for their behaviour, welfare and use in scientific procedures', *Altern Lab Animals* 32(2): 81–93.

Brace, Loring C. (1974) 'The "ethnology" of Josiah Clark Nott', in *Bulletin of the New York Academy of Medicine* 50(4): 509–527.

Bradshaw, Gay A. (2009) *Elephants on the Edge: What Animals Teach Us about Humanity.* New Haven and London: Yale University Press.

Bradshaw, Gay A. (2010) 'An ape among many: Animal co-authorship and trans-species epistemic authority', *Configurations* 18(1–2): 15–20.

Bradshaw, John (2012) *In Defence of Dogs: Why Dogs Need Our Understanding.* London: Penguin.

Bradshaw, John and Rooney, Nicola (2017) 'Dog social behaviour and communication', in J. Serpell (ed.), *The Domestic Dog: Its Evolution, Behavior and Interactions with People.* 2nd edn. Cambridge: Cambridge University Press, pp. 133–159.

Brand, Claire, O'Neill, Dan, Belshaw, Zoe et al. (2022) 'Pandemic puppies: Demographic characteristics, health and early life experiences of puppies acquired during the 2020 phase of the COVID-19 pandemic in the UK', *Animals* 12: 629.

Braude, Stan and Gladman, Justin (2013) 'Out of Asia: An allopatric model for the evolution of the domestic dog', *ISRN Zoology*, 841734.

Buchanan, Brett (2008) *Onto-Ethologies: The Animal Environments of Uexkull, Heidegger, Merleau-Ponty, and Deleuze*. New York: SUNY.
Buchanan, Brett (2015) 'The metamorphoses of Vinciane Despret', *Angelaki* 20(2): 17–32.
Buchanan, Brett, Bussolini, Jeffrey and Chrulew, Matthew (2014) 'General introduction: Philosophical ethology', *Angelaki* 19(3): 1–3.
Budiansky, Stephen (1992) *The Covenant of the Wild: Why Animals Chose Domestication*. New York: William Morrow.
Budiansky, Stephen (2001) *The Truth about Dogs: The Ancestry, Social Conventions, Mental Habits and Moral Fibre of 'Canis familiaris'*. London: Weidenfeld and Nicolson.
Buller, H. (2013) 'Individuation, the mass and farm animals', *Theory, Culture and Society* 30(7–8): 155–175.
Burghardt, Gordon M. (1985) 'Animal awareness: Current perceptions and historical perspectives', *American Psychologist* 40(8): 905–919.
Burkhardt, Richard W. (2005) *Patterns of Behavior: Konrad Lorenz, Niko Tinbergen, and the Founding of Ethology*. Chicago: Chicago University Press.
Bussolini, Jeffrey (2013) 'Recent French, Belgian and Italian work in the cognitive science of animals: Dominique Lestel, Vinciane Despret, Roberto Marchesini and Giorgio Celli', *Social Science Information* 52(2): 187–209.
BVA [British Veterinary Association] (2023) 'Extreme conformation'. Available at www.bva.co.uk/take-action/our-policies/extreme-conformation/ (accessed February 2022).
BWG [Brachycephalic Working Group] (2022) 'UK Brachycephalic Working Group – Strategy 2022–2025'. Available at www.ukbwg.org.uk/wp-content/uploads/2022/08/UK-BWG-strategy-2022–220822–1.pdf (accessed August 2022).
Byrne, Richard W. (1997) 'What's the use of anecdotes?', in R. Mitchell, N. S. Thompson and H. L. Miles (eds), *Anthropomorphism, Anecdotes, and Animals*. New York: SUNY, pp. 134–150.
Case, Linda P. (2022) *Feeding Smart with the Science Dog*. Mahomet, IL: AutumnGold.
Casey, Rebecca A., Naj-Oleari, Maria, Campbell et al. (2021) 'Dogs are more pessimistic if their owners use two or more aversive techniques', *Nature Scientific Reports* 11: 19023.
Cassidy, Rebecca and Mullin, Molly (eds) (2007) *Where the Wild Things Are Now: Domestication Reconsidered*. Oxford: Berg.
Castle, Julie (2019) 'Vicktory dog Curly passes away at age 13, less than two months after his best friend, Mya', Best Friends Sanctuary. Available at https://tinyurl.com/3us6s5hs (accessed October 2022).
Castle, Julie (2021) 'The last surviving "Vicktory dog"', Best Friends Sanctuary. Available at https://tinyurl.com/7ky53em3 (accessed October 2022).

Chaplin, Joyce E. (2003) *Subject Matter: Technology, the Body, and Science on the Anglo-American Frontier 1500–1676*. Cambridge, MA: Harvard University Press.

Charles, Nickie, Fox, Rebekah, Smith, Harriet and Miele, Mara (2021) '"Fulfilling your dog's potential": Changing dimensions of power in training cultures in the UK', *Animal Studies Journal* 10(2): 169–200.

Charmantier, Isabelle (2020) 'Linnaeus and race', Linnean Society of London. Available at https://tinyurl.com/5y6ph656 (accessed October 2021).

Chidester, David (2009) 'Darwin's dogs: Animals, animism, and the problem of religion', in *Soundings: An Interdisciplinary Journal* 92(1–2): 51–75.

Chrulew, Matthew (2018) 'My place, my duty: Zoo biology as field philosophy in the work of Heini Hediger', *Parallax* 24(4): 480–500.

Cladland, Douglas K. (1993) *Feral Children and Clever Animals: Reflections on Human Nature*. Oxford: Oxford University Press.

Clark, Nigel (2007) 'Animal interface: The generosity of domestication', in R. Cassidy and M. Mullin (eds), *Where the Wild Things Are Now: Domestication Reconsidered*. Oxford: Berg, pp. 49–70.

Clothier, Suzanne (2005) *If Dog's Prayers Were Answered ... Bones Would Rain from the Sky: Deepening Our Relationships with Dogs*. New York: Grand Central.

Clothier, Suzanne (2018) *Arousal, Anxiety and Fear: Empathy, Understanding, and Options for Anxious or Fearful Dogs*. Available at https://vimeo.com/ondemand/arousalanxietyfear (accessed February 2022).

Clutton-Brock, Juliet (2017) 'Origins of the dog: The archaeological evidence', in J. Serpell (ed.), *The Domestic Dog: Its Evolution, Behavior and Interactions with People*. 2nd edn. Cambridge: Cambridge University Press, pp. 7–21.

Collier, Stephen (2006) 'Breed-specific legislation and the pit bull terrier: Are the laws justified?', *Journal of Veterinary Behavior* 1: 17–22.

Collinson, Abi, Brennan, Marnie, Dean, Rachel and Stavisky, Jenny (2021) 'Priorities for research into the impact of canine surgical sterilisation programmes for free-roaming dogs: An international priority setting partnership', *Animals* 11(8): 2250.

Cook, Peter F., Prichard, Ashley, Spivak, Mark and Berns, Gregory S. (2016) 'Awake canine fMRI predicts dogs' preference for praise vs food', *Social Cognitive and Affective Neuroscience* 11(12): 1853–1862.

Coppinger, Raymond and Coppinger, Lorna (2001) *Dogs: A Startling New Understanding of Canine Origin, Behavior and Evolution*. New York: Scribner.

Coppinger, Raymond and Coppinger, Lorna (2016) *What Is a Dog?* Chicago: University of Chicago Press.

Coren, Stanley (2006) *The Intelligence of Dogs: A Guide to the Thoughts, Emotions, and Inner Lives of Our Canine Companions*. New York: Free Press.

Coulter, Kendra (2016) *Animals, Work, and the Promise of Interspecies Solidarity*. London: Palgrave Macmillan.
Coulter, Kendra (2020) 'Toward humane jobs and work-lives for animals', in C. E. Blattner, K. Coulter and W. Kymlicka (eds), *Animal Labour: A New Frontier of Interspecies Justice?* Oxford: Oxford University Press, pp. 29–47.
Crist, Eileen (2000) *Images of Animals: Anthropomorphism and Animal Mind*. Philadelphia: Temple University Press.
Crist, Eileen (2013) 'On the poverty of our nomenclature', *Environmental Humanities* 13(1): 129–147.
D'Souza, Renée, Hovorka, Alice and Neil, Lee (2020) 'Conservation canines: Exploring dog roles, circumstances, and welfare status', in C. E. Blattner, K. Coulter and W. Kymlicka (eds), *Animal Labour: A New Frontier of Interspecies Justice?* Oxford: Oxford University Press, pp. 65–87.
Darwin, Charles (1981) *The Descent of Man, and Selection in Relation to Sex*. Princeton: Princeton University Press.
Darwin, Charles (2008) *On the Origin of Species*. Ed. Gillian Beer. Oxford: Oxford University Press.
Darwin, Frances (ed.) (2009) *The Life and Letters of Charles Darwin*, Vol. I. Cambridge: Cambridge University Press.
Davies, Gail (2012) 'Caring for the multitude and the multiple: Assembling animal welfare and enabling ethical critique', *Environment and Planning D: Society and Space* 30(4): 623–638.
Davis, Barney (2021) 'Police dog "lucky to be alive" after being stabbed five times', *Evening Standard*, 2 June. Available at https://tinyurl.com/3hpsecen (accessed June 2021).
Day, Matthew (2008) 'Godless savages and superstitious dogs: Charles Darwin, imperial ethnography, and the problem of human uniqueness', *Journal of the History of Ideas* 69(1): 49–70.
Dayan, Colin (2016) *With Dogs at the Edge of Life*. New York: Columbia University Press.
De Waal, Frans (2019) *Mama's Last Hug: Animal Emotions and What They Teach Us about Ourselves*. London: Granta.
DEFRA [Department for Environment, Food and Rural Affairs] (2009) *Dangerous Dogs Law: Guidance for Enforcers*. London: Crown.
Deleuze, Gilles (1988) *Spinoza: Practical Philosophy*. Trans. Robert Hurley. San Francisco: City Light Books.
Deleuze, Gilles and Guattari, Felix (1987) *A Thousand Plateus: Capitalism and Schizophrenia*. Minneapolis: University of Minnesota Press.
Delon, Nicolas (2020) 'The meaning of animal labour', in C. E. Blattner, K. Coulter and W. Kymlicka (eds), *Animal Labour: A New Frontier of Interspecies Justice?* Oxford: Oxford University Press, pp. 160–180.
Derrida, Jacques (2008) *The Animal that Therefore I Am (More to Follow)*. Ed. Marie-Louise Mallet, trans. David Wills. New York: Fordham University Press.

Descola, Philippe (2014) 'All too human (still): A comment on Eduardo Kohn's *How Forests Think*', *HAU: Journal of Ethnographic Theory* 4(2): 267–273.
Desmond, Adrian and Moore, James (2009) *Darwin's Sacred Cause: Race, Slavery, and the Quest for Human Origins*. London: Penguin.
Despret, Vinciane (2008) 'The becomings of subjectivity in animal worlds', *Subjectivity* 23: 123–139.
Despret, Vinciane (2013) 'From secret agents to interagency', *History and Theory* 52: 29–44.
Despret, Vinciane (2015a) 'The enigma of the raven', *Angelaki* 20(2): 57–72.
Despret, Vinciane (2015b) 'Why "I had not read Derrida": Often too close, always too far away', in L. Mackenzie and S. Posthumus (eds), *French Thinking about Animals*. East Lansing: Michigan State University Press, pp. 91–104.
Despret, Vinciane (2016) *What Would Animals Say if We Asked the Right Questions?* Minneapolis and London: University of Minnesota Press.
Despret, Vinciane (2017) 'It is an entire world that has disappeared', in D. B. Rose, T. van Dooren and M. Chrulew (eds), *Extinction Studies: Stories of Time, Death and Generations*. New York: Columbia University Press, pp. 217–222.
Dickson, David (2009) 'Former fighting dog's legacy', Best Friends Santuary. Available at https://tinyurl.com/2xc9afjy (accessed November 2021).
Dietz, Lisa, Arnold, Anne-Marie, Goerlich-Jansson, Vivian and Vinke, Claudia M. (2018) 'The importance of early life experiences for the development of behavioural disorders in domestic dogs', *Behaviour* 155: 83–114.
Dinwoodie, Ian, Dwyer, Barbara, Zottola *et al.* (2019) 'Demographics and comorbidity of behavior problems in dogs', *Journal of Veterinary Behavior* 32: 62–71.
Doble, Josh (2020) 'Can dogs be racist? The colonial legacies of racialized dogs in Kenya and Zimbabwe', *History Workshop Journal* 89: 68–89.
Dona, Hiruni Samadi Galpayage and Chittka, Lars (2020) 'Charles H. Turner: Pioneer in animal cognition', *Science* 370(6516): 530–531.
Donaldson, Brianne (2013) 'Bad with names: Replacing "animal" with Whitehead's insistent particularity of bodies', *Process Studies* 42(2): 181–199.
Donaldson, Jean (2002) *Mine! A Practical Guide to Resource Guarding in Dogs*. Brentwood, CA: Academy for Dog Trainers.
Dugnoille, Julien (2018) 'To eat or not to eat: Symbolic value of dog meat and human–dog companionship in contemporary South Korea', *Food, Culture and Society* 21(2): 214–232.
Durston, Tamsin (2022) *Emotional Well-Being for Animal Professionals*. Wallingford: CABI.
Duster, Troy (2015) 'A post-genomic surprise: The molecular reinscription of race in science, law and medicine', *British Journal of Sociology* 66(1): 1–27.

Eisen, Jessica (2020) 'Down on the farm: Status, exploitation, and agricultural exceptionalism', in C. E. Blattner, K. Coulter and W. Kymlicka (eds), *Animal Labour: A New Frontier of Interspecies Justice?* Oxford: Oxford University Press, pp. 139–159.

Ereshefsky, Marc (2017) 'Species', in *Stanford Encyclopedia of Philosophy*. Available at https://plato.stanford.edu/entries/species/ (accessed October 2021).

Erikson, Paul A. (1986) 'The anthropology of Josiah Clark Nott', *KAS Papers* 65–66: 103–120.

Feller, David A. (2009) 'Dog-fight: Darwin as an animal advocate in the anti-vivisection controversy of 1875', *Studies in History and Philosophy of Biological and Biomedical Sciences* 40: 265–271.

Feuerbacher, Erica and Wynne, Clive D. L. (2011) 'A history of dogs as subjects in North American experimental psychological research', *Comparative Cognition and Behavior Reviews* 6: 46–71.

Fijn, Natasha (2018) 'Dog ears and tails: Differential ways of being with canines in Aboriginal Australia and Mongolia', in H. A. Swanson, M. E. Lien and G. B. Ween (eds), *Domestication Gone Wild: Politics and Practices of Multispecies Relations*. Durham, NH: Duke University Press.

Foucault, Michel (2003) *Society Must Be Defended: Lectures at the Collège de France 1975–1976*. Ed. Mauro Bertani and Arnold I. Davidson, trans. David Macey. New York: Picador.

Foucault, Michel (2009) *Security, Territory, Population: Lectures at the Collège de France 1977–1978*. Ed. Michel Snellart, trans. Graham Burchell. New York: Palgrave Macmillan.

Francione, Gary (2010) 'The abolition of animal exploitation', in G. Francione and R. Garner, *The Animal Rights Debate: Abolition or Regulation?* New York: Columbia University Press.

Francione, Gary and Charlton, Anna (2015) *Animal Rights: The Abolitionist Approach*. Logan, UT: Exempla Press.

Frantz, Laurent A. F. and Larson, Greger (2020) 'A genetic perspective on the domestication continuum', in C. Stépanoff and J.-D. Vigne (eds), *Hybrid Communities: Biosocial Approaches to Domestication and Other Trans-Species Relationships*. London: Routledge, pp. 23–38.

Fraser, Mariam (2006) 'The ethics of reality and virtual reality: Latour, facts and values', *History of the Human Sciences* 19(2): 45–72.

Freedman, Adam and Wayne, Robert (2017) 'Deciphering the origins of dogs: From fossils to genomes', *Annual Review of Animal Biosciences* 5: 281–307.

Freedman, Adam H., Gronau, Ilan, Schweizer, Rena M. *et al.* (2014) 'Genomic sequencing highlights the dynamic early history of dogs', *PLOS Genetics* 10(1): 1–12.

Fudge, Erica (2002) *Animal*. London: Reaktion Books.

Fudge, Erica (2004) 'Animal lives', *History Today* 54(10): 21–26.

Fugazza, Claudia and Miklósi, Ádám (2014) 'Measuring the behaviour of dogs: An ethological approach', in A. Horowitz (ed.), *Domestic Dog*

Cognition and Behaviour: The Scientific Study of 'Canis familiaris'. Heidelberg: Springer, pp. 176–200.

Fujimura, Joan H. and Rajagopalan, Ramya (2011) 'Different differences: The use of "genetic ancestry" versus race in biomedical human genetic research', *Social Studies of Science* 41(1): 5–30.

Futuyma, Douglas J. (1986) *Evolutionary Biology*. 2nd edn. Sunderland, MA: Sinauer.

Gannett, Lisa (2013) 'Theodosius Dobzhansky and the genetic race concept', *Studies in History and Philosophy of Biological and Biomedical Sciences* 44: 250–261.

Gantt, W. Horsley (1962) 'Factors involved in the development of pathological behavior: Schizokinesis and autokinesis', *Perspectives in Biology and Medicine* 5(4): 473–482.

Ghiselin, Michael T. (1987) 'Species concepts, individuality, and objectivity', *Biology and Philosophy* 2: 127–143.

Giambalvo, Emily (2019) 'The story behind the story of Michael Vick's dogs', *Washington Post*, 24 September. Available at www.washingtonpost.com/sports/2019/09/24/story-behind-story-michael-vicks-dogs/ (accessed August 2023).

Gilbert, Scott F., Bosch, Thomas C. G. and Ledón-Rettig, Cristina (2015) 'Eco-evo-devo: Developmental symbiosis and developmental plasticity as evolutionary agents', *Nature Reviews Genetics* 16: 611–622.

Gilbert, Scott F., Sapp, Jan and Tauber, Alfred I. (2012) 'A symbiotic view of life: We have never been individuals', *Quarterly Review of Biology* 87(4): 325–341.

Giraud, Eva and Hollin, Gregory (2016) 'Care, laboratory beagles and affective utopia', *Theory, Culture and Society* 33(4): 27–49.

Giraud, Eva and Hollin, Gregory (2017) 'Laboratory beagles and affective co-productions of knowledge', in M. Bastion, O. Jones, N. Moore and E. Roe (eds), *Participatory Research in More-than-Human Worlds*. London: Routledge, pp. 163–177.

Godfrey-Smith, Peter (2009) *Darwinian Populations and Natural Selection*. Oxford: Oxford University Press.

Godfrey-Smith, Peter (2016) *Other Minds: The Octopus and the Evolution of Intelligent Life*. London: HarperCollins.

Gould, Stephen J. (1996) *The Mismeasure of Man*. New York: W. W. Norton.

Greenhough, Beth and Roe, Emma (2019) 'Attuning to laboratory animals and telling stories: Learning animal geography research skills from animal technicians', *EPD Society and Space* 37(2): 367–384.

Griffin, Donald (1994a) *Animal Minds*. Chicago: University of Chicago Press.

Griffin, Donald (1994b) *The Question of Animal Awareness: Evolutionary Continuity of Mental Experience*. New York: Rockefeller University Press.

Gross, Charles G. (2005) 'Donald R. Griffin', in National Academy of Sciences, *Biographical Memoirs*, Vol. LXXXVI. Washington, DC: National Academies Press, pp. 188–206.

Guenther, Katja M. (2020) *The Lives and Deaths of Shelter Animals*. Stanford: Stanford University Press.

Guenther, Katja M. (2019) '"Taking the ghetto out of the dog": Reproducing inequality in pit bull rescue', *Ethnic and Racial Studies* 43(10): 1795–1812.

Gris, Silja, Riemer, Stefanie, Warembourg, Charlotte and Sousa, Filipe M. M. A. (2021) 'If they could choose: How would dogs spend their days? Activity patterns in four populations of domestic dogs', *Applied Animal Behaviour Science* 243: 1–11.

Grosz, Elizabeth (2004) *The Nick of Time: Politics, Evolution and the Untimely*. Sydney: Allen and Unwin.

Harari, Yuval N. (2011) *Sapiens: A Brief History of Humankind*. London: Vintage.

Haraway, Donna (1991) *Simians, Cyborgs and Women: The Reinvention of Nature*. London: Routledge.

Haraway, Donna (1997) *Modest_Witness@Second_Millenium.FemaleMan©_Meets_OncoMouse Feminism and Technoscience*. New York: Routledge.

Haraway, Donna (2003) *Companion Species Manifesto*. Chicago: Prickly Paradigm Press.

Haraway, Donna (2008) *When Species Meet*. London and Minneapolis: University of Minnesota Press.

Haraway, Donna (2016) *Staying with the Trouble: Making Kin in Chthulucene*. Durham, NH: Duke University Press.

Hare, Brian, Brown, Michelle, Williamson, Christina and Tomasello, Michael (2002) 'The domestication of social cognition in dogs', *Science* 298: 1634–1636.

Hare, Brian and Tomasello, Michael (2005) 'Human-like social skills in dogs?', *Trends in Cognitive Sciences* 9(9): 439–444.

Hare, Brian and Woods, Vanessa (2020a) *The Genius of Dogs: Discovering the Unique Intelligence of Man's Best Friend*. London: Oneworld.

Hare, Brian and Woods, Vanessa (2020b) *Survival of the Friendliest: Understanding Our Origins and Rediscovering Our Common Humanity*. New York: Random House.

Harmon, Kelli (2013) 'Vicktory dog Georgia says goodbye', Best Friends Sanctuary. Available at https://tinyurl.com/5n7uf4uz (accessed November 2021).

Hayward, Jessica J., Castelhano, Marta G., Oliveira, Kyle C. et al. (2016) 'Complex disease and phenotype mapping in the domestic dog', *Nature Communications* 7: 10460.

Hearne, Vicki (1991) 'What's wrong with animal rights: Of hounds, horses, and Jeffersonian happiness', *Harper's Magazine*, September: 59–64.

Hearne, Vicki (1993) 'Oyez à Beaumont', *Raritan* 13(2): 1–6.

Hearne, Vicki (2007a) *Adam's Task: Calling Animals by Name*. La Vergne: Skyhorse.

Hearne, Vicki (2007b) *Bandit: The Heart-Warming True Story of One Dog's Rescue from Death Row*. La Vergne: Skyhorse.

Heise, Ursula (2010) 'Lost dogs, last birds, and listed species: Cultures of extinction', *Configurations* 18: 49–72.
Held, Richard (1956) Review of Bertram Schaffner (ed.), *Group Processes: Transactions of the First Conference* (New York: Josiah Macy Jr Foundation, 1955), *American Journal of Psychology* 69(4): 690–692.
Hobson-West, Pru and Jutel, Annemarie (2020) 'Animals, veterinarians and the sociology of diagnosis', *Sociology of Health and Illness* 42(2): 393–406.
Hollin, Gregory, Forsyth, Isla, Giraud, Eva and Potts, Tracey (2017) '(Dis) entangling Barad: Materialisms and ethics', *Social Studies of Science* 47(6): 918–941.
Horowitz, Alexandra (2012) *Inside of a Dog: What Dogs See, Smell, and Know*. London: Simon and Schuster.
Horowitz, Alexandra (2014a) '*Canis familiaris*: Companion and captive', in L. Gruen (ed.), *The Ethics of Captivity*. Oxford: Oxford University Press, pp. 7–21.
Horowitz, Alexandra (ed.) (2014b) *Domestic Dog Cognition and Behaviour: The Scientific Study of 'Canis familiaris'*. Heidelberg: Springer.
Horowitz, Alexandra (2017) 'Smelling themselves: Dogs investigate their own odours longer when modified in an "olfactory mirror" test', *Behavioural Processes* 143: 17–24.
Horowitz, Alexandra (2019) *Our Dogs, Ourselves: The Story of a Unique Bond*. New York: Simon and Schuster.
Hovenac, Caroline (2018) *Animal Subjects: Literature, Zoology, and British Modernism*. Cambridge: Cambridge University Press.
Hubrecht, Robert, Wickens, Stephen and Kirkwood, James (2017) 'The welfare of dogs in human care', in J. Serpell (ed.), *The Domestic Dog: Its Evolution, Behavior, and Interactions with People*. 2nd edn. Cambridge: Cambridge University Press, pp. 271–299.
ICRC [International Committee of the Red Cross] (2022) 'No trace of you campaign: Families of missing migrants need to know', 25 August. Available at www.icrc.org/en/document/no-trace-you-missing-migrants (accessed October 2022).
Ingold, Tim (2013) 'Anthropology beyond humanity', *Suomen antropologi: Journal of the Finnish Anthropological Society* 38(3): 5–23.
Jackson, Zakiyyah Iman (2020) *Becoming Human: Matter and Meaning in an Antiblack World*. New York: New York University Press.
Jokinen, Olli, Appleby, David, Sandbacka-Saxén, Sofi et al. (2017) 'Homing age influences the prevalence of aggressive and avoidance-related behaviour in adult dogs', *Applied Animal Behavior* 195: 87–92.
Kalikow, Theodora J. (2020) 'Konrad Lorenz on human degeneration and social decline: A chronic preoccupation', *Animal Biology* 164: 267–272.
Kennel Club (2018) 'How our instant gratification culture is putting puppies at risk'. Available at https://tinyurl.com/2s8j6rbj (accessed August 2022).

Kennel Club (2021) 'Puppy farmers "exploiting confusion around pandemic restrictions", dog experts warn', 26 April. Available at https://tinyurl.com/2vpm75bn (accessed August 2022).

Kete, Kathleen (1994) *The Beast in the Boudoir: Petkeeping in Nineteenth-Century Paris*. Oakland: University of California Press.

Kim, Claire J. (2015) *Dangerous Crossings: Races, Species, and Nature in a Multicultural Age*. Cambridge: Cambridge University Press.

Kirksey, Eben (2015) 'Species: A praxiographic study', *Journal of the Royal Anthropological Institute* 21: 758–780.

Knoll, Elizabeth (1997) 'Dogs, Darwinism, and English sensibilities', in R. W. Mitchell, N. S. Thompson and H. Lyn Miles (eds), *Anthropomorphism, Anecdotes and Animals*. New York: SUNY, pp. 12–21.

Kohn, Eduardo (2013) *How Forests Think: Toward an Anthropology beyond the Human*. Berkeley and London: University of California Press.

Kubinyi, Enikő, Sasvári-Székely, Mária and Miklósi, Ádám (2011) '"Genetics and the social behavior of the dog" revisited: Searching for genes relating to personality in dogs', in M. Inoue-Murayama, S. Kawamura and A. Weiss (eds), *From Genes to Animal Behavior: Social Structures, Personalities, Communication by Color*. New York: Springer, pp. 255–274.

Latour, Bruno (1993) *We Have Never Been Modern*. Cambridge, MA: Harvard University Press.

Latour, Bruno (2005) 'What is given in experience? A review of Isabelle Stengers' *Penser avec Whitehead*', *Boundary 2: An International Journal of Literature and Culture* 32(1): 223–237.

Leach, Helen (2003) 'Human domestication reconsidered', *Current Anthropology* 44(3): 349–368.

Lehrman, Daniel S. (1953) 'A critique of Konrad Lorenz's theory of instinctive behavior', *Quarterly Review of Biology* 28(4): 337–363.

Lescureux, Nicolas (2020) 'Beyond wild and domestic: Human complex relationships with dogs, wolves, and wolf-dog hybrids', in C. Stépanoff and J.-D. Vigne (eds), *Hybrid Communities: Biosocial Approaches to Domestication and Other Trans-Species Relationships*. London and New York: Routledge, pp. 65–80.

Lestel, Dominique (2011) 'What capabilities for the animal?', *Biosemiotics* 4: 83–102.

Lestel, Dominique, Brunois, Florence and Guanet, Florence (2006) 'Etho-ethnology and ethno-ethology', *Social Science Information* 45: 155–177.

Lewontin, Richard C. (2006) 'Confusions about human races', *Social Science Research Council*. Available at http://raceandgenomics.ssrc.org/Lewontin/ (accessed March 2021).

Lindblad-Toh, Kerstin (2012) 'Canine genomics', in Elaine Ostrander and Anatoly Ruvinsky (eds), *The Genetics of the Dog*. 2nd edn. Cambridge, MA: CABI, pp. 255–274.

Lindblad-Toh, Kerstin, Wade, Clare M., Mikkelsen, Tarjei S. *et al.* (2005) 'Genome sequence, comparative analysis and haplotype structure of the domestic dog', *Nature* 438: 803–19.

Lindsay, Steven R. (2000) *Handbook of Applied Dog Behavior and Training*, Vol. I, *Adaption and Learning*. Iowa: Iowa State University Press.

Lindsay, Steven R. (2001) *Handbook of Applied Dog Behavior and Training*, Vol. II, *Etiology and Assessment of Behavior Problems*. Iowa: Iowa State University Press.

Livingston, Julie and Puar, Jasbir K. (2011) 'Interspecies', *Social Text 106* 29(1): 1–14.

Lo, Selina and Horton, Richard (2015) 'Everyone counts, so count everyone', *The Lancet*, Comment, 11 May.

London, Karen and McConnell, Patricia (2008) *Play Together, Stay Together: Healthy and Happy Play between People and Dogs*. Washington: DogWise.

Lorenz, Konrad (1950) 'The comparative method in studying innate behavior patterns', *Symposia for the Study of Experimental Biology* 4: 221–254.

Lorenz, Konrad (1970 [1937]) 'The establishment of the instinct concept', in *Konrad Lorenz: Studies in Animal and Human Behaviour*, Vol. I, London: Methuen, pp. 259–315.

Lorenz, Konrad (1970 [1942]) 'Inductive and teleological psychology', in *Konrad Lorenz: Sudies in Animal and Human Behaviour*, Vol. I, London: Methuen, pp. 351–370.

Lorenz, Konrad (2002a [1949]) *King Solomon's Ring*. London: Routledge.

Lorenz, Konrad (2002b [1949]) *Man Meets Dog*. London: Routledge.

Lorenz, Konrad (2002c [1963]) *On Aggression*. London: Routledge.

Mai, Dac L., Howell, Tifanni, Benton, Pree and Bennett, Pauleen C. (2021) 'Socialisation, training and help-seeking: Specific puppy raising practices that predict desirable behaviours in trainee assistance dog puppies', *Applied Animal Behaviour Science* 236: 105259.

Maier, Steven F. and Seligman, Martin E. P. (1976) 'Learned helplessness: Theory and evidence', *Journal of Experimental Psychology* 105(1): 3–46.

Manning, Aubrey (2005) 'Four decades on from the "four questions"', *Animal Biology* 55(4): 287–296.

Marx, Karl (1988) *The Economic and Philosophic Manuscripts of 1844; The Communist Manifesto*. Trans. Martin Milligan. New York: Prometheus Books.

Mays, W. (2013 [1959]) *The Philosophy of Whitehead*. London and New York: Routledge.

McCarthy, Daniel (2016) 'Dangerous dogs, dangerous owners and the waste management of an "irredeemable species"', *Sociology* 50(3): 560–575.

McConnell, Patricia (2017) 'Why don't dogs get angry more often?'. *The Other End of the Leash*, blog. Available at https://tinyurl.com/52jukm43 (accessed May 2022).

McEvoy, Victoria, Espinosa, Uri B., Crump, Andrew and Artnott, Gareth (2022) 'Canine socialisation: A narrative systemic review', *Animals* 12: 2895.

McWhorter, Ladelle (2010) 'Racism and biopower', in R. Martinez (ed.), *On Race and Racism in America: Confessions in Philosophy*. University Park: Pennsylvania State University Press, pp. 55–85.

Mech, L. David (1999) 'Alpha status, dominance, and division of labor in wolf packs', *Canadian Journal of Zoology* 77(8): 1196–1203.

Mech, L. David (2000) 'Leadership in wolf, *Canis lupus*, packs', *Canadian Field-Naturalist* 114(2): 259–263.

Meijer, Eva and Bovenkerk, Bernice (2021) 'Taking animal perspectives into account in animal ethics', in B. Bovenkerk and J. Keulartz (eds), *Animals in Our Midst: The Challenges of Co-Existing with Animals in the Anthropocene*. International Library of Environmental, Agricultural and Food Ethics 33. Cham: Springer, pp. 49–64.

Meyer, Iben, Forkman, Björn, Fredholm, Merete *et al.* (2022) 'Pampered pets or poor bastards? The welfare of dogs kept as companion animals', *Applied Animal Behaviour Science* 251: 1–6.

Miklósi, Ádám (2017) *Dog Behaviour, Evolution and Cognition*. 2nd edn. Oxford: Oxford University Press.

Miklósi, Ádám, Abdai, Judit and Temesi, Andrea (2021) 'Searching where the treasure is: On the emergence of human companion animal partnership (HCAP)', *Animal Cognition* 24: 387–394.

Miklósi, Ádám, Polgárdi, R., Topál, József and Csányi, V. (1998) 'Use of experimenter-given cues in dogs', *Animal Cognition* 1: 113–121.

Millan, Cesar (2020) 'Ten of the smartest dog breeds', *Cesar's Way*. Available at www.cesarsway.com/10-of-the-smartest-dog-breeds/ (accessed August 2022).

Morey, Darcy F. (2006) 'Burying the key evidence: The social bond between dogs and people', *Journal of Archaeological Science* 33: 158–175.

Morey, Darcy F. (2010) *Dogs: Domestication and the Development of a Social Bond*. Cambridge: Cambridge University Press.

Morgan, C. Lloyd (1886) 'On the study of animal intelligence', *Mind* 11(42): 174–185.

Morgan, C. Lloyd (1903) *An Introduction to Comparative Psychology*. London: Walter Scott.

Morris, Paul, Fidler, Margaret and Costall, Alan (2000) 'Beyond anecdotes: An empirical study of "anthropomorphism"', *Society and Animals* 8(2): 151–165.

Most, Konrad (2001 [1955]) *Training Dogs: A Manual*. Washington, DC: Dogwise.

Motamedi Fraser, Mariam (2012) 'Once upon a problem', *Sociological Review* 60(S1): 84–107.

Motamedi Fraser, Mariam (2019) 'Dog words – or, how to think without language', *Sociological Review* 67(2): 374–390.

Motamedi Fraser, Mariam (2023) 'Writing on the animal's side'. Review of Éric Baratay's *Animal Biographies: Towards a History of Individuals*. *Humanimalia* 14(1): 409–418.

Müller-Wille, Staffan (2014) 'Race and history: Comments from an epistemological point of view', *Science, Technology, and Human Values* 39(4): 597–606.

Munke, Sara (2023) Presentation at 'Clamping down on dangerous dogs: Protecting the public and promoting more responsible pet ownership' meeting. Organised by the Public Policy Exchange, 9 February.

Nance, Susan (2013) *Entertaining Elephants: Animal Agency and the Business of the American Circus*. Baltimore: Johns Hopkins University Press.

Niestat, Laura, Gupta, Maya, Touroo, Rachel and Brandler, Elizabeth (2022) 'Comparison of *Babesia gibsoni* infection in pit-bull type dogs with and without a known history of involvement in organized dog fighting', *Forensic Science International: Animals and Environments* 2: 100044.

O'Neill, Dan, Sahota, Jaya, Brodbelt, Dave C. et al. (2022) 'Health of Pug dogs in the UK: Disorder predispositions and protections', *Canine Medicine and Genetics* 9(4): 1–11.

Ostrander, Elaine A. (2012) 'Both ends of the leash – the human links to good dogs with bad genes', *New England Journal of Medicine* 367: 636–646.

Overall, Karen L. (1997) *Clinical Behavioral Medicine for Small Animals*. St Louis: Mosby.

Overmier, Bruce J. and Seligman, Martin E. P. (1967) 'Effects of inescapable shock upon subsequent escape and avoidance responding', *Journal of Comparative and Physiological Psychology* 63(1): 28–33.

Packer, Rowena, Brand, Claire, Belshaw, Zoe, Pegram et al. (2021) 'Pandemic puppies: Characterising the motivations and behaviours of UK owners who purchased puppies during the 2020 COVID-19 pandemic', *Animals* 11: 2500.

Patton, Paul (2003) 'Language, power and the training of horses', in C. Wolfe (ed.), *Zoontologies: The Question of the Animal*. Minneapolis: University of Minnesota Press, pp. 83–100.

Paxton, David W. (2000) 'A case for a naturalistic perspective', *Anthrozoös* 13(1): 5–8.

Paxton, David W. (2011) *Why It's OK to Talk to Your Dog: Co-Evolution of People and Dogs*. Brisbane: Paxton.

PDSA [People's Dispensary for Sick Animals] (2021) *PAW: PDSA Animal Wellbeing Report*. Available at www.pdsa.org.uk/media/12078/pdsa-paw-report-2021.pdf (accessed February 2023).

Pearson, Chris (2014) 'History and animal agencies', in L. Kalof (ed.), *The Oxford Handbook of Animal Studies*. Oxford: Oxford University Press, pp. 240–257.

Perri, Angela, Widga, Chris, Lawler, Dennis et al. (2019) 'New evidence of the earliest domestic dogs in the Americas', *American Antiquity* 84(1): 68–87.

Persson, Mia, Wright, Dominic, Roth, Lina *et al.* (2016) 'Genomic regions associated with interspecies communication in dogs contain genes related to human social disorders', *Scientific Reports* 6: 33439.

Peterson, Christopher (2004) 'Learned helplessness', in W. E. Craighead and C. B. Nemeroff (eds), *The Corsini Encyclopedia of Psychology and Behavioral Science*. 3rd edn. Hoboken, NJ: John Wiley & Sons, pp. 517–518.

Peterson, Christopher (2019) 'Races', in L. Turner, U. Sellback and R. Broglio (eds), *The Edinburgh Companion to Animal Studies*. Edinburgh: Edinburgh University Press, pp. 444–458.

Philo, Chris and Wilbert, Chris (eds) (2000) *Animal Spaces, Beastly Places: New Geographies of Human–Animal Relations*. London and New York: Routledge.

Pierantoni, Ludovica, Albertini, Mariangela and Pirrone, Frederica (2011) 'Prevalence of owner-reported behaviours in dogs separated from the litter at two different ages', *Veterinary Record* 169(148), 29 October.

Pierce, Jessica and Bekoff, Marc (2021) *A Dog's World: Imagining the Lives of Dogs in a World without Humans*. Princeton: Princeton University Press.

Pilley, John W., with Hinzmann, Hilary (2013) *Chaser: Unlocking the Genius of a Dog who Knows a Thousand Words*. Boston, MA: Mariner Books.

Platt, Belinda, Hawton, Keith, Simkin, Sue and Mellanby, Richard J. (2012) 'Suicidal behaviour and psychosocial problems in veterinary surgeons: A systematic review', *Social Psychiatry and Psychiatric Epidemiology* 47(2): 223–240.

Polgár, Zita, Blackwell, Emily and Rooney, Nicola (2019) 'Assessing the welfare of kennelled dogs – a review of animal-based measures', *Applied Animal Behaviour Science* 213: 1–13.

Porcher, Jocelyn (2014) 'The work of animals: A challenge for the social sciences', *Humanimalia: A Journal of Human/Animal Interface Studies* 6(1): 1–9.

Porcher, Jocelyn (2017) *The Ethics of Animal Labor: A Collaborative Utopia*. New York: Palgrave Macmillan.

Porcher, Jocelyn and Lécrivain, Élisabeth (2019) 'The wolf and the Patou dog: Freedom and work', in J. Porcher and J. Estebanez (eds), *Animal Labor: A New Perspective on Human–Animal Relations*. Bielefeld: Transcript, pp. 113–128.

Porcher, Jocelyn and Lécrivain, Élisabeth (2017) 'La louve et la chienne patou: La liberté et le travail', *Ecologie et politique* 54: 65–78.

Porcher, Jocelyn and Nicod, Sophie (2020) 'Domestication and animal labour', in C. Stépanoff and J.-D. Vigne (eds), *Hybrid Communities: Biosocial Approaches to Domestication and Other Trans-Species Relationships*. London and New York: Routledge, pp. 251–260.

Porcher, Jocelyn and Schmitt, Tiphaine (2012) 'Dairy cows: Workers in the shadows?', *Society and Animals* 20: 39–60.

Puurunen, Jenni, Hakanen, Emma, Salonen, Milla *et al.* (2020) 'Inadequate socialisation, inactivity, and urban living environment are associated with social fearfulness in dogs', *Scientific Reports, Nature Research* 10: 3527.

Pušić, Bruno, Gregorić, Pavel and Franjević, Damjan (2017) 'What do biologists make of the species problem?', *Acta biotheoretica* 65: 179–209.

Rich, Adrienne (1986) 'Motherhood: The contemporary emergency and the quantum leap', in *On Lies, Secrets, and Silence: Selected Prose 1966–1976*. New York: W. W. Norton, pp. 259–274.

Riskin, Jessica (2016) *The Restless Clock: A History of the Centuries-Long Argument over What Makes Living Things Tick*. Chicago: Chicago University Press.

Ritvo, Harriet (1987) *The Animal Estate: The English and Other Creatures in the Victorian Age*. Cambridge, MA: Harvard University Press.

Ritvo, Harriet (2000) 'Animal consciousness: Some historical perspective', *American Zoologist* 40: 847–852.

Roberts, Dorothy (2012) *Fatal Invention: How Science, Politics and Big Business Re-Create Race in the Twenty-First Century*. New York: The New Press.

Rollin, Bernard (1998) *The Unheeded Cry: Animal Consciousness, Animal Pain, and Science*. Ames: Iowa State University Press.

Romanes, George J. (2012 [1884]) *Animal Intelligence*. New York: D. Appleton.

Rosenberg, Meisha (2011) 'Golden retrievers are White, pit bulls are Black and chihuahuas are Hispanic: Representations of breeds of dog and issues of race in popular culture', in L. Kalof and G. M. Montgomery (eds), *Making Animal Meaning*. East Lansing: Michigan State University Press, pp. 113–126.

RSPCA [Royal Society for the Prevention of Cruelty to Animals] (2023) 'Recognising separation-related behaviour in dogs'. Available at https://tinyurl.com/2ptahfps (accessed February 2023).

Rugaas, Turid (2006) *On Talking Terms with Dogs: Calming Signals*. Washington, DC: Dogwise Publishing.

Salomon, Danielle (2010) 'From marginal cases to linked oppressions: Reframing the conflict between the autistic pride and animal rights movements', *Journal for Critical Animal Studies* 8(1–2): 47–72.

Savranksy, Martin (2016) *The Adventure of Relevance: An Ethics of Social Inquiry*. London: Palgrave Macmillan.

Sax, Boria (1997) 'What is a Jewish dog? Konrad Lorenz and the cult of wildness', *Society and Animals* 5(1): 3–21.

Scott, John P. and Fuller, John L. (1965) *Genetics and the Social Behavior of the Dog*. Chicago: Chicago University Press.

Schneider, Susan M. and Morris, Edward K. (1987) 'The history of the term *radical behaviourism*: From Watson to Skinner', *Behavior Analyst* 10(1): 27–39.

Seligman, Martin E. P. (1972) 'Learned helplessness', *Annual Review of Medicine* 23: 407–412.

Seligman, Martin E. P. and Maier, Steven F. (1967) 'Failure to escape traumatic shock', *Journal of Experimental Psychology* 74(1): 1–9.
Serpell, James (ed.) (2017) *The Domestic Dog: Its Evolution, Behavior and Interactions with People*. Second edition. Cambridge: Cambridge University Press.
Serpell, James and Duffy, Deborah (2014) 'Dog breeds and their behavior', in A. Horowitz (ed.), *Domestic Dog Cognition and Behaviour: The Scientific Study of 'Canis familiaris'*. Heidelberg: Springer, pp. 30–57.
Serpell, James, Duffy, Deborah and Jagoe, J. Andrew (2017) 'Becoming a dog: Early experience and the development of behavior', in J. Serpell (ed.), *The Domestic Dog: Its Evolution, Behavior, and Interactions with People*. Cambridge: Cambridge University Press.
Singer, Peter (2006) *In Defence of Animals: The Second Wave*. Oxford: Blackwell.
Singer, Peter (2015 [1976]) *Animal Liberation*. London: Bodley Head.
Skinner, Burrhus F. (1959) 'John Broadus Watson, behaviorist', *Science* 129: 197–198.
Skinner, Burrhus F. (1981) 'Selection by consequences', *Science* 213(4507): 501–504.
Smith, Justin E. (2015) *Nature, Human Nature, and Human Difference: Race in Early Modern Philosophy*. Princeton and Oxford: Princeton University Press.
Sokolov, V. E. and Baskin, L. M. (1993) 'Konrad Lorenz: A prisoner of war for three years', *International Journal of Comparative Psychology* 6(3): 178–182.
Spini, Maggie (2010) 'Q&A with Brian Hare', *The Chronicle*. Available at www.dukechronicle.com/article/2010/11/q-brian-hare (accessed April 2021).
Sports Illustrated (2008) 'What happened to Michael Vick's dogs …', *Sports Illustrated*, 23 December. Available at www.si.com/more-sports/2008/12/23/vick-dogs (accessed November 2021).
Star, Susan Leigh (1990) 'Power, technology and the phenomenology of conventions: On being allergic to onions', *Sociological Review* 38(1): 26–56.
Starkey, Mike P., Scase, Timothy J., Mellersh, Cathryn S. et al. (2005) 'Dogs really are man's best friend – canine genomics has applications in veterinary and human medicine!' *Briefings in Functional Genomics and Proteomics* 4(2): 112–128.
Stengers, Isabelle (1999) 'Whitehead and the laws of nature', *Salzburger theolgische Zietschrift* 3(2): 193–206.
Stengers, Isabelle (2000) *The Invention of Modern Science*. Minneapolis: University of Minnesota Press.
Stengers, Isabelle (2010) 'Including nonhumans in political theory: Opening Pandora's Box?', in B. Braun and S. J. Whatmore (eds), *Political Matter: Technoscience, Democracy, and Public Life*. Minneapolis: University of Minnesota Press, pp. 3–34.

Stepan, Nancy (1982) *The Idea of Race in Science: Great Britain 1800–1960*. London: Macmillan.

Stevenson, Rochelle and Morales, Celeste (2022) 'Trauma in animal protection and welfare work: The potential of trauma-informed practice', *Animals* 12: 852.

Steward, Helen (2018) 'Morgan's Canon: Animal psychology in the twentieth century and beyond', in P. Adamson and G. F. Edwards (eds), *Animals: A History*. Oxford: Oxford University Press, pp. 293–328.

Stilwell, Victoria (2017) 'Why I'm not (and never have been) a purely positive dog trainer', *Positively Victoria Stilwell*. Available at https://tinyurl.com/ymub684n (accessed August 2022).

Suen, Alison (2015) *The Speaking Animal: Ethics, Language and the Human–Animal Divide*. London: Rowman and Littlefield.

Swanson, Heather A., Lien, Marianne E. and Ween, Gro B. (eds) (2018) *Domestication Gone Wild: Politics and Practices of Multispecies Relations*. Durham, NH: Duke University Press.

Taylor, Sunaura (2017) *Beasts of Burden: Animal and Disability Liberation*. New York and London: New Press.

Thomas, Keith (1984) *Man and the Natural World: Changing Attitudes in England 1500–1800*. London: Penguin.

Thorndike, Edward (1911) *Animal Intelligence: Experimental Studies*. New York: Macmillan.

Tinbergen, Nikolaas (2005 [1963]) 'On aims and methods of ethology', *Animal Biology* 55(4): 297–321.

Tomasi, Suzanne, Fechter-Leggett, Ethan, Edwards, Nicole et al. (2019) 'Suicide among veterinarians in the United States from 1979 through 2015', *Journal of the American Veterinary Association* 254(1): 104–112.

Tomlinson, Maisie (2024) 'Emotional natives: The role of prey–animal ontologies in equine-assisted personal development', *Society and Animals*.

Topál, József, Miklósi, Ádám and Gácsi, Márta (2009) 'The dog as a model for understanding human social behavior', *Advances in the Study of Behavior* 39: 71–116.

Townshend, Emma (2009) *Darwin's Dogs: How Darwin's Pets Helped Form a World-Changing Theory of Evolution*. London: Frances Lincoln.

Trut, Lyudmila N. (1999) 'Early canid domestication: The fox farm experiment', *American Scientist* 87 (March–April): 160–169.

Tsing, Anna (2015) *The Mushroom at the End of the World: On the Possibility of Life in Capitalist Ruins*. Princeton, NJ: Princeton University Press.

Tuan, Yi-Fu (2004 [1984]) *Dominance and Affection: The Making of Pets*. New Haven, CT: Yale University Press.

Turner, Charles Henry (1892) 'Psychological notes upon the gallery spider – illustrations of intelligent variations in the construction of the web', *Journal of Comparative Neurology* 2: 95–110.

Van Dooren, Thom (2014) *Flight Ways: Life and Loss at the Edge of Extinction*. New York: Columbia University Press.

Van Dooren, Thom (2016) 'Authentic crows: Identity, captivity and emergent forms of life', *Theory, Culture and Society* 33(2): 29–52.

Van Grouw, Katrina (2018) *Unnatural Selection*. Princeton: Princeton University Press.

Van Sittert, Lance and Swart, Sandra (eds) (2008) *'Canis africanis': A Dog History of Southern Africa*. Leiden: Brill.

Vaterlaws-Whiteside, Helen and Hartmann, Amandine (2017) 'Improving puppy behavior using a new standardized socialization program', *Applied Animal Behaviour Science* 197: 55–61.

Vicedo, Marga (2009) 'The father of ethology and the foster mother of ducks: Konrad Lorenz as an expert on motherhood', *Isis* 100: 263–291.

Viegas, Jennifer (2008) 'World's first dog lived 31,700 years ago', NBC [National Broadcasting Company] News, 17 October. Available at www.nbcnews.com/id/wbna27240370 (accessed September 2022).

Vilà, Carles, Savolainen, Peter, Maldonado, Jesús E. et al. (1997) 'Multiple and ancient origins of the domestic dog', *Science* 276(5319): 1687–1689.

VonHoldt, Bridgett M., Shuldiner, Emily, Koch, Ilana et al. (2017) 'Structural variants in genes associated with human Williams-Beuren syndrome underlie stereotypical hypersociability in domestic dogs', *Science Advances* 3(7): 1–12.

Wadiwel, Dinesh (2002) 'Cows and sovereignty: Biopower and animal life', *Borderlands* 1(2). Available at www.borderlands.net.au/vol1no2_2002/wadiwel_cows.html (accessed March 2023).

Wadiwel, Dinesh (2015) *The War against Animals*. Leiden and Boston, MA: Brill.

Wadiwel, Dinesh (2016) 'Do fish resist?', *Cultural Studies Review* 22(1): 196–242.

Wadiwel, Dinesh (2018) 'Chicken harvesting machine: Animal labor, resistance, and the time of production', *South Atlantic Quarterly* 117(3): 527–549.

Wadiwel, Dinesh (2020) 'The working day: Animals, capitalism, and surplus time', in C. E. Blattner, K. Coulter and W. Kymlicka (eds), *Animal Labour: A New Frontier of Interspecies Justice?* Oxford: Oxford University Press, pp. 181–206.

Watson, Matthew C. (2016) 'On multispecies ethnography: A critique of animal anthropology', *Theory, Culture and Society* 33(5): 159–172.

Wauthier, Lauren M. and Williams, Joanne M. (2018) 'Using the mini C-BARQ to investigate the effects of puppy farming on dog behaviour', *Applied Animal Behaviour Science* 206: 75–86.

Weaver, Harlan (2013) '"Becoming in kind": Race, class, gender and nation in cultures of dog rescue and dogfighting', *American Quarterly* 65(3): 689–709.

Weaver, Harlan (2021) *Bad Dog: Pit Bull Politics and Multispecies Justice*. Seattle: University of Washington Press.

Weil, Kari (2012) *Thinking Animals: Why Animal Studies Now?* New York: Columbia University Press.

Wheat, Christina, van de Bijl, Wouter and Temrin, Hans (2019) 'Dogs, but not wolves, lose their sensitivity towards novelty with age', *Frontiers in Psychology* 10: 2001.

Wheeler, Roxann (2000) *The Complexion of Race: Categories of Difference in Eighteenth-Century British Culture.* Philadelphia: University of Pennsylvania Press.

Whitehead, Alfred N. (1967) *Adventures of Ideas.* New York: Free Press.

Whitehead, Alfred N. (1978) *Process and Reality: An Essay in Cosmology.* Corrected edn. Ed. D. R. Griffin and D. W. Sherburne. New York: Free Press.

Whitehead, Alfred N. (1985) *Science and the Modern World.* London: Free Association Books.

Wilde, Nicole (2006) *Help for Your Fearful Dog: A Step-by-Step Guide to Helping Your Dog Conquer His Fears.* San Clarita: Phantom Publishing.

Wilkins, John S. (2017) *Species: The Evolution of the Idea.* 2nd edn. Boca Raton, FL: CRC Press.

Williams, David L. and Hogg, Sarah (2016) 'The health and welfare of dogs belonging to homeless people', *Pet Behaviour Science* 1: 23–30.

Williams Syndrome Foundation (2023) 'Williams Syndrome explained'. Available at https://williams-syndrome.org.uk/what-is-williams-syndrome-6-2/

Włodarczyk, Justyna (2018) *Genealogy of Obedience: Reading North American Dog Training Literature, 1850s–2000s.* Leiden: Brill.

Wolfe, Cary (2009) 'Human, all too human: "Animal studies" and the humanities', *PMLA* 124(2): 564–575.

Wolfe, Cary (2010) *What Is Posthumanism?* Minneapolis: University of Minnesota Press.

Wollaston, Sam (2021) 'Rescue me: Why Britain's beautiful lockdown dogs are being abandoned', *Guardian*, 1 December. Available at https://tinyurl.com/5n9abt7f (accessed March 2022).

Woodhouse, Barbara (1997 [1954]) *Dog Training My Way.* New York: Berkley.

Worboys, Michael, Strange, Julie-Marie and Neil Pemberton (2018) *The Invention of the Modern Dog: Breed and Blood in Victorian Britain.* Baltimore: Johns Hopkins University Press.

Wynne, Clive D. L. (2020a) *Dog Is Love: Why and How Your Dog Loves You.* Boston, MA and New York: Houghton Mifflin Harcourt.

Wynne, Clive D. L. (2020b) 'What makes dogs special?', presentation at the 29th International Society for Anthrozoology Annual Conference (virtual), University of Liverpool, 31 August–6 September.

Yin, Sophia (2009) *Low Stress Handling, Restraint and Behavior Modification of Dogs and Cats: Techniques for Developing Patients who Love Their Visits.* Davis, CA: CattleDog Publishing.

Young, Robert (2003) *Environmental Enrichment for Captive Animals*. Oxford: Blackwell.
Zelinger, Amir (2019) 'Race and animal breeding: A hybridized historiography', *History and Theory* 58(3): 360–384.

Index

ableism 133, 135
affect 33, 35, 55, 134, 136, 175, 176, 231
affirmative biopolitics 17, 33, 55, 56
Afghan Hounds 30, 32
Agassiz, Louis 191
agencement, concept of 175, 176, 177
agency 4, 8, 134, 135, 146, 147, 152, 155, 156, 165, 174–177 *passim*, 179, 182
aggression 13, 14, 44, 48, 51, 52, 60n13, 145, 153n6, 159
agility 33, 34
Alex (parrot) 164–165
Allen, Colin 118, 119, 120
Ambruster, Karla 234
American Kennel Club (AKC) 30, 32, 59n4, 213
Anderson, Virginia DeJohn 31, 209
anecdotalism 19, 20, 91, 93, 114, 117, 162
anecdotes 94, 100, 101, 106, 107, 108, 109, 110–118 *passim*, 119, 162, 184n10, 192
  see also parasol anecdote; Senta (dog); Senta's howl
animal–human relations 80, 123, 151
animal intelligence *see* intelligence
animal labour *see* labour

anxiety 37, 47, 48, 51, 52, 53, 57, 159
  see also separation anxiety
archaeology and dogs 7, 18, 65, 71, 73, 74, 87
Aristotle 86, 149, 187, 189, 216n2, 221
artificial selection 67, 75, 76, 88, 88n4, 110, 158, 169, 170, 217n9
  see also natural selection
assistance dogs 45
autism 134, 143

Babesia gibsoni 214
Baratay, Eric 87
Basenjis 32, 75
bats 66, 117
Battaglia, Carmen 40, 45, 47
Beagles 32, 134
behavioural problems 18, 29, 45, 47, 51, 52, 55, 56, 60n9, 143, 159, 235
behaviourism 32, 33, 91, 93, 104, 153n4, 177, 178
  see also radical behaviourism
behaviour patterns *see* instinctive behaviour patterns
Bekoff, Marc 2, 3, 6, 22, 60n9, 82, 94, 117, 118, 119, 120, 148, 155, 156, 161, 166, 167, 168, 169, 170, 171, 172, 173, 175, 182, 184n7, 184n8

Berns, Gregory 6, 45, 131, 133, 134, 142, 143, 148, 153n7, 153n8, 160
Besky, Sarah 149
Best Friends Animal Society 213
Beth (dog) 1, 137, 140, 149, 227
Birke, Lynda vii, 24, 144, 219, 220, 224, 225, 227, 231, 232
black men 207, 208, 209
Blanchette, Alex 149
Blattner, Charlotte 123, 150, 152, 220
Bloodhounds 32
Boakes, Robert 68, 105, 106, 110, 111–112, 113, 114, 115, 198
Boardman, Holly 52
Boas, Franz 194
Bob (dog) 66, 192
Boer dogs 31
Boisseron, Bénédicte 230
Boltanski, Luc 229, 230
bonding *see* dog–human bond
bonobos 125, 130
Border Collies 30, 34, 169
Borzois 32
Boxall, Jackie 45
Boxers 46, 61n17, 184n3
Boyle, Robert 222
Bradshaw, Gay 205, 206
Bradshaw, John 47, 51, 62, 154n15, 163
Brand, Claire 49, 50, 51, 52, 60n13
Braude, Stan 76, 77, 78
breeding, dog 40, 49, 50, 51, 66, 67, 73, 74, 75, 83, 88n6, 95, 107, 134, 170, 192
breed-specific legislation (BSL) 207, 211, 216n1, 217n13
brood-defence instinct 14, 100, 101
brood-tending instinct 14, 101
Buchanan, Brett 8, 9, 26n7, 26n8, 164, 165, 166
Budiansky, Stephen 76–77
Buller, Henry 228, 229, 237n7
Burghardt, Gordon 117

Burkhardt, Richard xiv, 10, 11, 12, 13, 16, 26n10, 93, 95, 96, 101, 121n6
Bussolini, Jeffrey 8, 9
Byrne, Richard 118

cage-reared dogs 181, 182
Callie (dog) 153n7, 160
Campebell, John 31
canine racism 207, 210
Canine Science Collaboratory 125
Canis aureus 12, 89n14
Canis familiaris 65, 67, 70, 80, 81, 86, 104, 115, 134, 146, 158, 211, 219, 231, 236
Canis lupus 12, 71, 80
Canis lupus familiaris 71, 80
captive dogs 3, 11, 25n2, 62, 90n19, 98, 99, 147, 170, 172, 173, 184n8
cardiac studies 131–132
cats 66, 106, 111, 158, 167, 184n12, 233
Cavalier King Charles Spaniel 50, 60n17
Charlton, Anne 135
Chaser (dog) 160
chemical studies 132
  see also neurochemistry; oxytocin
Chidester, David 23, 196, 200
Chilterns Dog Rescue Society 54
chimpanzees 32, 125, 126, 127, 128, 129, 194
Chrulew, Matthew 26n7, 147
citizenship 213
Cladland, Douglas 111
Clark, Nigel 235–236
classification
  animals 32, 67, 114, 193, 228, 231, 232
  dogs 80, 81, 113, 115, 168, 190
  humans 189, 190, 193, 194
  pets 160
  plants 114
  species 139, 187, 204, 206
  see also Linnaeus, Carl

cleverness 108, 109, 153n6
Close, Susan xi, xiii, 162
Clothier, Suzanne 45, 48
Clowes, Adam 52
cognitive ethology 94, 117
colonialism 5, 67, 149, 190, 200, 217n10
commercial breeding establishments (CBE) 51, 52, 53
companion animals 36, 37, 57, 59n1, 89n12, 143, 158, 235
companion dogs 30, 32, 33, 37, 45, 52, 58, 70, 75, 82, 86, 123, 124, 133, 134, 142, 147, 148, 150, 151, 152n1, 163, 168, 169, 171, 172, 184n8, 218n16, 234
companionship 5, 20, 25n4, 147, 154n12, 172
connectivity, principle of 128
continuity, evolutionary *see* evolutionary continuity
Coppinger, Raymond and Lorna 19, 76, 77, 80, 81, 82, 83, 84, 85, 86, 90n17, 90n19, 90n20, 124, 159
coprophagia 47, 60n10
Coren, Stanley 29, 30, 32, 35, 137
Corgi 68
Costall, Alan 107, 122n9
Coulter, Kendra 8, 151
COVID-19 pandemic 18, 29, 49, 52, 53
see also pandemic puppies
cows 15, 16, 138, 140, 146, 150, 176, 181, 209
coyotes 72, 84
Crist, Eileen 92, 96, 97, 102, 111, 116, 122n13, 192

dangerous dogs 23, 207, 208, 209, 210, 211, 212, 214, 215, 217n13
Darwin, Charles 6, 19, 23, 65, 66, 67, 68, 69, 70, 85, 88n4, 88n5, 88n6, 91, 93, 94, 95, 104, 110, 112, 114–117 *passim*, 158, 185–201 *passim*, 217n6, 217n8, 217n9
see also Bob (dog); continuity, evolutionary; essentialism; natural selection; parasol anecdote; tree of life
Day, Matthew 196, 198, 199, 200
death
 animals 5, 8, 82, 150, 187, 230
 dogs 1, 23, 24, 25, 28, 37, 59n5, 133, 140, 183, 186, 187, 192, 201, 205, 211, 212, 213, 214, 215, 218n17, 228, 229
 in general 135, 211
 humans 230
deathlessness of species 4, 24, 187, 211, 215
degeneration 11, 12, 189
Deleuze, Gilles 231
Delon, Nicolas 25, 25n5, 138, 139, 151, 233, 234
dependence on humans 37, 45, 63, 79, 135, 136, 161, 168, 236
see also independence of dogs
deportation 13, 206
Derrida, Jacques 202, 225, 230
Descartes, René 221, 222, 224
Descola, Philippe 9
Desmond, Adrian 65, 66, 67, 190, 191
despair, dog 29, 55, 171
Despret, Vinciane 8, 9, 15, 21, 22, 26n7, 92, 103, 118, 126, 139, 157, 163, 164, 165, 166, 173, 174, 175, 176, 177, 180, 181, 226, 228, 229, 230, 237n4
see also polite research
destiny of dogs 18, 28, 126, 152n1
developmental periods, dog 10, 39, 49, 51, 53
devouring impulse 101, 102, 103
Dietz, Lisa 45, 51
dingoes 14, 84, 90n19, 100, 101, 102, 103, 121n7

Index 263

Dinwoodie, Ian 45, 47
disability and dogs 133, 134, 135, 136
discontinuity, principle of 68, 71, 102, 194, 198
  see also continuity, evolutionary
disease 47, 51, 57, 60n8, 82, 132, 201, 214
  see also Babesia gibsoni; Williams-Beuren syndrome (WBS)
Doble, Josh 59
dog despair see despair, dog
dog fighting see fighting, dog
Dog Hub, The xi
dog–human bond 5, 21, 28, 29, 34, 35, 37, 49, 53, 58, 78, 86, 123, 125, 126, 132, 137, 138, 139, 140, 147, 148, 149, 152, 155, 156, 159, 160, 168, 171, 172, 173, 234, 235
dog–human relations 17, 28, 29, 32, 33, 36, 37, 38, 54, 56, 59, 78, 85, 125, 156, 163, 167, 171, 172, 174, 184n4, 236
dog-is-wolf thesis 62, 64, 81, 85
dogness 34
dognition 128, 131
Dognition.com 59n3, 125, 127, 183n2
dog paper boom 6, 157, 158
dog preferences see preferences, dog
Dogs Trust 52, 61n17
dog trainers see trainers, dog
dog training see training, dog
domestication 10, 11, 12, 18, 46, 64, 65, 70–80 passim, 81, 82, 88, 89n15, 89n16, 124, 130, 139, 153n6, 158, 159, 167, 171, 173, 233
Donaldson, Brianne 227, 230, 231, 232
Donaldson, Jean 44, 57

doubly inductive method 107
D'Souza, Renée 150, 151
Du Bois, William E. B. 17
ducks 92, 94, 102, 110, 121n6
Duke Canine Cognition Center 125, 143
Durston, Tamsin 57

echolocation 117
ecological evolutionary developmental biology (eco-evo-devo) 223
Eisen, Jessica 150–151
elephants 174–175, 205–206, 232
emotions 8, 17, 38, 44, 45, 51, 55, 63, 64, 65, 66, 115, 124, 126, 127, 131, 151, 153n4, 155, 159, 168, 174, 178, 179, 192, 199, 234
Endangered Breed Association 212
endangerment 203
endurance, concept of 225, 227–228
enduring percipient, concept of 4, 24, 225–226
English civilisation and dogs 10, 14, 31, 209, 217n6
enrichment 34, 48, 147, 151
essence of dogs 21, 34, 133, 171, 187, 193, 199, 226
essentialism 85, 122n12, 187, 188, 192, 193, 194, 210
ethics 3, 33, 34, 99, 133, 135, 136, 143, 150, 156, 173, 208, 224, 232
ethology xiv, 5, 7, 8, 9, 11, 15, 16, 19, 26n8, 27n11, 91, 92, 94, 95, 100, 110, 112, 117, 118, 120, 121n5, 157, 161, 183n3
euthanised dogs 1, 46, 54, 60n13, 137, 149, 212, 213, 214, 227
evolutionary continuity 70, 102, 115, 117, 189, 197, 198, 200, 201, 209
  see also discontinuity, principle of

evolutionary developmental biology (evo-devo) 24, 223
evolutionary theory 6, 70, 105, 110, 168, 193, 196, 222
exceptionalism 8, 81, 149, 187, 200
exercise 30, 133, 141, 170, 172, 234
expectations of dogs 1, 35, 40, 44, 45, 48, 87, 125, 224
exploitation of animals 3, 56, 123, 133, 135, 150, 170, 208, 230, 233
extinction 12, 135, 189, 203, 205, 226, 233
extreme conformation 58

family dogs 64, 90n19, 151, 160, 161, 162, 234, 235
fancy hobby pet dogs 82, 83, 85
Farnworth, Mark 52
fascination with dogs 18, 54
fear in a dog 37, 39, 45, 46, 47, 48, 51, 52, 53, 55, 60n13, 148, 159, 199
Fidler, Margaret 107, 122n9
fighting, dog 23, 170, 185, 207, 208, 212, 214
   see also Vick, Michael
food, need for 114, 128, 131, 133, 141, 153n7, 170
fossil research 72, 73, 74
Foucault, Michel 23, 193, 201, 209
Fox, Michael 40
foxes 31, 89n13, 130
Fox Terrier 66, 94, 106, 111
Francione, Gary 135, 233
Franjević, Damjan 202
Frank (heron) 4
Freedman, Adam 70, 71, 72, 73, 74
freedom for dogs 172, 173, 175, 183, 233
   see also captive dogs; unfreedom of dogs

Fudge, Erica 154n7, 160, 182, 183, 215
Fujimura, Joan H. 74, 203
Fuller, John 38, 39, 59n6, 160
fun 17, 29, 33, 34, 35
functional magnetic resonance imaging (fMRI) 131, 134, 143, 153n7, 160
Futuyma, Douglas 188

Galambos, Robert 117
Gantt, W. Horsley 161, 184n4
gate latch trick 106, 107, 110, 111, 130
generalisation, in science 21, 22, 112, 116, 117, 118, 119, 155, 156, 160, 162, 163, 166, 167, 168, 169, 170, 182
genetics and dogs 5, 7, 11, 18, 21, 38, 46, 51, 60n8, 65, 70, 71, 72, 73, 74, 75, 77, 81, 87, 132, 134, 136, 140, 141, 142, 153n4, 170, 183n3, 194, 195, 197, 202, 203, 204, 222
genius of dogs 21, 54, 126, 127, 128–131 *passim*, 134, 136, 137
genocide of animals 206
German Shepherds 147
gestures, human 127, 130, 132, 133, 155, 159
Ghiselin, Michael 202
Gilbert, Scott 24, 222, 224, 226, 236n1, 237n2
Giraud, Eva 124, 134
Gladman, Justin 76, 77, 78
Gliddon, George Robbins 191, 193, 216n3, 216n5
Global North 1, 18, 29, 37, 58, 125, 140, 169, 235
Gobineau, Joseph Arthur de 191
golden jackal *see Canis aureus*
Gould, Stephen J. 189, 191
Greenhough, Beth 232
Gregorić, Pavel 202
Griffin, Donald 117, 118, 119

Grosz, Elizabeth 68, 70, 193, 195–196, 199
guard dogs 32
Guenther, Katja 35, 186, 212, 213
Guide Dogs National Breeding Centre, UK 40

happiness 17, 33
Haraway, Donna 2, 5, 25n4, 33, 79, 154n10, 222, 223, 224, 225, 226, 227, 228
Hare, Brian 6, 20, 106, 124, 125, 126, 127, 128, 129, 130, 131, 133, 136, 137, 142, 143, 146, 148, 153n6, 158
Hartmann, Amandine 39, 40, 43
Hayes, Ed 51
Hayward, Jessica 60n8
Hearne, Vicki 1, 60n16, 154n10, 161, 165, 212
Hediger, Heini 147
Heinroth, Oskar 13, 89n14, 95, 96
Held, Richard 92, 93, 104, 121n3
Hobson-West, Pru 162
Hollin, Gregory 124, 134
Holocaust 13
Homo sapiens 64, 70, 77, 78, 79, 86, 194, 195, 203, 228
Horowitz, Alexandra 6, 64, 123, 128, 147, 157, 158, 166, 183n3, 205
horses 7, 8, 62, 66, 107, 231, 233
Hovorka, Alice 150
Hribal, Jason 174
Hubrecht, Robert 37, 38, 45
human–dog bond *see* dog–human bond
Human Genome Project 194, 195
Huxley, Julian 95, 115, 116
Huxley, Thomas 115, 116

imprinting 99, 121n6
independence of dogs 3, 32, 81, 129, 137, 167, 168, 178
see also dependence on humans
Indian dogs 31, 209

individuality of dogs 4, 22, 24, 120, 124, 155, 156, 161, 162, 173, 181, 183, 185, 206, 214, 223, 225, 226, 227
individual selection 76, 77
individuation 23, 185, 207, 211, 212, 213, 214, 215
Ingold, Tim 144
instinctive behaviour patterns 93, 95, 96, 97, 98, 100, 103
instincts 6, 10, 14, 17, 20, 33, 63, 92, 96, 101, 103, 121n5, 141, 142, 149, 174
intelligence
 animal 12, 32, 105, 111, 112, 113, 189
 dog 17, 29, 30, 31, 32, 35, 115, 116, 137, 146, 147, 169
 in general 6, 30, 93, 129
 obedience 29, 30
intentionality 8, 17, 76, 109, 126, 129, 131, 133, 153n6, 163, 174, 175, 176

jackals 12, 74, 75, 81, 84, 89n14
see also Canis aureus
James, William 115
Jewish people 13, 230
Jutel, Annemarie, 162

Kaiser (dog) 147, 148
Kalikow, Theodora 10, 11, 12
keeping animals 11, 92, 94, 97, 98, 99
Kennel Club 50, 51, 66, 83
Kim, Claire Jean 207, 208, 209, 210, 211, 212, 215, 218n16
Kirkwood, James 45
Kis, Anna 132
Knox, Robert 191, 192
Kohn, Eduardo 9, 224
Kubinyi, Enikő 160, 161, 162

labour
  animal 15, 20, 21, 123, 137, 138, 140, 141, 145, 149, 150, 151, 233
  dog 20, 36, 138, 139, 141, 144, 146, 150, 151
  see also working dogs
lawless dogs 31
law of effect 111
Leach, Helen 79, 89n16
learned helplessness 22, 156, 158, 163, 177, 179, 181, 184n11, 184n12
  see also Seligman, Martin
Lécrivain, Élisabeth 141, 142, 145, 146
Le Guin, Ursula 219, 231
Lehrman, Daniel S. 92, 121n1
Lestel, Dominique 26n7, 120, 162, 181
Levi, Primo 13, 14
limitations on dogs 2, 25n1, 35, 109, 138, 141, 147, 176, 181, 192, 203, 215, 221, 224
Lindsay, Steven 37, 38, 39, 40
link, the (concept of) 21, 137, 138, 139, 140, 142, 146, 148, 150, 151
Linnaeus, Carl 65, 80, 187, 189, 190, 194
living together 138–141 *passim*, 142, 144, 146, 148
Locke, John 149
London, Karen 34
Lorenz, Konrad 6, 10–14 *passim*, 26n8, 26n9, 26n10, 27n11, 75, 76, 81, 89n14, 91, 92, 94–103 *passim*, 121n2, 121n3, 121n6
  see also Canis aureus; *Canis lupus*
lost dogs 128, 129
love 21, 25, 55, 56, 66, 126, 127, 128, 131–137 *passim*, 141, 172, 199, 233–236 *passim*
Lucy's Law 50

Mai, Dac 45
Manning, Aubrey 15, 92
Marchesini, Roberto 26n7
Martin, Joanne xiii
Marx, Karl 138, 144, 145, 149
McConnell, Patricia 34, 44
McEvoy, Victoria 38, 39, 49, 50, 51, 59n6
Meyer, Iben 44, 45, 46
migration, human 74, 78
Miklósi, Ádám 6, 72, 73, 74, 75, 76, 81, 153n2, 157, 158, 159, 161, 162–163, 179, 180
military dogs 40, 45, 63, 141
Millan, Cesar 63, 64
Mills, T. Wesley 111
mirror self-recognition (MSR) test 128, 153n5
mitochondrial DNA (mtDNA) 72, 88n11
Monk xiii, xv
monogenism 188, 189, 190, 191, 192, 196, 217n6
Moore, James 65, 66, 67, 190, 191
Morales, Celeste 57
Morey, Darcy 70, 71, 81
Morgan, Conwy Lloyd 6, 91, 93, 94, 104, 105, 106, 107, 108, 109, 110, 111, 112, 113, 114, 115, 121n8, 122n10, 128, 130
  see also cleverness; gate latch trick; Tony (dog)
Morgan's Canon 94, 104–106, 108, 109, 111, 115
Morris, Paul 107, 122n9
Morton, Samuel George 191, 216n5
Most, Konrad 63
Müller-Wille, Staffan 194, 202
Munke, Sara 49, 53, 57
mutations 72, 73, 227

Nance, Susan 174–175
National Institutes of Health (NIH) 203

Nationalsozialistische Deutsche Arbeiterpartei (NSDAP) 10
natural selection 11, 65, 67, 68, 75, 77, 88n4, 88n5, 90n20, 110, 136, 192, 197, 227
  see also artificial selection
Nazi ideology 10, 11, 13, 14, 26n10, 121n1
Neil, Lee 150
neurochemistry 132, 136, 153n4
Nicod, Sophie 138, 139, 148, 233
northern wolf *see Canis lupus*
Nott, Josiah Clark 191, 192, 193, 198, 216n3, 216n5

obedience 17, 29, 30, 32, 35, 145
obedience ring 30
obituaries, dog 95, 213, 214
Office for Race Policy 10
O'Neill, Dan 58
operant conditioning *see* dog training
Oreo (dog) 127
out group, definition 72, 129
Overall, Karen 38, 39
Overmier, Bruce 178
owners
  dog 28, 34, 37, 39, 44, 45, 47, 48, 49, 50, 51, 54, 55, 56, 57, 58, 59, 60n12, 62, 63, 87n1, 156, 161, 172, 173, 235
  pet 107, 108, 109
oxen 231
oxytocin 132, 168

Packer, Rowena 49, 53, 60n11
pandemic puppies 18, 29, 48–53 *passim*, 60n11, 60n12
  see also COVID-19 pandemic
parasol anecdote 23, 186, 196–201 *passim*
parrots 164–165, 166, 180
Patous 141, 142, 144, 145, 146, 147, 149, 233
Paxton, David 78, 79, 87n2, 155

Pearson, Chris 174
People's Dispensary for Sick Animals (PDSA) 49, 52, 60n12
Pepperberg, Irene 164, 166
  see also Alex (parrot)
perspective 174, 175, 177
Persson, Mia 132, 134
Peterson, Christopher 177, 184n11, 190, 201, 218n14
pets 49, 65, 82, 83, 107, 153n9, 160, 167, 171, 215, 235
Pierantoni, Ludovica 38, 51
Pierce, Jessica 2, 3, 22, 60n9, 82, 148, 155, 156, 161, 167, 168, 169, 170, 171, 172, 173, 175, 182, 184n7, 184n8
Pilley, John W. 160
Pinocchio hypothesis 76, 77
pit bulls
  black 207–213 *passim*
  in general 185, 186, 187, 218n15
  pit bull types 23, 216n1, 217n13, 227
  white 212–214 *passim*
  see also Beth (dog)
Plato 187, 216n2
Platt, Belinda 57
Pointers 47
Polgár, Zita 37, 48
police dogs 63, 141, 147
politeness 164, 165
polite research 21, 155, 156, 163, 164, 165, 166, 173, 174, 175, 180, 182, 184n10
polygenism 190, 191, 192, 193, 196, 198, 200, 217n6
population thinking 23, 186, 188, 193, 194, 202
Porcher, Jocelyn 15, 20, 21, 26n7, 123, 137, 138, 139, 140, 141, 142, 144, 145, 146, 148, 149, 150, 151, 152, 153n9, 154n10, 173, 176, 181, 233
  see also link, the (concept of)

positive reinforcement training *see* dog training
posthuman dogs 167–174, *passim*
preferences, dog 34, 60n6, 153n7
problem dogs 35, 37, 38, 137
programming of dogs 131, 149
protection 57, 142, 145, 203
Public Policy Exchange 54
Pugs 57, 58, 60n17
Puurunen, Jenni 45
puppy farms 50, 51
puppy mills 51, 170, 184n8
Pušić, Bruno 202
puzzle box experiment 111

Rabanal, Lisa xiii, 144
race, concept of 3, 11, 13, 19, 22, 23, 32, 67, 68, 80, 84, 85, 88n4, 89n14, 185, 186, 188–204 *passim*, 207–210 *passim*, 213, 216, 217n7
racialisation of dogs 23, 80, 185, 186, 187, 195, 196, 201, 204, 208, 209, 210, 211, 212, 213, 215
racism 3, 14, 17, 23, 80, 83, 84, 85, 185, 186, 187, 188, 195, 197, 200, 201, 203, 204, 207, 208, 209, 210, 215–216, 217n10, 218n14 *see also* canine racism
racist science, nineteenth-century 32, 188, 203
radical behaviourism 33, 178
Rajagopalan, Ramya 74, 203
rats 13, 14, 128, 184n12, 234
ravens 164, 175, 230
Ray, John 114
reductionism 14, 15
relationality 25, 64, 136, 155, 156, 167, 176, 182, 220, 221, 222, 223, 224, 225, 232, 237n4
remains, dog 73, 168
reproduction 36, 74, 82, 171, 201

resistance, forms of 22, 37, 40, 56, 123, 148, 149, 154n13, 155, 156, 157, 174, 177, 179, 180, 181, 182, 183, 223
responsiveness to humans 1, 35, 163, 166
Revitalisation Act 203
rewards for dogs 55, 131, 139, 147
Rich, Adrienne 58, 59
Riskin, Jessica 221
Ritvo, Harriet 31, 32, 65, 66, 113, 114
Roberts, Dorothy 194, 195, 203, 204
Roe, Emma 232
Rollin, Bernard 104, 116, 178, 179, 180
Romanes, George 6, 19, 90, 93, 106, 110, 111, 112, 113, 114, 115, 116, 117, 118 *see also* anecdotes
Rooney, Nicola 47, 163
Royal Institution 115
Royal Society for the Prevention of Cruelty to Animals (RSPCA) 53, 61n17, 217n13
Royal Veterinary College (RVC) 51, 53, 58, 61n17
Rugaas, Turid 34

Sapp, Jan 222
Savransky, Martin xiii, 225
Sax, Boria 11, 13, 26n10
Scanlan, Lawrence 8
Schmitt, Tiphaine 15, 139, 140, 173, 176
Schneirla, Theodore C. 17, 121n3
Schönbrunn Zoo 100
sciences
 animal xiv, 6–10 *passim*, 71, 107
 biological 8, 223
 life 6, 9, 15, 16
 natural 9, 15
 social ii, 8, 9, 25, 89n15, 112, 163, 169, 174, 195, 203, 220, 223, 228

Scott, John 38, 39, 59n6, 160
Second World War 5, 11, 194
Seligman, Martin 22, 156, 157, 158, 163, 177, 178, 179, 180, 181, 183, 184
  see also learned helplessness
senses, dog 79, 82, 140, 170, 171, 172
sensitive periods in canine development 38, 39, 50
Senta (dog) 14, 100, 101, 102, 103, 104
Senta's howl 14, 103–104
separation anxiety 45, 51, 52, 53, 55, 60n12
  see also anxiety
Serpell, James 21, 47, 81, 140, 160, 229
service dogs 107, 143, 148
sheep 117, 138, 140, 141, 145
sheep dogs 141, 142, 145
shelters 50, 127, 133, 152n1, 170, 186, 212, 213, 218n15, 236
shepherds 31, 141, 142, 144, 145, 146, 147, 149
Shiba (dog) 34
sign language 132
Singer, Peter 135
singularity 4, 22, 94, 100, 120, 155, 157, 166, 177, 180, 181, 182, 183, 204, 212, 218n17, 225, 226, 227, 230, 231, 232, 237n7
Skinner, Burrhus F. 33, 60n16, 93, 110, 111, 178
slavery 5, 190, 191, 200, 210, 217n6
slothful dogs 31
Smith, Justin 189, 192, 193, 196, 203, 204, 207, 216, 217
social bonding *see* dog–human bond
social competence of dogs 158–159
socialisation 5, 18, 29, 34, 35, 36, 37, 38, 39, 40, 41, 44, 45, 46, 47, 48, 49, 50, 51, 52,
53, 59n1, 59n6, 86, 142, 151, 159
socialisation programme 39, 40, 41, 42, 43, 44, 57
solidity, principle of 128
speciation 2, 18, 19, 20, 64, 67, 70, 73, 75, 77, 78, 79, 80, 81, 85, 86, 87, 87n2, 116, 124, 125, 129, 130, 159, 171, 205
species identity 13, 87, 92, 100, 166
speciesism 3, 23, 186, 200, 203, 206
species representative 74, 94, 100, 106, 109, 111, 118, 125, 181, 189, 205, 206, 211, 229
species thinking 3, 4, 5, 10, 16, 25, 91, 93, 94, 106, 109, 112, 118, 185, 186, 187, 206, 210, 215, 216, 229, 231, 232
species-typicality 58, 99, 100, 118, 119, 120
spiders 16, 149
Spini, Maggie 143
Starkey, Mike 60n8
Stepan, Nancy 189, 193, 194, 197, 198
Stevenson, Rochelle 57
Steward, Helen 104–105
stray dogs 83, 145
street dogs 59n1, 83, 85, 90n19
stress, resistance to 40, 51, 73
Swart, Sandra 31, 59n5
Sweat, Eddie 7–8
Sweet Jasmine (dog) 214
symbiosis 222, 223, 224, 231, 237n3

Tasha (dog) 47, 184n3
Tauber, Alfred 222
Taylor, Sunaura 132–133, 135, 136
Thévenot, Laurent 229, 230
Thomas, Keith 7, 66, 113, 114, 191
Thorndike, Edward 17, 93, 94, 110, 111, 112, 114, 115
  see also law of effect; puzzle box experiment

time, concept of 8, 19, 21, 65, 68, 71, 75, 85, 102, 151, 152, 169, 196, 197, 198, 200, 210
Tinbergen, Nikolaas 15, 26n8, 27n11, 92, 95, 96, 162
Tomasello, Michael 126, 127, 129
Tomasi, Suzanne 57
Tony (dog) 93, 94, 106, 107, 108, 109, 110, 111, 128, 130
trainers, dog 29, 34, 54, 55, 56, 57, 148
training, dog
  affirmative biopolitics 17
  dominating a dog 28
  encouraging a dog 28
  fun and training 34
  obedience training 32
  operant conditioning 55, 56
  positive reinforcement 55, 56, 60n14
  punishment 55, 56
  purely positive dog training 55, 60n14, 60n15
  training–science relationship 7
  see also Dog Hub, The
tree of life 68, 69
tricks 30, 106, 108
Tschock (jackdaw) 94
Turner, Charles H. xiii, 16–17

Udell, Monique 133
unfreedom of dogs 123, 147, 148
  see also freedom for dogs
un-owned dogs 134
utility of dogs 31, 32, 33, 35

van Dooren, Thom 9, 87, 99, 124
van Grouw, Katrina 67, 68, 88n6, 116
van Sittert, Lance 31, 59n5
Vaterlaws-Whiteside, Helen 39, 40, 41, 43
Vicedo, Marga 11, 92, 97
Vick, Michael 23, 185, 208, 210, 211, 212, 213, 214, 215
Vilá, Carles 72

village dog scenario 77, 83, 90n19
von Frisch, Karl 17, 26n8
vonHoldt, Bridgett 132

Wadiwel, Dinesh 36, 37, 150, 151, 152, 179, 187, 216
Wallace, Alfred Russell 197
Washburn, Margaret 17
Watson, John 93, 178
Watson, John Broadus 17
Watson, Matthew 9
Wauthier, Lauren 51
Wayne, Robert 70, 71, 72, 73, 74
Weaver, Harlan 1, 23, 35, 137, 212, 213, 218n15
welfare, dog xi, 5, 37, 38, 44, 45, 51, 54, 57, 58, 59, 60n17, 134, 150, 177, 235
Western breeds 82, 83, 90n19
Wheat, Christina 45
Wheeler, Roxann 189, 190, 198
white fang model 76
Whitehead, Alfred North 4, 5, 24, 220, 221, 222, 225, 226, 227, 237n5, 237n6
  see also endurance, concept of; enduring percipient, concept of
Whitman, Charles Otis 12, 95, 96
Wickens, Stephen 45
Wilde, Nicole 46, 47
Wilkins, John 86, 88n10, 187, 188, 189, 191, 202
Williams, Joanne 51
Williams-Beuren syndrome (WBS) 132, 134
Williams Syndrome Association (US) 132
Williams Syndrome Foundation (UK) 132
Włodarczyk, Justyna 7, 17, 18, 28, 32, 33, 34, 54, 55, 56, 57, 60n16
Wolfe, Cary 15, 149, 225
Wolfinger, Raymond 119
Wollaston, Sam 52

wolves 12, 13, 19, 31, 62, 63, 64, 68, 70, 71, 72, 73, 74, 75, 76, 77, 78, 80, 81, 82, 83, 84, 85, 88n8, 128, 129, 131, 132, 141, 145, 158, 168, 233 *see also Canis lupus*; dog-is-wolf thesis
Woodhouse, Barbara 63, 87n1
Woods, Vanessa 20, 106, 124, 125, 126, 127, 128, 129, 130, 131, 133, 136, 137, 142, 143, 146, 148, 153n6
working dogs 30, 37, 55, 58, 63, 83, 123, 124, 125, 137, 138, 140, 141, 142, 145, 151, 152n1, 169, 184n8, 218n16, 233
Wynne, Clive 6, 20, 124, 125–128 *passim*, 131–137 *passim*, 140, 141, 142, 146, 148, 153n4, 172, 184n4

Xephos (dog) 127, 128

Yin, Sophia 63–64
Young, Robert 45, 235

Zelinger, Amir 190

EU authorised representative for GPSR:
Easy Access System Europe, Mustamäe tee 50,
10621 Tallinn, Estonia
gpsr.requests@easproject.com

www.ingramcontent.com/pod-product-compliance
Ingram Content Group UK Ltd.
Pitfield, Milton Keynes, MK11 3LW, UK
UKHW021345310725
461408UK00008B/40